62 - 63

H. G. WELLS

A BIOGRAPHY BY VINCENT BROME

H. G. WELLS

H. G. WELLS

A Biography by
Vincent Brome

 BOOKS FOR LIBRARIES PRESS
FREEPORT, NEW YORK

First Published 1951 by Longmans, Green and Co.

Reprinted 1970 by arrangement with Vincent Brome and his
literary agents, David Higham Associates, Ltd.

INTERNATIONAL STANDARD BOOK NUMBER:
0-8369-5547-1

LIBRARY OF CONGRESS CATALOG CARD NUMBER:
78-133515

PREFACE

"When a really objective biography of Wells will be written, instead of the enormous reel of self-justification which he is still producing, where his very cunning art of feinting, his very subtle trick of inaccuracy in confession, have again succeeded in blinding his audience to the nature of his play, it will be discovered that he has wounded and injured often beyond cure . . . ."

(ODETTE KEUN—*Time and Tide*, 1934)

DISENCHANTMENT is a curious thing. One may regret or revile the passing of an illusion which has helped to sustain the burden of earthly woe, and yet go on living as if it were still there, intact. The idolatrous do not easily throw down their idols. I have never worshipped H. G. Wells, but as this long pilgrimage into his personality progressed, it led me to believe that there might be something in Miss Keun's passionate criticism of him; and then, very soon, I felt a compulsion to interpose between him and half the evidence, because the judgment pronounced by so many of his detractors turned out to be highly personal. And in the end, the man who sent sparkling winds into many a mental slum, the cheerful, friendly soul whose personality threatened to explode from its own vitality, was still, it seemed to me, at my elbow undiminished. And yet, another Wells had grown up beside—or was it inside—him? Whether this other Wells was capable of overwhelming his alter ego, whether one subdued the other before the book was out, I must leave the reader to decide. There were, in fact, before long, many Wells. Having nine lives, he craved and achieved a tenth.

I can only add that there were for me extravagant compensations in that "enormous reel of self-justification," the *Experiment in Autobiography*. Practised with sufficient patience, rationalisation becomes more revealing than reality in those few places where he uses it, and if he does occasionally evade responsibility by describing himself as a journalist, that saddles his biographer with a journalistic frankness. It is, in any case, very clear that this book could never have been written without the *Experiment in Autobiography*, and there were so many chapters in it which bore for me an odd resemblance to honesty and others where I had no choice but to interpret the mood as fierce, unrelenting integrity.

To this book, and to Geoffrey West's *H. G. Wells* I owe a considerable debt, which brings me to the sole reason for writing a preface at all; there are so many people who made my own book possible, and so many generosities I have to acknowledge. An unpleasant feeling troubles me that their number is overwhelming for so slight a preface. Let me isolate a few: Fenner Brockway, Baroness M. Budberg, Ritchie Calder, Frank Frost, John Guest, Angela Harling, Joan Hitchcock, Frank Horrabin, Gertrude Hutchinson, Eirian James, Professor Harold Laski, H. W. Leggett, Robin Lawrence, Kingsley Martin, Cecily de Moncheaux, Jack T. Murphy, Hermon Ould, Edward Pease, Hugh Pilcher, Dorothy M. Richardson, Ralph Straus, Dennis Sullivan, Eric Trist, Michael Young.

I should also have been at a loss without permission to quote from the *Experiment in Autobiography* published by Victor Gollancz Ltd. and The Cresset Press Ltd.; *H. G. Wells* (Geoffrey West) published by Gerald Howe, Ltd., and *Pilgrimage* (Dorothy Richardson) published by J. M. Dent & Sons Ltd., and The Cresset Press Ltd. Neither Mrs. Geoffrey West, widow of the late Geoffrey West, nor Dorothy M. Richardson would wish me to stress their generosity over this biography. I can only say that it was of a very special kind—as was the work of Eirian James.

For the rest, grateful acknowledgment and thanks are due to the following for permission to quote from their publications: Mrs. Cheston Bennett and the Viking Press for extracts from *The Journals of Arnold Bennett*; Messrs. Chatto & Windus for material from the *Book of Catherine Wells* preface by H. G. Wells; Miss Collins for a letter from G. K. Chesterton to H. G. Wells; Messrs. Constable & Co. Ltd. for extracts from *First and Last Things* by H. G. Wells; Messrs. J. M. Dent & Sons Ltd. for quotations from *Pilgrimage* by Dorothy Richardson; Messrs. William Heinemann Ltd. for extracts from *Mind at the End of Its Tether* and *The Time Machine* by H.G.Wells; the Representatives of the late Henry James for use of material from letters written by Henry James to H. G. Wells; Messrs. Longmans Green & Co. Ltd. for material from *Our Partnership* by Beatrice Webb; Mr. Somerset Maugham and Messrs. Doubleday & Co. Inc. for extracts from *A Writer's Note-book* (copyright, 1949, by W. Somerset Maugham); the Rev. T. Ormerod for a letter written to the Author; Mr. Hermon Ould for a letter written to H. G. Wells; Messrs. Sheed & Ward Ltd. for quotations from *G. K. Chesterton* by Maisie Ward; and Mrs. A. M. Wells and Messrs. John Lane the Bodley Head Ltd. for extracts from *H. G. Wells* by Geoffrey West.

V. B.

CONTENTS

PLATES

Chapter One

PROFILE

ANY summer day in the sun-trap of No. 13 Hanover Terrace the old man sat, a panama hat jammed down on his head, dark glasses to protect his eyes and sometimes a notepad on which he recorded symptoms for the doctors he did not entirely believe in. Amongst the scattered callers one found him inattentive and was injudicious enough to point it out. 'Don't interrupt me,' said Wells, 'can't you see I'm dying ?'

To the last his courage and irascibility, his primitive furies and hatred of tact did not desert him. He was a wreck of his old self, a loosely knit affair of skin and bones with his barrel of a forehead standing out like the hull of a ship, but he continued—incongruously—to loose off broadsides in the same reedy Cockney voice, and remained pathologically sensitive to the lightest breath of criticism. He pottered now mentally and physically. He wrote sporadic pages, dallied in the garden and when nothing seemed to grow in the square yard of earth complained bitterly of that 'bloody' sycamore tree next door which drained the life out of everything.

There were those who came to No. 13 Hanover Terrace to see whether the aged prophet still had something to say. Some found him intolerable, but his friends were not to be duped by the outward display of irascibility, or the eloquent vituperation with which he still occasionally violated, enraptured or merely reduced to silence those who dared his company. One, a very small man, shorter even than Wells and infinitely pompous, incited him to say, 'He's so near the ground he's unhygienic.' He could be quite choleric. But there were many softer moods when he wandered across Regent's Park and played with the children, or fell to painting idly on a convenient strip of wall, or just talked, not in the same torrential fashion as before, but still with vivacity.

By normal standards No. 13 Hanover Terrace was an odd house. Deliberately chosen to incense the gods of superstition, its number delighted Wells who had dedicated half his days to fighting obscurantist nonsense. Soon after he took it, he raced a friend around the house like a spoilt child, showing him the big

I

four-poster bed with canopy and curtains, the photographs of the women deeply part of his emotional life, and the special picture of Catherine his second wife, accorded the place of honour amongst what his enemies referred to as the graceless concubinage. The crimson curtains belonged to the Victorian age which he so much despised, and for unaccountable reasons he proudly displayed on the mantelpiece of the drawing-room the large Chinese terra-cotta horse to which he gave undying devotion. There were occasional gadgets which he revealed as a gleeful child performing conjuring tricks. The lavatory seat set at a special angle, the private telephone exchange by which he could call Margaret the maid or Mrs. Johnston the housekeeper. On the first floor was the famous ladies' room lined with mirrors, a gesture from the heart of Wells, for his warm feminine subtle mind enjoyed women—even if he did not really understand them—better than men. Just outside the house the garage walls had suffered, at his hands, artistic onslaughts which lacked the flair of the *Picshuas* he drew for his wife Catherine almost until her death, but depicted the dawn of civilization from the beetle-like Trilobites to Man, with something of the elemental vigour of our prehistoric forbears. Above the crude sketches he wrote: 'Limitless energy for good or evil. . . . Now distance is abolished. . . .' And finally in pencil, 'Have you the wits, have you the will to save life . . . ?'

Whatever he said, wrote or drew was still news. He was still the popular oracle. Living in a fierce limelight, he issued judgments—which always read like last judgments—on kings and princes, prime ministers, politicians, Bernard Shaw and the divinities. At a hundred pounds a thousand words he told humanity in the *Evening Standard* and Sunday newspapers that it was a parcel of sweeps. He became less abashed than usual in his old age. He had ceased to enlighten his readers about science and interplanetary struggles, and dealt now only in ultimate destinies. Eminent men in every walk of life remained his friends but he saw less and less of them, preferring to rebuke some of them, from time to time, from the isolation of his room. Low cartooned him. Whispers about his health were murmured in very high places. Malicious gentlemen of the old tradition raised a fascinated eyebrow when they heard the incredible list of ailments still trying to kill a man who should have died at thirty. 'A little wonder . . . But perhaps it is time . . .' Others shuddered at the very name. The newspapers were prepared for his death and many elaborate obituaries waited in the files. He had by now written his own obituary. Despite a dash of optimism about his age—he thought he would die at 97—groundless fears of political violence, and a well-nigh irresistible temptation to give it artistic pattern, it bore certain resemblances to reality: 'He occupied an old, tumble-down house upon the border of Regent's Park,' he wrote, 'and his bent, shabby, slovenly and latterly somewhat obese figure was frequently to be seen in the adjacent gardens, sitting and looking idly at the boats on the lake, or the flowers in the beds, or hobbling painfully about with the aid of a stick . . . "Some day," he would be heard to say, "I shall write a book, a real book. . . ."' (1)

He knew he was dying. 'Among the complications of his never very sound body is a fatty degeneration of the heart which ended the lives of his father, his eldest brother and a long line of their ancestors for a number of generations. The machine stops short and the man drops dead unaware of his death. . . .' (2) Sitting in his sun-trap he cheerfully told how his grandfather leaned over a gate to admire the sunset at 82 and ceased to live. His father at the same age, woke up briskly one morning, gave his housekeeper explicit instructions for cooking a suet pudding, finished reading his *Daily Chronicle*, stretched his legs out of bed, slid down and died. His brother rose from a good breakfast at 77, reeled and collapsed. . . . 'And that's how it will be with me. . . .'

It wasn't, in the end. The enormous courage he brought to bear on the wrong way of death had its element of tragedy. H. G. Wells died a long-drawn-out death, far less pleasant than anything his forbears suffered, but just when it seemed insupportable that this man—whose demonic *life* had once driven a whole generation, blazingly, along new and daring paths—should fall to pieces before their eyes, a wheezy chuckle came out of the depths and the same reedy voice asked, with the old Cockney impudence, 'Did I ever give you my lecture on the virtues of promiscuity?'

Some demon in him insisted to the end that people should run the gauntlet of his iconoclasm, and there were moments of quite childish tantrum when he flew into inexplicable rages, but the thought of death itself did not disturb him and he saw no terrors in the approach of encompassing darkness. 'I shall hate to leave the spectacle of life but go I must at last.' (3) It was a pity to die; worse to die painfully; worse still to know that the full rich fantastic cauldron of his life would soon run cold. He had drunk his fill at a hundred perilous pools, it was clear the vessel was worn and exhausted, and there were moments now when he would suddenly stop in mid-career of a sentence, grope for a word and miraculously fall asleep.

Waking from one such short nap he said to Ritchie Calder, a frequent visitor in the last days, 'One life's enough for little H. G. . . .' He smoked and drank moderately, but performed wonders with his diabetic diet which seemed to break all the rules while observing them. 'I am a stoic,' he said, a moment before shrilly denouncing some fresh fool who had given little cause for attack. He still hankered after the laboratory career he had forsaken for literature, and sometimes talked of a life squandered on writing which had failed to convert people to his persuasions and left them glorying in their ignorance. Until the last eighteen months his incandescent vitality remained, and even though his physical strength was failing fast, he would still ring up a friend at 2 o'clock in the morning, ask 'What's the opposite of peroration ?' and getting the answer 'exordium,' say: 'That's it. Come round in the morning, we must find an exordium.'

Signs of the man he had been were still very plain in the last five years of his life. The romantic, the iconoclast, the novelist, the person who could so plausibly convert 'intellectual debate into a private quarrel,' (4) the socialist with a vigorous belief in individualism, the man who preached co-operation with a passion he seldom brought to its practice, a maker and breaker of worlds and ideas and conventions, who periodically dusted the contemporary scene from his hands and cut loose to horrify the young beyond their highest hopes. And the lover, yes still the lover, very aware of beautiful women and feminine subtlety, a lover who had once been so 'careless about paternity. . . .' (5)

Wells remained in his later years a king of chameleons, with somewhere at the heart a noble core, the final assurance of continuity of personality, which when they found it even his enemies respected. But how he could change ! One moment the privileged author in the Ivy Restaurant, throwing out his arms to a lady—'But my dear you're glorious'—and the next the outraged prophet attacking his critics with primitive fury, a dumpy irascible little man who carried a shrivelled stomach on two short legs and tiny feet, with the big forehead jutting above and overhanging it all,

still possessing the world in his own right, still eloquently vituperative. There was no holding the ageing H. G. Wells. He ran
away with whatever he wanted. Sometimes he eschewed all dignity and pretences. Granted nine lives he craved a tenth and
occasionally, in his search for it, would brilliantly abuse whatever
frustrated him. 'There was no malice in his attacks,' Bernard Shaw
said. 'They were soothed and petted like the screams and tears of
a hurt child.' (6) But heaven help the man who tried to collaborate
with him in some of his missions, even far into life, when age
might have softened the edge of acerbity, and the search for the
Rights of Man should have asserted the first right of tolerance
for one's fellows. Collaboration with him was difficult. Many
said Wells could only work with himself. 'I never met such a
chap,' Shaw wrote. 'I could not survive meeting such another.' (7)

The cheery friendly soul people found in Wells' writings, the
prophet and exuberant novelist, seemed to have little resemblance
to the man himself, but his moods were kaleidoscopic and it
would just be another piece of exhibitionist futility to judge him,
as Shaw sometimes did, by any one of them. The inevitable gaiety
and good humour of everything else Shaw wrote redeemed his
attacks on Wells. Shaw could knife somebody and laugh them out
of feeling it. There were others who burst into wrathful denuncia-
tion of a Wellsian mood with blunter weapons. 'He warned his
friends,' Shaw wrote about his tantrums, 'that he went on like
that sometimes and they must not mind.' (8)

But sometimes they did mind and then hell broke loose, a hell
saturated with the gall of Swift, and inflamed by floods of temper
which ceased and were forgotten with almost the same self-
contained abruptness as the moods of a child.

Kingsley Martin, editor of *The New Statesman,* tells how, during
the war, he met Wells unexpectedly at a luncheon one day and
greeted him with a warmth so genuine that the impression remained in the great man's mind. At the end of the same week a
blistering attack on Wells' latest novel appeared in the literary
pages of *The New Statesman*, and on Monday morning a card
arrived from H. G. which began, 'Dear Judas Martin, So you
really had that stinker up your sleeve did you, when you met me so
warmly on Tuesday?' Instantly Kingsley Martin replied that he
had not seen the review before it was in page proof, but if he had
done so, what difference would H. G. have expected that to make?

Would anyone want an editor of standing to remove the sting before releasing a piece of criticism on poor defenceless authors like his old friend Wells? Kingsley Martin did not put it in precisely those words, but generally, that was the gist of what he said. Wells at once replied with a postcard more explosive than the first: 'Now you're pretending you don't edit your own paper.'

At this point correspondence ceased. But some weeks later they met again at a party, H. G. held out his hand with a sheepish grin, seeking reconciliation, and with a sweetness far more infuriating than his original rancour, bubbled into brilliant conversation, good-humoured, alive, oblivious of anything untoward having happened. That was his special gift. His storms evaporated quicker than the morning dew. He would bounce happily like a pleased boy a second after slaughtering the person now the cause of his pleasure. In an age when masterly conversationalists—Chesterton, Belloc, Wilde, Shaw—abounded, he was a brilliant talker who used his gift, without the least sign of virtuosity, to dissolve sudden black thunders of his own making. 'Nobody was ever sorry to see him'; (9) except perhaps the pompous.

Woe betide the pompous, the stuffy, the smug who had the effrontery to maintain their masks in his presence. There was the very serious-minded young writer who came to worship at his shrine one week-end, bringing the stiff politeness of formal adoration, until Wells, suffocating under the carefully chosen words, made occasion to throw some buttered buns about, narrowly missing the disciple with great skill, pouring out torrents of wit and laughter under which solvent granite itself might have chuckled to life. By the time the disciple left on Monday morning, he was practically throwing buns himself. There was the man who fell into pseudo-scientific discussion of inferiority complexes, assuming very solemn airs about it all. 'I never quite know,' said Wells, 'what constitutes an inferiority complex, but I suspect you have one.'

Possibly it was nearer the knuckle than Wells cared to admit. Busy assessing what, in his 77th year, H. G. Wells amounted to, it was automatically assumed by a number of critics that half his splenetic eruptions were the fruit of a carefully nurtured inferiority complex. He sprang so unnecessarily to defend himself. He was touchy to the point of insanity, they said. It was all the result of that voice, the common accent, the huge pit of inferiority from which he had so painfully and so articulately climbed into the serene upper air. They would even have you believe that his books were little more. In a violent state of reaction—he was too much, too constantly in a state of instant reaction—he threw it all down on paper, eased his pathological condition with a course of words. Passion was as natural to him as the tide to the sea. It seized, shook and convulsed him. It engulfed him in one affair after another, affairs which the normal personality would have survived intact, but which led him into the most explosive pits. It was this which so complicated his private life—or so the story ran—and for half of it some critics went to the same class-conscious, embittered Wells, unnecessarily aware of his ancestry. It was his class-consciousness, they said, which made him turn on royalty. He hated kings and queens. At last confined to his room, he summoned Kingsley Martin one day and said, 'I want you to tell your readers what I feel about royalty.' He had written a letter. Together in the sickroom they agreed on a few small changes which stripped from the letter unnecessarily offensive trappings, Kingsley Martin published it and there were those who waited apprehensively for the results. But nothing happened. No whiff of the barricades came out of the East End, no hint of treason returned to Hanover Terrace. Everyone kept a well-bred silence. The one person it disturbed was H. G. Wells. Had the public at last lost interest in his pronunciamentos, dead echoes of a once great thunder ?

* * *

In matters other than World States, politics, sociology, war and religion, Wells remained far into life an intransigeant realist. It was his realism in the wrong fields which all but brought him down. One could be realistic about most things in England with reasonable chances of survival, but to challenge sex, patriotism and motherhood, to shout view halloo and let loose a glittering rush of words to hound the life not from vice but from what was considered to be virtue, was to invoke the darkest gods of social taboo. Once they tried to refuse him admission to London's most exclusive literary club, they banned and abused him, they attempted to browbeat him into silence, and once there were questions in the House of Commons about his activities; but he continued to talk about sex, love-making and royalty in terms which blenched the cheek of bishop and harlot, and unlike Godwin or the average heretic of his time, continued to live after the fashion of his talk.

7

It is easy to exaggerate Wells, the *enfant terrible*. A far bigger and more important Wells will appear later in this book: a man who cared passionately for the state of the world, who devoted half his life to re-affirming the rationality of man, who exhausted himself in a sustained exposition of a rational world-state, who was sometimes beside himself with his own illumination. But Wells never conformed.

Most people live by permission of other people's opinions. H. G. Wells did not. He did not because he was never in any conventional sense of the word a gentleman. Twist and turn it as you will the word does not fit. Wells qualified far more easily as a genius than as a gentleman, and if he was not *consistently* a genius —what man is ?—he most certainly had moments when he knew what the experience meant. Sometimes in books when words themselves took charge, sometimes in talk when sheer inspiration brought up a dazzling flood of ideas which left his audience aghast with admiration—for they were usually of breath-taking unconventionality; but most disturbingly he knew genius in those deep, passionate moods when one felt in contact with a primitive vision and fury capable of clothing profound experience in beautiful language, and an odd, gnome-like Wells would suddenly peer out from behind the everyday author, a sprite drawing life from some ancient spring, granted incredible vitality. He would have loathed any such fancy. The ineffable mysteries were anathema to him. But at bottom Wells was a primitive, a passionate particle from the deepest caverns of creation.

It is difficult to suffer primitives gladly. They make one feel like the least star in interstellar space. And for all there was the other lovable, endearing Wells, Wells the warm-hearted humanist always ready to consider his fellows, his primitive genius simply did not permit him to behave like, imitate or resemble the average idea of a gentleman. His very physical appearance was against it. If the word has any relation to the thoroughbred people who carry beautifully tailored bodies about the less leprous haunts of London with the natural authority of aristocracy, he was half a world away. He had short arms, a rather shapeless torso and tiny feet. Tailors did not quite know what to do about him. His appearance bothered him a great deal when he was young. But the massive forehead and personality gave unmistakable power to his presence, and the eyes brimming with warmth and intelligence were very fine. His manners could, when he chose, be very bad. They distressed Beatrice Webb deeply on one occasion, and although he had met everyone and everyone knew him, it seemed to render him even less amenable to everyday gentility, until it was as well not to ask anyone to lunch with him until you knew whether they were still on talking terms.

Nor was his brain any help. It encouraged dark investigations of a most ungentlemanly character, and his pre-occupations with its habits had half the makings of indecency. He persisted to the end with excessive affectation that it was a not very extraordinary brain and in the same breath deeply desired to know the nature of its convolutions. He thought it would be interesting to have his brain dissected when he was dead to see where it differed from other brains. But his son Gip pointed out that brain tissue decays at such a rate that it might be pointless unless he was prepared to 'commit suicide in a hardening solution.' (10)

He could always encourage his friends by the simple expedient of wearing their hats. Usually they enveloped his head and settled on his ears. His head was small, but the brain which it carried had a brilliant gift for grasping form and relation, was astonishingly equipped to generalize, to find an outline which held together under strain of appalling stresses, and yet it was a brain quite incapable of anything more than the simplest mental arithmetic, hopelessly inferior at card games demanding memory, and bad, very bad, at chess. He played a brand of patience called 'Miss Milligan' for 25 years without breaking into any very new patterns. He had several goes at mastering French, and lived in France for years, but a fluent Frenchman still baffled him. London was the city he knew and loved best, a city he had tramped for many years, and yet at 65 he confessed, 'If I wanted to walk from Hoxton to Chelsea without asking my way I should have to sit down to puzzle over a map for some time.' (11) He could not remember names, dates and places with any ease. His attention slackened easily, he could fall into facile boredoms, and he insisted in the end, 'For all my desire to be interested I have to confess that for most things and people I don't care a damn.' (12)

*　　　*　　　*

It has been said of Wells that his greatness lay in his ordinariness; take a common or garden person, quicken his pulses, grant him more perceptive vision, make him immensely articulate and you have the twin brother of Wells if not Wells himself. But even in his decline it wasn't true. As the panama hat and the dark glasses became more necessary, his expeditions to the park more shambling, his breath shorter, he remained, in private, a person who could talk and enchant and invent odd little games, but still with the nerve endings of a Strindberg, still capable of attacking anyone who had the temerity to agree with him, and so swift in his change of attitudes that Saturday would find him worshipping Unesco and Monday flaying it alive. But ordinariness—no—except perhaps in moments of unadulterated bad temper.

In those last years the moods were as multi-coloured as ever. He referred, on occasion, to the Royal Society as a lot of bastards, he said the Roman Catholic Church was his *bête noire* and the Labour Party his *bête rouge*, he wandered, remained magnificently irascible, and sometimes—out of nowhere, with no revelance to the present—he brought back bits of the past, brought them back not so much into life as into magic, those enchanted hours which had meant as much to him as all the rest.

The moment by the light of the paraffin lamp in Sevenoaks when *The Time Machine* was first written. The unimaginable goddesses who constantly haunted his imagination until he clothed Catherine Robbins in their likeness. The first magical intimations that illimitable leisure could be his, and the world a great treasure house to be rifled at pleasure. The lovely woman eternally sitting on the wall of his imagination come down at last into life. The discovery of song implicit in words and people and science, a great warm undercurrent with lyrical depths. And talking to Bob Stevenson in the dusk of a Chiswick garden. . . . And W. E. Henley 'red-faced and jolly like an October sunset leaning over a gate at Worthing after a long day of picnicking at Chanctonbury Ring . . . or blue-shirted and wearing the hat that Nicholson has painted . . . laughing and talking aside in his bath-chair, along the Worthing esplanade. . . .' (13)

It was all done with now. He sat in his sun-trap at Hanover Terrace, with the panama hat pulled well down over his head, he sat nodding in old age and reflected it was all gone, dead, done, and they could measure him as they would. Already, measuring Wells had become a national pastime.

Chapter Two

THE SMALL YEARS

HERBERT GEORGE WELLS was born into a world where Lord Palmerston's queer metallic laugh had ceased to register, Lord Derby was too aged to matter and Lord John Russell was beginning to totter. The scene had changed abruptly. The country now watched a new battle between the redoubtable Gladstone and Mr. Disraeli, urbane, witty, quite prepared to flatter his way into power. The year of Wells' birth, 1866, brought the Conservatives into office, and saw Disraeli established as Chancellor of the Exchequer to the delight of Queen Victoria whose intellectual limitations had made hard going of Mr. Gladstone and his dundreary habits.

The General Election of 1874 followed, routed Mr. Gladstone and his Liberals, and brought Dizzy falling on one knee to kiss the Queen's hand, romantically murmuring, 'I plight my troth to the kindest of *mistresses*.' Disraeli understood the old lady's psychology too well. . . . 'You have heard me called a flatterer,' he said to Matthew Arnold, 'and it is true. Everyone likes flattery; and when you come to royalty you should lay it on with a trowel.' As Prime Minister he now wrote Her Majesty daring letters, dramatized the debates in the House for her consumption, and never failed to assure her that Britain was moving towards a time of even greater prosperity and power. Looking back over the century there was some evidence for this.

The first quarter had been consumed by war, the second saw great new forces liberated and growing in the railway engine, factory machines and an untried electorate able to express its will under the Reform Bill for the first time. The third quarter looked for a wave of prosperity which would give Britain cheap food in abundance from the industrial revolution, political stability from the freedom to vote, and scientific powers capable of dominating Nature itself. The Hero as a figure now had a key place in society. Self-reliance, silent martyrdom, the pioneer spirit and a conviction that the British were the Lord's anointed—these were the sustaining precepts of a society which dared not yet admit the full powers of reason in the 1880's. Women needed chaperons, father was infallible, sex something exclusively animal, thinking in women a sign of unbalance, property venerated as a god.

But presently the expectations for the third and last quarters of the century began to flag. Something had gone awry with that benediction which marked out the British for special dispensation. The wheels turned faster, the chimneys grew, a red brick tide invaded the countryside and production reached unprecedented heights; but new and deep divisions developed under the smooth surface, and occasionally, a rumble came out of the depths to the confusion of Established Order.

Romantically, the soothsayers had seen a land of plenty rising from the industrial revolution, and when they were confronted with far too much sweated labour and poverty, they turned to politics for a new panacea. The vote; this would re-affirm the stars of social justice in their courses. But put to the immediate test, the illumination of the vote proved a poor thing. Science then, and all its wizardry, must now be summoned to change the ways of man; but Darwin's theory of natural selection had already undergone certain modifications, and it was rapidly becoming clear that the powers of science held no certain promise of prosperity. Far more disturbing, the deep divisions between wealth and poverty, worker and employer, individual and union, once happily hidden below aristocratic surfaces, now showed signs of volcanic life and could no longer be quelled with blandishment or blarney.

Blatchford's *Merrie England* was to sell a million copies, the Fabian Society to appear in 1884, the Independent Labour Party in 1893. And if a great culture flowered cheek by jowl with brutish living, if there were no mistaking a high inspiration in certain quarters of the land, and moral passion found its place in the least likely corners, Britain was soon faced with growing social confusion in an ideological vacuum.

Nature does not abhor a vacuum more than society. While the new political factions were sorting out their differences and the clash between the classes producing its own ferment, it was left to the artists and the writers to try to fill the gap. Oscar Wilde languidly detached himself from reality and took refuge in a scented palace of art. In his wake he bedevilled the life of many a handsome beau fully at home on a horse, but hard put to it when asked to live *fin-de-siècle*. And then there appeared the far more robust figures of Kipling, Wells, Shaw and Chesterton, each with an invigorating message, each highly skilled in the art of communication, and all flatly contradicting one another in such resounding language as to excite the attention of half the Western world.

Kipling's message was plain and unequivocal for all to see. Lay the flattering unction of Empire to your soul with all its disciplines, renunciations, wealth and humanity, and the desired miracle would be wrought. Chesterton—who with his confederate Hilaire Belloc once rode into the Savoy Hotel on donkeys, demanding food, drink and shelter for man and beast—besought mankind to drop the machines, and march back to the Middle Ages where a Catholic Socialist State would somehow overcome the pestilence and poverty which had troubled those days.

The messages of Shaw and Wells were very different. Fresh, keen and vigorous they came, looking forward not backward. They brought the Rational Word down from the mountain, but unlike Shaw, the Word of Wells had its roots right back in his early beginnings, in those spacious certain days of the middle eighties when the universe of England still seemed timeless for the fortunate, and Wells, a weakly, snub-nosed infant, born of lowly parents, trapped in a dungeon of lower-class stupidity, was not of the fortunate.

*　　*　　*

It is more than eighty years now since Wells' brain first 'squinted and bubbled at the Universe and reached out its feeble little hands to grasp it,' in a bedroom over a china shop in Kent. The year 1866, the bedroom part of a badly built house in Bromley High Street with the dusty shop at the front, full of china and glassware, and—outward evidence of Mr. Wells' deepest preoccupation—an array of cricket accessories. A steep staircase with a murderous twist at its middle ran down to a cavern of a kitchen which relied for light largely on a grating at street level. Abovestairs were two small bedrooms, the front occupied by Mr. Wells and the back by Mrs. Wells, their way of propitiating the gods of reproduction and stopping the family from getting out of hand. Outside a yard. H. G. Wells remembered the yard very clearly till his death. It was 30 feet square, had an earth closet within 20 feet of the well from which they drew their drinking water, and a cement runnel which took the waters from the kitchen sink and allowed them to seep into the earth at a spot where they stood every chance of meeting the closet accumulation and encouraging closer acquaintance with the well. . . .

It was a depressing, impoverished household, where the furniture looked worn to the point of exhaustion, sheets were grey in the interests of economy, the wooden bedsteads bred a particularly vicious brand of bug which smelt worse when slain than when living, and the whole uncertain organism was sustained by a flow of trade in the tiny shop so feeble that it threatened to expire even before competition came, in the form of multiple stores, which assumed, for them, the proportions of a Colossus.

If man is made by his environment, and the question was to haunt H. G. Wells half his life, then Herbert should have been a sorry specimen. His world was for a long time a world of boots. Sagging, shining, broken boots, boots with buttons, boots with grins, dumb, defeated boots, all passing along the pavement within the limited vision offered by the grating above the kitchen, a strange, sub-human world where people did not exist above their knees, and the tread of feet took the place of the human voice.

He wrote about it later, as he wrote about everything, *This Misery of Boots*, by a man who knew boots for what they really were, the key to the material universe, a slip-shod, sickening universe where you had to sell a set of cricket stumps or go hungry; and even when you had sold them, some malignant stroke of fate might bring them back with bitter complaints. Whatever light fell on this grey inward world was shed by an unending array of oil lamps, the one luxury made certain by taking lamps out of stock, bright and beautiful and newly trimmed, and duly returning them whenever a customer appeared.

His mother lived in permanent fear of pregnancy, not because the processes of birth alarmed her, but because it meant another mouth to feed. She was a little pink-cheeked woman with a round innocent face, as incapable of original sin as she was of questioning her conviction that the good God would in the fullness of time remember her plight. Half her energies went to sustaining what Wells considered this sham. She repeated all the dogmas, patiently, unendingly. She was a pious parrot, fearful of escaping from her cage into the outer world, in case there were no angelic wings to bear her. She prayed, Wells said, to Our Saviour, Our Father, the

Holy Ghost and many other magnificent abstractions, to bring a little trade, a little money, a little more attention from husband Joe who had a habit of patting her on the head with masculine solidity—'There now, Saddie'—and then going off to hold communion with his own cricketing gods. Mr. Wells was no mean cricketer. His name will be found in *Wisden's Almanac* at the top of the list of those who have taken, in first-class cricket, four wickets with four successive balls, and names like Lockwood, Ulyett, Brearley, Mold and Trott, kings of the cricketing world, stand beside it. But his cricketing did not get him very far.

The one big answer which came out of the infinite in answer to Mrs. Wells' so persistent prayers was the sudden death, in three days, of her darling sweetest child Fanny, Herbert's sister, and as happy a baby girl as Mrs. Wells was ever likely to see. And did she revolt? Were the incantations empty nonsense from thence on and the universe hostile, godless, beyond comprehension ? No. Quite obviously this little boy Herbert, the flaxen-haired, snub-nosed infant who so successfully scowls out of early photographs, a flurry of petticoats, ribbons, bare legs and curls, was sent to compensate her, and from now on must have all her attention. Somewhere there was a touch of nobility in it all. No matter what happened, she always had an answer, even though the mind contorted itself out of all recognition to get one. But Wells himself has recorded in *Experiment in Autobiography*, 'It is my conviction that deep down in my mother's heart something was broken when my sister died . . . before I was born. . . .'

Hell in the first few years of dawning consciousness was an awful reality to Herbert. It frightened him. It was drummed into him along with the Devil. For Mrs. Wells not only reflected, with slavish devotion, every convention of the day, but was determined that no child of hers should grow into the sceptical, heathen, fanatically anti-clerical person which Herbert did in fact become once he burst out into the light of day. Her strictures must have encouraged his emancipation. Certainly it happened with Queen Victoria. This lady was second only to God in the estimation of Mrs. Wells. She searched out and swallowed, like a beautiful drug, every scrap of information she could muster about the Queen. Words, acts, clothes, goings and comings, lyings-in, court duties, nothing escaped her attention until it became quite clear that this regal person, also a diminutive woman, was Mrs. Wells' idealized self, the lady she so very much would like—fantastically—to be. But Herbert ? Nothing would persuade him to bend his knee to the over-clothed, rather ordinary, vain old lady who dominated England, and caused him to undertake exhaustive journeys just that mother might see the top of her head above a milling crush of people, whispering excitedly 'She's coming . . . she's coming. . . . Take off your hat, Bertie dear . . . !' Seeds of the man H. G. Wells are plainly scattered in his childhood. The Republican born of too much Queen Victoria, the atheist who had heard his mother's appeals to God go unanswered, and the scientist, direct descendant of the young star-gazer who projected his fantasies into interstellar space and tried to make sense of a vast, incomprehensible universe, for the moment drearily hostile.

Both his parents were born to a world where King George IV, the horse and the sailing ship were still supreme. It was a Britain where great estates remained intact, carriages drove through lavender-scented evenings, and touching one's cap to one's betters was a law of nature. Beautiful wayside inns and windmills made up the English countryside, and even if a distant rumble in the lowest caverns of society produced the suspicion of a frown on aristocratic brows, it was not sufficiently prolonged to disturb the essential timelessness of the scene. This was immutable. It would go on. God had willed it so. Joined together in weary wedlock, Sarah Wells, of remote Anglo-Irish stock, and Joseph Wells, who came of a long line of Kentish people, had no reason to suspect that England, one hundred years from the day they took over the shop in Bromley, would be any different from the England they knew, walking soberly to church of a Sunday with everything in its appropriate place. . . . Unless perhaps, unexpectedly, Joseph Wells stole off after a hard day's gardening, to throw himself on the midnight turf beyond the big house of Uppark, in an effort to read the riddle of the stars wherein lay some doubt of England's immortality. It happened occasionally and no one was quite sure whether these midnight excursions revealed unsuspected states of consciousness in Wells senior, or just so much adolescent romanticism. Joseph remarked on this star-gazing habit to his son, a son already alive to his own insignificance against the backcloth of the universe. Wells remembered it right up to his death. That his father bought him books of a kind, and provided an odd collection for him to read, he also occasionally remembered.

In later years he tried to reconstruct what occupied his mother's mind in the long lonely evenings at Atlas House when Joe was away at his inevitable cricket, and it was steadily borne in on her that a dreary perspective of worry, pinch and scrape stretched away to every horizon. Reverie, Wells believed, was at that time the opium of the people. Life became intolerable without it. His mother was a hopeless addict. But in what did her reveries consist? He had more chance to discover when a boisterous son of the landlord of the Bell Inn picked him up one day, tossed him in the air, demanded—'Whose kid are you?'—and failed to catch him as he came down. It was all done in the friendliest fashion, but Wells broke a tibia, there followed a great hullabaloo and he was carried back to be enthroned on the sofa in the parlour where he remained for many days, king of the household for the first time in his life, able to command undreamed of delicacies from brawn, jellies and fruits sent by the landlord's wife to books, books of all kinds, books which suddenly and beautifully rolled the fog away and revealed a landscape, exciting beyond anything he had so far known. What a joy that broken leg turned out to be. It was badly set and had to be rebroken and set again. He yelled long and loudly whenever they touched him. But without it all Wells swore he might easily have remained an inhibited shop assistant, dying long before his time from boredom, exhaustion and appalling frustrations. For now he was away to China and Tibet and the Rocky Mountains, with a book about the stars opening the heavens, and the first dim ideas of evolution becoming clear through a handful of animal drawings, until—most disturbing of all—a flicker of sexuality, aroused with magnificent incongruity by the pictures in *Punch*, first stirred in him passions which were to become so powerful.

The tall and lovely feminine figures of Britannia, La France, Columbia and Liberty, conceived in the untrammelled medium of art, were able to discard the smother of clothes and flounces inspired by the hypocrisies of the day, and open to the world a glory of bosom and shining thigh which entranced Herbert on his lonely sofa in the parlour of Atlas House. Later in life Wells never saw eye to eye with Freudian psychology: 'I cannot detect any Oedipus complex or any of that stuff in my make-up. . . .' He believed that the evidence provided by Austrian and Eastern European people for early psycho-analysis was admissible only in a limited context. The mother-babe reaction might blaze an unmistakable trail in Southern and Eastern European people, where the pattern of kiss and caress was more intimate and more sustained than in Western Europe, but could it be made to explain the staid British, or the puny little boy Wells who 'found no more sexual significance about my always decent and seemly mother than I did about the chairs and sofa in our parlour.' (1) Wells was probably wrong. His open-air healthiness about sex made him suspect any too-subtle explanation, for fear it would complicate what he wanted to remain simple, and whatever variation there might be between the emotional patterns of Eastern and Western Europe, they appeared to differ more in degree than in kind.

But clearly and unmistakably the first stirrings of those strong passions which were to remain so vividly with him for the greater part of his life, were achieved by none other than *Punch*. His dreams quickly took him into the monstrous arms of Tenniel's political divinities, and now at night he often fell asleep across a great swell of breast, made beautiful by a quickening imagination . . . and in the process created a huge and far more satisfying mother figure than the timid, inhibited little woman who sat so many nights beside a dying fire, straining her ears to catch the murmur of acclaim from the multitude as they cheered the figure of Queen Victoria in a striking likeness to Mrs. Sarah Wells.

Chapter Three

DRAPER'S DEVIL

SCHOOL, Mr. Morley, gross revelations about sex, a glory of books, and somewhere behind the bewildering torrent of new experience, a dimly sensed notion that perhaps he was not cast in the same mould as other boys; all this now swept down upon the under-nourished little boy of seven who made his way every morning, in a holland pinafore, up the High Street, desperately gripping a green baize satchel, desiring above all things to slip back again into the world which his books and reading revealed.

But Mr. Morley, his first schoolmaster, would have none of it. Life was real, life was earnest. One had to earn a living. That shadow loomed continuously at the back of Morley's teaching, for all the most intensive course at his grandiloquently named Morley College rarely led to higher flights than clerking at thirty shillings a week. Never had a college been cramped into such confined quarters. It was one room built out over a scullery. The boys left their coats and caps in the scullery, kicked and clattered upstairs, and there confronted, in person, the large bewhiskered apparition of Mr. Morley, one-time usher at an old-established local school, but now launched into education on his own account with the intention of teaching 'Writing in both plain and ornamental style, Arithmetic logically, and History with special reference to Ancient Egypt.' Desks in this one-roomed school were ranged around the walls with a stove at the centre. Mr. Morley's bedroom conveniently overlooked both the schoolroom and his own desk on which stood a huge well of ink where all the pots were refilled, a heap of slates and a cane. What a persistent part that cane was to play in the next year, with Mr. Morley laying about him luxuriously on the slightest provocation, using his hands when the cane was out of reach, and occasionally falling back on rulers, but never failing, whatever the weapon, to pour scorn on his victims while beating them. 'You *imp*-udent, *ill*-iterate, *sni*-vellers —that will *teach* you to laugh behind my back. . . . You chumble-pumpennies. You cardistographers . . . You HOUNDS!' (1)

The only alternative punishment, not recommended by hardened offenders, was standing on a form with arms outstretched holding a slate until one's arms were deadened by the ache.

Thirty pupils attended Morley's college. The more industrious ones eventually sat for an examination organized by an association of private schoolmasters 'for their mutual reassurance, known as the College of Preceptors.' And then clerking, or, final heaven of distinction, book-keeping. Profit and loss, balance sheets, double and single entry played a big part in the evil-smelling afternoons of Morley College, on those occasions when 'old man Morley' did not drop off to sleep and the whole class fell into a fantastic mime of the most outrageous kind wherein the more vulgar the gestures, the more daring one was considered . . . until with a snort, a start and an eye half opened, Morley put his spectacles straight and glanced ferociously round only to find an industriously scribbling class. If he was so unwise as to leave the room it released a series of mysterious missiles and whispered insults, steadily swelling in number and volume until pitched battles started between the bolder boys, and before Morley's footsteps heralded his return, the ring-leaders of the class were locked in mortal combat on the floor in clouds of dust. With the opening door everyone was back in his place, the roar cut off abruptly, and only the settling dust bore testimony to any sort of strife. What Mr. Morley knew about the habits of his pupils and never bothered to reveal; how much he learnt about human nature without coming any nearer to understanding it. . . . Yet his strawberry nose was not entirely lost to the finer scents of learning. In whatever it consisted, he did get something across to Bertie Wells once he found the boy interested in analysing sentences and in mathematical problems. Very soon he discovered that Bertie could make quick little sketches which showed critical insight, that his memory appeared to work without effort, and there were moments when Morley looked sharply at this thin, pale child, in case he hadn't heard aright and later, in the pub, over a glass of something, said to Joseph Wells, his father, that was a smart lad of his. Bertie himself—rated something of a mother's boy, uninterested in games, not very good to look at, precocious, ragged, dominated when it came to street battles by his elder brother Frank, and driven by a wholesome fear of the cane—read widely at home or in the local Literary Institute, running through Humboldt's *Cosmos,* Grote's *History of*

Greece, some of Hume and Chaucer, Captain Cook's *Travels,*
Wood's *Natural History* and *The Lady of the Lake.*

At length came his first examination. Finding his accounts
refused to balance in the last few minutes, Wells prayed dis-
tractedly to the Divine Being he had been taught to regard as
omnipotent, but the bell went and his accounts still seemed awry
and in a burst of heathen resentment he muttered, 'All right God,
catch me praying again.' In the end Wells tied with a second pupil
as top of all England for book-keeping—heaven alone knows
what precise part of England the College of Preceptors covered—
and retired at the age of thirteen covered in doubtful glory 'with
his French crippled for life.'

One other impression remained deeply with him from the days
at Morley's College. Wells recognized, for the first time, his
middle-class status when the boys of the nearby elementary school,
Bromley Water Rats, met in pitched battle on Martin's Hill,
Morley's Bull Dogs, including his own most unbulldog-like self,
and nobody quite knew who carried the day except that Wells
went off with a sweet sense of superiority born of some consciousness of class distinction. He never 'believed in the superiority of
the inferior. . . .' He hated his mother's deference towards her
betters and was prepared to challenge many of them on their own
ground, but that did not lead him to suppose 'the lower orders'
should replace the 'higher' or that anyone had divine rights
because they were downtrodden. Lenin later called him incurably
middle class. If it was not true when Lenin met him, now, at the
age of thirteen, the essential product of a class-conscious shop-
keeper, a scrupulously precise mother and a school-master with
infinite distaste for the 'illiterate rabble,' he was in every sense of
the phrase, 'petty bourgeois.' The rest of his mental attitudes
matched. The English were the Lord's anointed, his head was
full of great battles in which he out-generalled lesser breeds within
the law, made enormous alliances, deployed a devastating line of
fire and never, for a moment, paused to consider the tedious business of economics, social security, unemployment or poverty. It
has been said that he was victimized at home, that he suffered at
the hands of his two brothers, both older than himself. The evidence points the other way. He survived the outrages of Frank and
Freddy without serious pain or injury because he was known to be
delicate and they could never, with an easy conscience, press their

more horrible designs to the final point. Indeed he took a heavier toll than they expected. Once he flung a fork at Frank which stuck into his forehead and left a scar for years. Thereafter Frank and Freddy took to silencing him by the simple process of smothering him with pillows.

Otherwise he continued to eat his meals in the underground kitchen, use the earth closet, watch the boots eternally passing the grating, and read. But he was growing in many ways. Sexually he now underwent much the same experiences as overtake any boy in early, lower middle-class adolescence, although some of them were then socially taboo, and the idea that any boy under twenty-one—when the law created him man—had any profound physiological experience, was considered coarse, except by a handful of people who thought it better to keep what they knew to themselves. For most of the boys adolescence brought black pits of shame, or if not shame, then dirty whispering. With Wells it appears there was shame but no dirtiness. The gathering forces of sex expressed themselves naturally. Things happened to him: 'I had so to speak a one-sided love affair with the bedding'. (2) But he never told a soul.

Even the holidays spent with Uncle Tom at his Thames-side inn Surly Hall, where two strapping daughters shared the duties of the barmaids, did not bring his sex life to the surface or make real any one of his now disturbing fantasies. They liked him at Surly Hall. He was bright and amusing, he said unexpected things, and he could make the most outrageous little drawings of people which sent Clara off into peals of laughter if her sister Kate was more interested to get Herbert reading. Surly Hall was heaven indeed: a beautiful scent on the air when you rose in the morning, the lawn running down to the river, boats and trees and young people ripe for mischief, and great adventures possible in infinite woods and thickets.

Back in Bromley it all seemed impossible again. The underground kitchen, the book-keeping and his mother's secondhand strictures were bad enough, but there were times when the district itself became, after the country, the river and Surly Hall, unendurable. Born on the outskirts of a London still very much as Dickens described it, Wells saw in his childhood and early working days, the ugly stucco streets run riot, crawling squalidly over the countryside. In his student days came the decline and fall of the Victorian era, and with it a further swelling of the cheap brick tide, muddled, confused, unaware where it was going. He was a 'Country-Cockney.' He was born and grew up on the outskirts of London, one of the first citizens of Greater London. Bromstead in *The New Machiavelli* draws the picture perfectly: 'That age which bore me was indeed a world full of restricted and undisciplined people overtaken by power, by possessions and great new freedoms, and unable to make any civilized use of them whatever; stricken now by this idea and now by that, tempted first by one possession and then another. The whole of Bromstead as I remember it, and as I saw it last . . . is a dull, useless boiling-up of human activities, an immense clustering of futilities. It is as unfinished as ever; the builders' roads still run out and end in mid-field in their old fashion. . . . Well, we have to do better. Failure is not failure, nor waste wasted, if it sweeps away illusion and lights the road to a plan. . . .' (3)

To a plan. The phrase, as Ivor Brown has written, came from the very heart of Wells and was to illumine his life, but there was precious little trace of a plan in those first boyhood days, or if it could be described as a plan it was one he loathed. From the start his mother was set on making him a draper, but what black stroke of commerce ever put the company of Rodgers and Denyer in a position to break into his life he never quite knew, for even Morley's College was more palatable to him than what followed. It was not in any case commerce alone. Fate contrived a whole chain of accidents to deliver him into the toils of drapery in his early teens. His father fell from a ladder and broke his leg; his mother, in urgent need of money, became housekeeper to Miss Featherstonhaugh at the big house called Up Park; his brothers Frank and Freddie launched themselves into the only world where Mrs. Wells thought success worth-while—drapery—and the question at last arose what was to be done with pale-faced sickly Herbert, the precocious prattling brat who could not be left alone in Atlas House with an invalid father. Slowly, irrevocably, the only solution available to Mrs. Wells' limited imagination forced itself on her—Drapery!

In the 1870's, Mrs. Sarah Wells worshipped the world where tight little men in coat tails paced their shops, observing younger men, measuring and packaging and persuading. It was a sober certain world where you knew exactly what to-morrow would bring, and now it seemed the only solution to the problem of Herbert. He would be permitted to answer the high call of Drapering, he would learn the trade, earn his living, and blossom into who knew what heaven of haberdashery. So one morning, after 'an evening of sacrificial solemnity,' Herbert bade farewell to his books and his paints and his free-running imagination, was set down from a dog-cart with his absurd portmanteau at the side door of the establishment of Rodgers and Denyer, and the colour went out of everything. Life had been a drab enough business before, Morley's College sometimes an insufferable hell, but once he was ensconced on the high stool of the cash desk and began taking money, giving change, and stamping receipts, an awful fog came down on everything.

Messrs. Rodgers and Denyer were a civilized firm. Work began at half past seven in the morning and finished around eight in the evening. They provided a dormitory of eight to ten beds. There was an underground dining-room. Dusting, almost at dawn, began the day, followed by a bread-and-butter breakfast, preparation of the cash sheets, and the intolerable monotony of taking other people's money for goods in which he had no interest. After eight in the evening Herbert was free for two hours until ten. Lights went out at 10.30.

Very soon it became clear that he must set his own stamp on this routine or fall into unutterable misery. Long spells developed when he disappeared from his high stool and nobody thought to search for him behind the bales in the warehouse where he sat reading for as long as he dare, enthralled by a world which—idiotically—became so much more exciting once conveyed to the printed page. But there was no avoiding the hour of reckoning, that appalling climax each day when the contents of the till were compared with his cash sheets and the two differed with a dreary consistency which sent the manager into great silent rages. Always the till was short. Always something called a 'discrepancy' could not be accounted for. Either large-handed Herbert was doling out change too generously or his makeshift arithmetic had gone awry. If it had happened once or twice with some variation in the symptoms, all might have been well but when, day after day, the till was short without any visible explanation, awful suspicions began to mount in the minds of his employers who set their heads together to concoct a plan while Herbert, half-absent in another world, went his lonely way. He continued to slip off whenever he could to his cousins at Surly Hall and a world where there was music and shaded lamps, people laughed at what he said, and he did not feel a lower form of life without any real justification for existence. The journey had its hazards. A luxuriant imagination and undernourished body created unimaginable ogres in hedge and wood on that last terrifying stretch to the river when the world seemed emptied of life and the inn impossibly remote. . . . But oh the joy, the enormity of relief, when at last the door opened on that other world and his cousins greeted him with warmth and affection. He continued to draw pictures for them. His talk ran full of sparkle. He peeped at the jostling people drinking many-coloured liquids which seemed to open magic casements on worlds closed to him. He wondered at the alchemy of a simple wineglass. The universe reeled at the amount of money poured down delicate feminine throats. And when he tired of watching the drinking, he wandered off to the lawn by the river, threw himself on the turf like his father before him, and stared at the stars, bewildered by their brilliance and some unfathomable message which he could not apprehend.

Each time the shock was the greater when he returned to Rodgers and Denyer. Each time the world of drapery became a blacker hell. Soon he was vowing to smash his way out from the headless effigies, the pin bowls, the wrappered blocks, and the awful permeating smell of cloth which clung about him when he was far away from anyone resembling a shop walker, until it seemed the atmosphere of drapery had penetrated his very being. Perhaps if he ran amok, did something violent, crowned Mr. Denyer with a roll of cloth, split the skull of a difficult customer, kissed a pretty girl in full view of Mr. Rodger or Mr. Denyer or both. . .

In the end it was his employers who took action. They practically accused him of pilfering and though it left Herbert unmoved, his Uncle Tom came bounding to his defence—'Be careful what you are saying now!' The superficial evidence against him was black indeed, with a long chain of deficiencies in the cash desk, but nowhere could they find one shred of evidence to prove that Herbert himself had benefited, and he never, to the end of his drapering career, discovered where the money went. For the moment, in a burst of Christian magnanimity born of prospering trade and lack of evidence, Messrs. Rodger and Denyer said that they were prepared to give him another chance, but now—whether deliberately or not—Herbert irremediably wrecked his career in the world of drapery by crossing the path of the porter and getting his eye blacked in the most determined midnight hue. To slack at his job was bad enough; to give the wrong change, show no reasonable interest in the subtleties of his profession, and inexplicably vanish like a phantom at a crucial point of salesmanship, almost insupportable; but a brawl, with the porter, under the very eyes of the shop-window! This was anti-Christ. Mr. Wells must go. Mr. Wells was not refined enough for the world of drapery.

Chapter Four

GOD OF SCIENCE

THERE followed a brief and glorious spell at Up Park where his mother's work as housekeeper to Miss Featherstonhaugh already showed signs of the deterioration which was to bring her down. He went there soon after his defeat at the hands of drapery —the only place left to take refuge in—and watched with wonder the intricacies of a world remote from anything he had known before, where a whole community recognized the authority of the big house and mimicked its manners and behaviour. Up Park was the unquestioned centre of the universe. Its habits were, immutably, the most desirable habits. It produced snobberies in the servants' quarters at least as subtle and extravagant as anything practised above-stairs, and built a world of hierarchies where everyone knew and kept his place. Nobody dreamed in the immediate environs of Up Park that this way of life, where the Squire and the big house dominated everything, was being sapped, until presently the last vestiges of the feudal system would crumble under the ramshackle weight of modern capitalism. They were already crumbling. But no-one at Up Park wanted to know. Any disturbance to the even flow of life was better ignored unless starvation threatened, and no-one at Up Park came within a mile of any such vulgar experience, or even suffered a sense of shame when the urge to ape the poise of their superiors sprang so obviously from a desire to impress their 'equals.'

It was at Up Park that Wells met half the characters later to sustain the story of *Tono-Bungay* through its length, although the person of Mrs. Mackridge—who painted hair on the bald part of her head, and should surely have had some equivalent in Up Park life—is difficult to trace. 'Her leddyship' comes through clearly. A thing of jewellery rattling on old bones, multiple black skirts, and constant preoccupation with aristocratic lineage, she was drawn from the life, a vivid caricature of Miss Featherstonhaugh.

At Up Park, Wells also made his first incursion into journalism. He produced a daily newspaper, *The Up Park Alarmist*. As striking as its title, it was written from top to bottom by Herbert and scandalized that half of the household which bothered to read it. He plundered the library, discovered a hidden hoard of books in the attic, and gave himself up to Tom Paine's *Rights of Man, Gulliver's Travels,* and many another piece of scepticism not calculated to encourage anyone in the easy persuasions of the day. A telescope held him fascinated for hours at a time, watching the procession of the stars and planets with a lordly sense of reaching unscathed into space, chastened a little by awe at what he found.

But it was Plato's *Republic* which most impressed him, a book he discovered in the library of Sir Harry Featherstonhaugh, a bold free-thinker in his day who had left a wealth of literature to the mercies of his descendants, and unwittingly provided young Herbert with his first glimpse of a society changed not by minor adjustment or creaking legislation, but by imaginative sweeps. Plato dazzled him. He said things which were outrageous beyond Herbert's darkest thoughts. The book was to remain a touchstone to him for years, to become indeed one of the sources of his own *Modern Utopia.*

Many years later in *Tono-Bungay* Up Park suffered badly at Wells' hands, but as a boy he would have given much to lengthen his stay. The house was full of fascinations. There were unexpected rooms and forbidden territories to be explored, there were endless adventures possible in the grounds, there were strange personalities, people who carried beautiful scents wherever they went, servants unendingly entertaining, and books he could read with no thought of sudden discovery behind the bales in the warehouse, and no voice to bellow 'Wells' at moments of deepest reverie. But drapery lay in wait for him just around the corner all over again, drapery, cold and malignant after another swift reversal at the hands of a slightly less arduous apprenticeship. By January 1881 his mother, full of the fear that he would never 'settle down,' decided that he must avail himself of an opening in chemistry, considered of secondary importance, in her eyes, to drapering. So once again the pathetic little portmanteau was filled with his few tawdry belongings, there were tear-stained farewells, and Up Park with its beautiful grounds and books and leisure, faded away.

Wells joined the establishment of a certain Mr. Samuel Evan Cowap, a chemist of Church Street, Midhurst, the drowsy Sussex backwater which later reduced Ponderevo in *Tono-Bungay* to morbid frustration. There, in a not uninteresting world of great coloured globes, pills, quackery, gossip and rabid ambition, he learnt how to roll a beautifully symmetrical pill without wasting his materials, but failed to unravel the deeper mysteries of pharmacy for the simple reason that he had no Latin. Repairing this shortcoming with the help of Mr. Horace Byatt, M.A., headmaster of Midhurst Grammar School, he astonished his tutor by mastering in four or five hours the greater part of Smith's *Principia (I)* which took the tradesmen's sons a year. This feat helped to solve the troubles which again dogged his efforts to settle down as an apprentice. The inner joys of chemistry remained closed to Herbert in the one month it took him to discover that he was little more than a bottle-washer whose grander moments involved 'minding' the shop. But at the end of the month the now familiar head-shakings on both sides were not repeated with Mr. Cowap. Herbert, in fact, quite liked the bright little shop with its multiple drawers filled with mysterious charcoals and sulphurs, and it was only the cost of becoming a dispenser which checked his ambitions and prevented him from ending his days as manager in Timothy White's or Head Dispenser in Boots, given of course to fantastic experiment, but never dreaming of the untapped talents straining beneath the surface. His mother agreed that the way to dispensing was too expensive and the study involved seemed immense. So Wells retreated from behind the coloured globes and the patent medicines as he had from the cash desk. But Mr. Byatt of Midhurst Grammar School had been deeply impressed with his pupil's performance, and now Mrs. Wells decided he might as well become a boarder at the school for a spell, until with the help of God, a great deal of ingenuity, and that stroke of luck which had so far viciously eluded her, she could settle this fractious son of hers in a Good Position. It seemed a little miracle to Herbert. It was more than he had ever dared to hope. It was as if the dungeon walls of drapery and chemistry dissolved about him to let flooding in the warmth of fellowship, fellowship with books and unhurried people in the pleasant ivy-coloured house at the far end of the town where Byatt had his school; but once again it was shortlived. He became the thirty-third pupil on February 23rd, 1881. Still a blushing, uncertain, undernourished boy of fourteen with a tendency to gabble everything he said, he was continually possessed by spurts of high spirits which he relieved in wild larks undertaken with one or two friends, or by the sudden appropriation of a fellow student's exercise book in which he dashed down a few lines resembling one or other of the pupils in such comic disarray as to excite the laughter of half the class. He was lively and popular. He wrote an interesting essay or two. He romped and enjoyed himself but he did not learn very much. For seven happy weeks this way of life went on. Then his mother's consuming passion to see him safely settled in the world rose up with renewed urgency. Like a knell came the news that he was to go back once again into the jungle from which he had so lately escaped. It was a prison sentence. This time he was condemned to four years' incarceration in another drapery establishment. What manner of thing was this to do to a mind growing fit to fill the universe, possessed by intellectual appetites more voracious than sex? But his protests went unheard. Nothing it seemed could stop his return to drapering now.

Yet even as he entered Hyde's Drapery Stores in Southsea on that first abysmal day in the summer of 1881, a voice kept repeating at the back of his mind: 'Brother Fred went this way—Don't let it engulf you too—There must be a way out—You must not *succumb*. . . .' For another year and more than a year he did succumb. He sank back into the routine of moving headless effigies about the shop with just sufficient consideration for their postures to avoid any hint of indecency, he replenished interminable pin-bowls, he panted with malignant lengths of cloth intent on wrapping themselves around him, and listened to calls, an unending cacophony of calls which he remembered half his days and could hear years afterwards as though they were still on the air. . . . 'Where is Wells ?—Idiot ! Show the lady the silk !—Haven't I told you before, boy !—Late Wells !—Late again !—Why is it always *you* !—Why ? Wells ! Wells ! BRING ME WELLS !' At night in the stuffy dormitory it sometimes became a great bellow of sound which went reeling down infinite corridors of the mind until it burst and he awoke with a shout—'Wells !'—on his lips, and his fellow assistants said he was a nasty type who dreamt about himself. Maybe Hyde's Drapery Store had its enlightened people. Herbert was not disposed to appreciate them. Every day drapery became a more ruthless device for crushing the spirit. With less than two of his four years' sentence served, he knew it could not go on. The voice of his genie was now high-pitched: 'At any cost get out. . . .'

'I suppose,' he said addressing the Shop Assistants' Conference many years later, 'if I had had a normal ability to pack parcels and respect my shopwalker I should have been a draper's assistant all my life. What got me out of the business was nothing but incompetence. I couldn't handle the stuff skilfully, and I couldn't keep bright and attentive for long spells. I can work pretty well in short spells but then I must knock off for half an hour or so before I can go on, and the staying power of my colleagues filled me with envy and astonishment. . . .' (1)

It wasn't only that. Wells hated actively and with venom this world of insufficient food, drudgery and abominable dormitories, the way of life where ignorant tight-lipped little men with half his brain tried to tyrannize him with their shouts of 'Wells! Idiot! Show the lady the silk!' He had enormous reserves of nervous energy and little physical strength. Where bursts of violent activity in reading, larks or drawing held him enthralled, he was bored, bored to the uttermost, by steady slogging attention to goods and customers. Half his nervous energy he now threw into his private world which became more animated every month, a world where he kept notebooks to record great primaeval questions—'What is matter? What is Time? What are WE?'

Lying awake at night he read by candlelight a popular book of education which may have been Cassell's, Chambers' or some other; his own memory was blurred. It led him into fascinating speculations about the nature of light, the wonders of metaphysical flights, the simple differences between subjective and objective thinking. But the grip of drapery could not be broken by notebooks, great questionings of the universe or the burning of midnight oil. That 'hell of a life' it all became, until many years later he released it in the novel *Kipps,* the unfortunate Kipps, driven by a job he hated, harried by small cruelties and terribly aware of interminable hours when merely to be present so long in a drapery store was unmitigated misery. It all reached a pitch where he contemplated suicide. 'The cool embrace of swift-running, black deep water on a warm summer night couldn't be as bad as crib-hunting or wandering about the streets with the last of one's courage gone. . . .' (2) He used the threat to shake his mother's determination to keep him at drapery. The voice of his genie, now beside itself, had become hysterically insistent on escape somehow, somewhere, at any price.

And then he ran away. At the age of sixteen, one summer morning in August 1883 when the balmy air and the sun lured him —as it later lured Mr. Polly—down the open road, he suddenly knew he would choke if he did not dodge under the hand of Messrs. Hyde's Drapery Stores and answer the call. He ran away one Sunday morning and tramped seventeen miles to tell his mother that he would rather die than go on being a draper.

It needed the awful sense of pursuing vengeance in the likeness of a monster draper and a steadily increasing ache in the pit of his stomach from lack of food, to drive him along those unending seventeen miles. One other hope sustained him—that he would meet his mother before he met anyone else. If the evidence of *Tono-Bungay* means anything, and it is closely autobiographical, he planned to intercept his mother on her way home from church. So it happened. Coming within sight of the real Up Park, he lay in wait in the bushes with a queer feeling of brigandage, wondering with near terror in his heart what reception he would get.

Presently they came out of church, in straggling groups, the servants first and the laundry maids and the footmen, and then the prim figure of his mother clad in sober Sunday black. His heart leapt at sight of her. Then he was on his feet shouting in schoolboy fashion, 'Coo-ee mother—coo-ee,' running towards her. 'My mother looked up, went very white and put her hand to her bosom. . . . I suppose there was a fearful fuss about me. . . . But I held out stoutly. "I won't go back . . . I'll drown myself first." ' (3)

In the end drowning was not necessary. His mother said she would do everything she could if only he would return to the shop. Herbert made the ignominious journey back again, expecting far worse trouble at Hyde's Drapery Store. But an unexpected solution quickly presented itself. Mr. Horace Byatt, headmaster of Midhurst Grammar School, must have had a high respect for Herbert's potentialities. Ill-educated, under-nourished, and still very slip-shod in his speech, he was hardly the best material to become a student master in any school, but Byatt now offered him a job as student assistant at £20 a year. Sarah Wells cried and wrangled. She had set her heart on giving Herbert the good sound start in life which drapery alone could offer, she had pinched and scraped to that end, and he must take this into account before he ran off on such a wild impulse as schoolmastering. Herbert did take it into account, but he knew that what appeared to Mrs. Wells as a simple decision to be made according to family precedent was in fact a major crisis in his life. He had been driven and harried too long. Now he made up his mind and sat tense and white and silent. Nothing would move him. This time, whatever the cost, he was breaking the yoke of drapering. The battle, says Wells, taught him two guiding principles, which are interesting portents of the person he was to become and astonishing in a man who professed —at that stage at least—a profound sympathy with the claims of others: 'If you want something sufficiently, take it and damn the consequences. . . .' 'If life is not good enough for you, change it. . . .' Always supposing one was richly endowed, like Herbert Wells, with special gifts for breaking the Universe to one's will.

Now grown into a thin fair youth of seventeen with badly fitting clothes, pale face and highly impulsive ways, Wells was about to undergo the metamorphosis he so much craved when a final obstacle arose which struck fresh fear into his heart. The Endowed Schools Act insisted that he must be confirmed by the Church of England before he could become a student assistant in any sort of school. A 'young sceptic,' scornfully aware that his own childhood made nonsense of the ways of the Almighty, he had gone to church often enough with his mother and brothers, but doubt, if not downright disbelief, was strong in him. Hume, Humboldt and Spencer were not the best nourishment for the unquestioning Christian. He had fed at their tables and starved in the underworld of drapery. The Devil of his own underworld was much more real to him than any red-fanged monster conceived by the Holy Books, and if he refused to accept the mumbo-jumbo of religious confirmation, he risked, it seemed to him, a hell at least as flaming as any other. 'The result was that I committed the first humiliating act of my life. I ate doubt and was confirmed and lost my personal honour.' His surrender was not quite so abject. The young curate who initiated him into the rites of confirmation was first subjected to a merciless cross-examination about the exact date of the Fall, what transubstantiation really meant, why the bread and wine carried mystical significance, and several other highly sceptical questions quite beyond rational answer. Having heard the answers, Wells said 'So that is what I am to believe.'

33

There was a pause. Then he asked, would it do if he accepted them in spirit, and the eager young curate immediately responded, 'It is much better that way. . . .' (4)

So Wells was confirmed, drapery put behind him and life in Byatt's school began. As a teacher he did not excel. He was competent, hard-working, sympathetic to his pupils. But as a student he performed acrobatic feats of learning to win the ambitious Byatt a number of awards which he badly needed. The process became almost farcical. Solemnly every evening a special class took place at Midhurst Grammar School, with Byatt the master, and Wells the solitary pupil, one ensconced at his high desk correcting the exercise books of a totally different class, the other sitting in the body of the room, splendidly isolated, swotting from one textbook after another. They were in effect bogus classes of one. They enabled Byatt to win £2 or £4 for every award which Wells captured. They enabled Byatt to teach human physiology, vegetable physiology, geology and many another subject of which he knew little or nothing, by the simple expedient of buying his sole, star, indefatigable pupil an elementary text book in each of them, and letting his enormously swift mind soak up the necessary quota of facts. The Board of Education was broadminded in those days. But it had, it transpired, advantages for Wells as well as Byatt. An audacious idea born of the awards presently occurred to him. Could it be that he was equipped to try his luck for a scholarship as a teacher-trainer in the Normal School of Science, London ? Was it possible that he could escape from Midhurst to a quite different way of life ? His minute bedroom at Midhurst, with its dormer windows and bulging walls, the ugly schoolroom and its forty-five pupils, Mr. Byatt and the backwater existence in this forgotten mid-Sussex town, seemed impossibly apart from the Olympian habits of South Kensington and the god-like figure of T. H. Huxley, still startling the world with his mechanistic heresies; but at this point the Board of Education took things into its own hands. It was impressed with the performance of H. G. Wells. And one day an egg-shell blue document arrived from London. He opened it with trembling fingers and read of things he never really believed could come into his life. To be paid £1 1s. 0d. a week while other people talked to him ! To work in the same college as Huxley—T. H. Huxley, the god of English biology, the holy presence who permeated half of scientific thought. To be allowed to sit at his feet and listen to his lectures. To live at the expense of the Government in London. . . . The world reeled a little as these unbelievable things swam into certainty, and he read on down the page until the stilted English grew warm, colourful and very nearly beautiful.

*　　*　　*

He came to London for the first time in the summer of 1884. The city fascinated him. He lost his heart to London at a very early age and never quite recovered it. He was to roam the cities of Russia, know the Riviera, wander widely in America and Europe and the Mediterranean, but always he came back to London, and the grimy, splendid Cockney life. For the moment it was a harsh, hostile London, not prepared to compromise with young science students trying to live on a guinea a week. But 'one day, one September day in that vanished incredible past, before the telephone and incandescent light, when men still rode on ordinary bicycles and Gladstone prevailed, I found myself with a black bag and beating heart amidst a great tumult in the hall of the Science Schools, seeking Huxley in an unobtrusive manner.' (5)

He found the laboratory first, sat himself on a little round stool and opened his Parker's *Zoology*, there being no time to waste if he was to become, as he fiercely intended, a great scientific man. But a barrage of students breaking through the little black door constantly distracted his attention, the page blurred, the wonder of it all broke over him afresh, and he gave himself up to the enormity of—research—research going on now, around him, 'research which might at any minute make a Discovery !' 'A man with a lot of gummed labels and a voice asking for his name' brought him to earth again. And then from the door of the preparation room emerged another figure, 'carrying many warm and twitching rabbits. He carried them by the hind legs and flopped one down in front of each student.' Wells' turn came. 'Whop it went on the desk and there was a terrifying mess waiting dissection.' (6) Brought at last to the actual cutting, considerably perturbed because the rabbit continued to twitch, he suddenly became aware, looking downwards as he was, of a pair of feet approaching with an assurance not customary in the ordinary student. He looked up and drew breath sharply. There was the man, no longer a name, no longer an awesome abstraction, but in the flesh, with deep-set brown eyes shining underneath the great eyebrows, and a mane of hair receding from the 'wall of a forehead,' preoccupied, pacing, not very aware of H. G. Wells or what he was doing.

'Possibly he might in a moment speak to me or look at the gory mess before me. . . . I pretended to be absorbed and not particularly aware of his presence. I consulted my Zootomy and scrutinized those bowels, then, with elaborate delicacy and a certain air of concentrated attention I made a little cut that meant neither harm nor good—and pricked a hole in the main branch of the portal vein !' (7) When he looked up out of this horror, expecting pure fire from those magnificent eyes, he saw only the receding back of Huxley. He had passed on.

Wells found in T. H. Huxley a figure into whose likeness as a great scientist he desired to step from the moment of meeting. Hero-worship, rabid and unashamed, began and lasted far into life. Huxley's teaching gripped and held his imagination. It was the teaching of the supreme rationalist which said that nothing became a fact until it was susceptible of proof, and faith remained a pointless delusion without organized evidence to support it. The logical outcome of Darwin and the days when the question—is man ape or angel ?—convulsed Victorian society, Huxley's answer was very different from the urbane utterance of Disraeli, 'I am, my Lords, on the side of the angels.'

These were the days when the inheritance of acquired characteristics had fallen into serious doubt and the evidence of Weissman was in the ascendant, the days when the 'phylogeny of the invertebrata was still in a state of wild generalization, vegetable morphology concerned itself with an elaborate demonstration of the progressive subordination of the oophore to the sporophore and even the fact of evolution as such was still not universally conceded. . . .' (8)

Huxley had arrived at his mechanistic universe by scientific processes, by testing inductive conclusions against actual experiment, and in those days it seemed to fix our methods of thought for all time, and Wells rose excitedly to it. Here was the key to a new way of thinking. Here was a higher organization of evidence and experience. Apply it to the feckless sordid scramble of everyday living, and the distortions would fall smoothly into place, into a higher pattern which Wells was already coming to believe to be implicit. It was unfortunate, perhaps, that his own life was later to produce massive denials of the rationalist philosophy when matters he detested temperamentally were happily obliterated without rational analysis, but for the moment the cold, scientific star shone untarnished.

As a student, in the Christmas examinations he took a first class in biology, a second class in the February botany examinations, and a first class again in advanced zoology. But with the new session Huxley was gone, overtaken by a breakdown in health, and Wells' student universe echoed emptily even though the uneasy, irritable, black-bearded G. B. Howes, later Professor Howes, so brilliantly took his place. But Howes, Judd, Lockyer and Guthrie could never excite Wells' imagination like Huxley. His concentration relaxed. It was still comparatively easy to distinguish himself whenever he chose to make the effort, but his discursive mind disliked being tied too long to one subject and it soon became clear that he lacked the ability to blot out extraneous attractions and canalize his efforts into one stream. Soon, a new and disastrous habit had grown in him. He took to disappearing from the laboratory—as he had disappeared from the draper's stool—into the Dyce and Foster reading room where it quickly seemd to him that men like Blake and Carlyle had far more to say than Judd and Lockyer, and the rhythms of their style lured him away from his note-books into a world of noble language and idea, uninhibited by weight or measurement. The habit grew. Words and their inner music began to fascinate him. Presently, every day, he went through the ritual of swearing to do two hours on physics or anatomy before giving way to the Reading Room, and with hardly one hour gone found himself back deep in Carlyle, Blake or another. Slowly it dawned on him that he was slipping. Presently he knew he was not going to fulfil his brilliant promise as a scientific student. Within a year something far more serious had happened. By 1887 his chances of doing research had died, he was in distinctly bad odour with his lecturers, and looked like going to the scientific bad. But what limited his success in applied science widened it in literature. A mind temperamentally hostile to the slow minutiæ of the scientific approach was perfectly at home with word pictures and sweeping visions. If only he had realized this and not forever hung on the coat-tails of science, craving distinctions he could only achieve by choking the very roots of his personality, he might not have died a disappointed man. As it was, he emerged from the Normal School with a comprehensive picture of the Universe which no ordinary education would have given him, and a treasure trove of ideas for anyone who wanted to become a writer. He understood the long painful processes of gestation, knew how 'the ancestral caecum . . . shrank to that disease net, the appendix of to-day,' had traced the development of man's lungs, watched the transformation of gill into ear, spent long months studying physics, biology, astronomy, geology and palaeontology, and had come at length to place man in the perspective of the Universe, to understand his relative importance in the scheme of things. It was a vast unfolding of a quite new view of life, exciting, fascinating and promising yet more remarkable discoveries—if only one pressed on into new fields.

The quality of Wells' *élan vital*, which sustained him through many exhausting years, became very evident in the student, an alarmingly thin apparition, always under-nourished and eternally trying to make ends meet on his one guinea a week. Lodging, food, clothes, fares, sometimes a doctor, less often a dash of entertainment, had all somehow to be squeezed from the guinea. Sometimes it meant a fourpenny lunch of dead lettuce, doubtful tomato and a few mouthfuls of bread. Laundry was an impossible luxury, the theatre rarely achieved by a great struggle to get a seat in the gallery. It was a squalid harassed existence. Only the most vital brains could overcome the physical lethargy induced by lack of food, air or exercise which was the common lot of poor science students in those days. Yet Wells' brain sparked and bubbled increasingly, sometimes thrown into great glooms and depressions, sometimes driven on by the sheer fascination of what might happen next into tremendous bursts of work, hilarity and larking.

Around him the London of the middle eighties went its way enlivened by beautiful carriages, fine houses and rich living, pressing back into the gutter the less fortunate, the poor and sometimes starving. These were dismaying times. The gap between rich and poor steadily widened. Rioting occasionally disturbed the scene and a nasty odour of destitution too often came up from the depths of the city as though its culture were built on human drains. While labour leaders protested that strikes were not a revolutionary weapon, the Social Democratic Federation disseminated its gospel which came close enough to revolution for the difference not to matter. It was a London of beautiful mansions and grey slums, of leisured men and women determined to preserve their ignorance of the social underworld intact, and working people who only dimly apprehended that God had not irrevocably cast them for their lot. Despite the unemployment and depression abroad, solid British business men spread themselves spaciously, certain of their right to do just as they pleased and supremely unaware of any threat to their security, because supremely unimaginative. The telephone had yet to appear with a touch of sorcery, and there was never a car on the streets. In the advertisement columns of *The Times* teachers were called for by the hundred at salaries which sound like pittances to-day, huge advertisements for Wincarnis repeated insensibly down the whole length of many pages 'Wincarnis is Good for You,' and Carlsbad Powder was Recommended by the Clergy with a fine disregard for spiritual discrimination. Englishmen remained curiously convinced that they were the Lord's anointed, that right would prevail even though their gods—Dickens, Darwin, Gladstone—were shifting in their courses. The staid mid-Victorian period was about to give place to the more restless late Victorian, the upper classes would soon be living rather deliberately *fin-de-siècle*, the lower classes already showed signs, alarming signs, of truculence and Queen Victoria approached the zenith of her power with just the right touch of divinity. Kipling caught and developed the spirit of Empire in books and poems which found a lofty destiny in the shabbiest colonial outpost and fired the youth of Britain to carry the White Man's Burden. If a little later Kipling suffered occasional misgivings they were quickly swamped by national smugness; if his moral purpose was sometimes mistaken for Imperial patriotism, in the end it became Imperial patriotism, yet there was no mistaking an authentic ring about his work which went back down the ages to the Hebrew poets of old.

But Kipling, Queen Victoria and *The Times* advertisements did not reveal a glimmer of the great tides which were moving under the surface of London; indeed they helped to obscure them. There is nothing more calculated to reconcile people to their lot than the flattering unction of Empire. Yet smothered though it was, the conflict between capitalism and labour, between worker and employer, trade union and individuals, threw up occasional flashes which the intellectuals at least read aright. All ran smoothly on the surface except for those impossible occasions when the rioters disturbed the quiet of the clubs in Pall Mall itself, and looking out from their windows clubmen observed unmannerly clashes between police and demonstrators. The Royal Commissions to investigate all this were yet a year or so away, and somehow Royal Commissions seemed utterly remote to the man in the street with his immediate problems; even more so to the unfortunates who didn't know where their next meal was to come from, and to science students trying to live on £1 1s. 0d. a week. There was a deep contradiction at the heart of this society, but for all the pettiness, for all the heedless money-drunk ideas, there was no mistaking an essential greatness in the scene. The fog-bound capital influenced half the world, moral passion found its place in unexpected quarters, the everyday workmen showed a statesmanlike calm when they might have become a rabble, and if irrevocable forces were driving society along its path into a new way of life, Britain refused to be hurried or flustered in the process.

Wells had to be a Socialist. No-one bred in such a background, living on so little, could escape the creed. And wearing a violent red tie, he hurried through the gas-lit streets of London to hear William Morris on Socialism, Bradlaugh on Atheism, Graham Wallas on Classical Philosophy, Gladstone on Home Rule, and 'that raw aggressive Dubliner' George Bernard Shaw on everything—although 'I object to Bernard Shaw rather: he is such a giddy creature.'

Intermittently Socialism came and went in the rest of his life, fluctuated and changed, sometimes came close to disgusted annihilation, but never quite died. For the next few years he was fiercely, sarcastically Socialist. Neither it nor his comparative failure in the Normal School prevented his becoming, at length, a teacher of sorts, erratically brilliant in zoology, and capable of improvising wherever else the need arose. His abilities varied according to his mood and how much he had eaten, but Mr. T. Ormerod, one of his pupils in those days, says of him:

'I have a very clear recollection of the man himself, somewhat below average height, not very robust in health, and with evident signs of poverty, at least disregarding any outward appearance of affluence. In dress, speech, and manner he was plain and unvarnished, abrupt and direct with a somewhat cynical and out-spoken scorn of the easy, luxurious life of those who obtained preferment and advantage by reason of social position or wealth. He quoted more than once the couplet:—

> When Adam delved and Eve span,
> Who was then the gentleman ?

It came in quite naturally in his teaching about the classification of species, and asides in which he frequently indulged. He lectured for an hour each morning, and this was followed by a period of two hours in the laboratory, when he came round to each student in turn to explain and correct his dissections, and it was here that we really got to know the man. He was extremely painstaking and evidently anxious to help each student. He was very satirical about the highly coloured drawings in which some of us indulged, and indicated by a few bold lines inserted in our drawings the essential points of importance. He insisted that education consisted in the ability to differentiate between things of real importance and those of secondary or trivial import. Behind the biting satire of which even in those early days he was a master, there were a real kindli-ness and a very evident sympathy towards his pupils, many of whom were struggling to obtain a university degree, an achieve-ment not so easy and straightforward as it is to-day. Wells had a profound regard amounting almost to a reverence for Huxley. . . .'

But although Huxley remained his god, and conditioned his thinking for years to come, science, teaching and Kensington were not much more than very uncertain stepping stones which led him in a direction quite opposite from the Normal School of Science. Wells did not yet know where he was going.

Chapter Five

FIRST WIFE

HE had gone to live with his aunt in the Euston Road. It was arranged that he should have an upstairs room to sleep in, and study at night in the gas-lit, underground room. But the whist, piano-playing, darning of socks and constant exchange of tiny superficialities which went on in the front room, night after night, drove him time and again to his bedroom where by candlelight, in an overcoat, with his feet stuck in a drawer to avoid the draught, he tried to concentrate on physics and geology. Aunt Mary, a bright-eyed little woman, lovably disposed towards him, brought a new warmth and affection into his life, and it was all very different from the hard-faced landladies he had known, who believed that students were the devil's brood to be accepted on sufferance. But the move to his aunt's house changed his life in another way.

He was sitting one afternoon having tea with Aunt Mary and her sister, reflecting that they both looked grimy from eternally emptying ashes and slops, scrubbing and dusting, when a pretty dark-eyed girl came into the room, confused with shyness, and was introduced as cousin Isabel. Her appearance made a sudden silence in Herbert's mind. Isabel was lovely. The broad brows, the grave expression, the simple easy carriage. . . . All the repressed urges of adolescence rose up in him with enormous power. He had no idea of what lay behind the face, but he knew she was infinitely desirable, the only lovely thing he had encountered for months in a squalid world of cheap clothes, poor food and warped minds.

Presently, in the mornings, he joined Isabel as she set out for the photographer's shop where she worked as a retoucher, leaving her at Regent Street to go on across the Park to the Normal School of Science. From the enchantment of her company he sometimes walked on in a state of near exaltation, and between Regent Street and Exhibition Road, was frequently overtaken with the vision of a world stripped of shabbiness, a noble world where everyone could read the message of the stars, at the moment a shining, indivisible Socialist message, permeated somehow with the presence of Isabel. Presently, they kissed in the shadow of the stairs.

It was gauche, inexpert. Isabel resisted with a sense of sin. But it happened again, and now there was no mistaking a warmth in the embrace, which quickly carried them into a world of fantasy where all the repressed urges in Herbert insisted that he was deeply devoted to his cousin and that she, in her own queer, hesitating fashion, was ready to respond. Sheer hunger forced on them an infatuation which had at first no validity in itself; or very little. They were attracted by some kindred spark, and for the moment a web of magic ran glistening into the darkest corner of Euston Road, but 'I think from the beginning we should have been brother and sister to each other, if need, proximity and isolation had not forced on us the role of lovers . . . ,' he wrote fifty years later.

Lovers indeed. A stifled kiss in the shadow of the stairs and all real urgencies resisted still did not break the spell elaborately spun in Herbert's mind. Every evening he set off to meet her and bring her home. They walked back whispering in darkened squares. There was magic in a lamp seen amongst the trees. And on Sundays they went to Regent's Park where Herbert babbled valiantly about the vision already growing in his mind, an artist's vision of the new world, enthralled by its light and colour, and hopelessly failing to impress it on the kind conventional universe of Isabel, firmly cast in the role of a pretty young woman walking out in her Sunday best. Their temperamental difference was obvious to the least observant eye. But not to Herbert's: 'She was to be my woman whether she liked it or not. . . .' And in the end it seems they were in love with one another.

Two incidents now intervened which threatened not only the glow Isabel had brought into his life but his everyday habits, career and very bread-and-butter. Leaving the Normal School of Science he found himself without career or future, and a mood of near panic seized him as he looked out on the world and wondered what was to become of him next. He had neglected his studies, failed to develop his interest in literature, done everything to land himself in a mess at the very moment when Isabel seemed most desirable. But there must be a job for him somewhere. Surely, half-educated as he was, a scientific dolt, with literary sirens continually luring him away from the obvious path of duty, he could find something to do in this black, benighted world? Surely there would be something one day in the advertisement columns . . . and at last there was. A job in an Academy close on the borders of Wales. He applied and was accepted. The job had appalling drawbacks. It meant leaving London, it destroyed the beautiful dream of quickly making Isabel his own, and there was other fascinating company just beginning to open out to him which would have to be abandoned; but he must earn some money or face far worse hazards, and the thought of country air and food had its attractions.

Three weeks later he concluded that there were some experiences worse than unemployment, slum air and a lost career. Holt turned out to be a squalid ill-run travesty of the word Academy, where the boys slept three in a bed, lessons took place with the uncertainty of April showers, and downright disorder threatened with such persistence that the headmaster freely advocated in private the physical punishment he abhorred in public. The girls in the school, young enough to have been sweet, were prematurely soured, and the village of Holt which should have had some pretensions to the picturesque in the year 1887, was blandly overlooked by a gasworks. From the first few weeks Wells knew he would have to find some way of escape from this grey, flat, desolate land, the dirty school and Presbyterian habits, and very soon the way was clear. His Scripture lessons on Sunday afternoons became erratic, his weekday lessons gim-crack, and an inordinate quantity of cricket and football began to fill the gaps. As his school work slackened he turned inward for his satisfactions. Presently he slipped into the habit of writing and, finding the exercise easy and exciting, wrote more. Living in the world of fiction was like living in another dimension. People, events, landscapes, could be summoned to serve one's will. They now served Wells prodigally. He wrote several short stories and almost completed a novel, *Lady Frankland's Companion*, and if *The Chronic Argonauts* was not first written at Up Park—it is in doubt—it was written here.

And then, in the middle of one hot August afternoon, dragged from the depths of his imaginative fortress to take part in a football match, someone knocked him down in the most ungentlemanly manner. It was an abusive foul. It sent him sprawling. Badly shaken, he staggered off the field to the derisive cries of his pupils whose implacable code permitted no retreat while any player stood on two feet or even one. But he went off, was violently sick, and presently, answering the need to urinate, found himself looking into a pot with a considerable quantity of blood. He became delirious. He remembered at one point crawling over the floor in search of water. Then the doctor arrived, there was much head-shaking and the headmaster grew suddenly anxious. Still white and shaken and aware of the peculiar tang of blood in his mouth—a taste he soon came to dread—Wells heard the doctor tell the headmaster that he must be suffering great pain, and contrived to play the part of stoical endurance under the torments of hell, when in fact he felt no discomfort. At first his heroism improved the very doubtful quality of the school nursing system, but soon the headmaster grew impatient, overcame his awe at Herbert's courage and suggested, with some preliminary attempts at sympathy, that he should return to London. Grimly determined to earn the £20 due to him when he had completed six months' teaching, Wells refused and a few hours later went back, pale, stiff and unhappy, to the schoolroom. A second haemorrhage followed. This time the doctor murmured something about consumption and said that he must have careful nursing, proper food and constant attention. It was clear now that he could not stay at Holt. Once more there was only one place left in the world and he quickly arranged to join his mother again at Up Park. There she remained for the moment as housekeeper to Miss Featherstonhaugh, refusing to admit by now advanced deafness and a wild confusion in her housekeeping. And there, very soon, Wells was burning gore-laden handkerchiefs to avoid reducing his already distressed mother to the point of panic, and beginning to realize that this was no passing accident.

The affair of the trampled kidney had in it all the makings of tragedy, and Wells, not slow to draw the worst conclusions, drew them with such gusto, irony and high spirits that perhaps the very resilience of his attitude defeated disaster—or so it appears from his letters. At any rate, very soon he contrived to twist every other symptom into a glittering shape of words, making mock of his disorganized lungs until—with a sort of sepulchral laugh that illness should find him so hard to kill—he foresaw the grave in one letter after another. From 'The House of Captivity, Valley of the Shadow of Death,' he wrote that the doctor promised something interesting in the way of a tumour if he remained a conscientious patient, held out hopes of dyspepsia given time and perseverance, and hinted—with the sinister note of the assassin—that if he,

Wells, found this trifling with life too much, he could always sit in a draught for a few hours and lure pneumonia into his lungs. Wells thought himself a good thing for the doctors. He didn't doubt that they would wish to encourage his type, even to giving football lessons for those who found direct entry to the surgery slightly vulgar. But Up Park was a very different place for him now. He had grown out of its early excitements, he had learnt and seen a great deal, and try as he would to resist it, Up Park plainly and simply bored him. The people were impossible, conversation negligible, half the life of the place anachronistic, and continually he fell to moaning. .. . . . O God, this damned, dreary desert! O God, why couldn't I be sick in the Science School. Oh God, it's dull . . . dull . . . dull. . . . By February the end seemed much nearer. 'I was going into the dark and I was not afraid . . . with ostentation . . .' he recorded. 'For nearly four months I was dying with immense dignity. Plutarch might have recorded it. I wrote—in touchingly unsteady pencil—to all my intimate friends and indeed to many other people. I saw the littleness of hate and ambition. I forgave my enemies and they were subdued and owned to it. . . .' (1) When his lungs were wheezing and whispering with the beginnings of congestion, he wrote to a friend that forty-eight hours would send him out on the long journey or leave him a still more sickly wraith unable to produce even the ghost of a laugh. Two weeks later: 'I may drag on a maimed existence in this accursed land of winds, wet ways and old women for three or four years yet. . . .'

So it went on. One moment making elaborate obeisance to the shadow of death, the next cheerfully reconciled to a few more years' spitting, coughing and cursing, interspersed with bouts of writing; for he continued, at the gates of a particularly nasty hell, to read omnivorously and write. The results were not calculated to improve his health. One year's account is shown on the opposite page. (2)

There were times when—the strain of writing under such a sickness apart—he would have thrown it all up. He found it a heartbreaking game. It was bad enough that people seemed stolid, without taste, sold to established gods, but to reach that pitch of indifference where they could not bother to return his manuscripts, as some of them did, was close to humiliation. It needed the crippling limitations of his lungs, which kept him from most other forms of work, and the persistent encouragement of friends like A. T. Simmons and Elizabeth Healey, before he screwed his courage to the sticking place after each fresh rebuff, and tried again, in between bouts of coughing,

Item	1 short story	Sold	£1	0	0
Item	1 novel	Burnt	–	–	–
Item	1 novel unfinished	Burnt	–	–	–
Item	Much Comic Poetry	Lost	–	–	–
Item	Some Comic Prose	Sent away, never returned	–	–	–
Item	Humorous essay	Globe did not return	–	–	–
Item	Sundry Stories	Burnt	–	–	–
Item	1 story	Wandering	–	–	–
Item	Poem	Burnt	–	–	–
			£1	0	0

He never really shook off ill-health for the next ten years and its effects on his character and writings were multiple, but it failed to produce in him any of those symptoms so inseparable from the invalid's life when, looking continuously into the face of pain, he finally makes out the lineaments of God. In his talk and writing Wells remained intransigeantly atheistic. More, he wanted to tell the world there was no God, write excessively about it. Illness gave him time for much reflection on men, God and writing. Most men he decided were a combination of self-deception, humbug, saintliness and sin. Their lives so easily became a continuously sustained lie. He wanted henceforward to live and write the truth, be himself, be utterly one with primal feelings as they arose from the innermost recesses, even in the face of recurring haemorrhage and not unlikely death. The real death he knew would overtake him when the recording angel should scrawl across his page— insincere. So from now on he would pursue what he considered the austere path of self-discovery, allowing no community with easy-going conventions, avoiding the sweets of conciliation, accepting unquestioningly the disciplines of finding one's true self, and perhaps putting some of it on paper, if paper would stand it. It was curious perhaps that, eschewing dignity and deception, devoted to the paths of primal truth, his letters to his friends

gave no hint of the dread, dismay, sometimes despair which over
took him, and the asseverations of remaining absolutely true t
himself were sicklied o'er by a great deal of what can only b
described as posing in his letters; gay and vastly entertainin
posing maybe, but too sustained to be true, and never disclosin
to a soul the black pits which sometimes engulfed him. Illnes
prolonged, painful illness, could become insupportable, and il
ness when it threatened death to a young man still virgin, wh
had known only a fraction of the joys of living, made every sigh
sound and hint of young women maddeningly exciting.

These searchings and lofty commotions quietened a little as th
summer of 1888 reached its full splendour. His health showe
signs of mending, and he went to stay with an old schoolfriend i
the Midlands. The haemorrhages subsided, energy came back, an
his mental exuberance, never entirely suppressed by the wor
that illness could do, developed a physical counterpart. Very soc
he was laughing and joking and beginning to employ his brillia
gifts as a mimic, launching into nimble-witted debate, never at
loss for something to say, and positively gambolling now as l
guyed one person after another, making mock of every trick ar
habit, throwing every available cap into the air—and occasional
writing. He was getting better. Life was beginning to be worth
Life was exciting. Perhaps after all, the austere disciplines of sel
discovery could wait a while. 'The medical profession which ha
pronounced my death sentence, reiterated it steadily,' he wrot
'Towards the end of those four months, however, dying lost i
freshness for me. I had exhausted all my memorable remar
upon the subject. . . .

'One day in the spring-time I crawled out alone, careful
wrapped, and with a stick, to look once more—perhaps for t
last time—on sky and earth, and the first scattered skirmishers
the coming army of flowers. . . . Quite casually I happened up
a girl clambering over a hedge, and her dress had caught in
bramble, and the chat was quite impromptu and most idyllic. .
And we talked of this and that. . . . I quite forgot I was a Doom
Man. . . .' (3)

He also wrote the first three instalments of *The Chronic Ar
nauts*, later to become *The Time Machine*.

*　　*　　*

Back in London by 1888, with £5 capital, he found work dangerously elusive. Once it meant renting a room which wasn't a room—a lodging in Theobalds Road for four shillings a week which turned out to be half a room, so thinly partitioned that he could hear the intimate life of the lodgers behind it, and was left wondering at the sturdy fibre of city dwellers who seemed to spend their lives in a permanent state of being overheard. Once he was down to a halfpenny in ready cash and realized that he had broken the last postal link with any of his relations, because a postcard cost three farthings. But he came through somehow, and at last landed a job with the University Correspondence College— an organization designed to coach students in a variety of subjects, at first by post and later by direct tuition. Already he had sought out Isabel again and the combined demands of teaching and Isabel pushed his writing into the background. But before he reached the verge of those volcanic emotional eruptions which had been gathering force all these years and were ready to explode with appalling violence, something happened in his sexual life which needs recording.

Some time in his early twenties, during his second stay in London, Wells was suddenly overcome with a secret shame at his virginity and brooded on it until he was driven out into the streets and went 'furtively and discreetly with a prostitute.' She was hopelessly unimaginative. She left him in a state of horrible recoil from the festering slums on the edge of sex, and drove him to find a drift of beautiful creatures in his own imagination, cloudy visions capable of ravishing ugly reality. They appear to have attained an astonishing vividness. They occasionally stepped down into everyday life, only to dissolve in the London crowds before he could know them, but when he set eyes on his cousin Isabel again in all her fresh young womanhood, it was inevitable that he should quickly transfer to her some of the attributes which belonged to one at least of his goddesses. Still a pretty dark grave young person not calculated to set the senses afire, her effect on Herbert was deeply disturbing. For his senses were starving, crying out for satisfaction and every feminine line held an appalling lure. He suddenly knew with overwhelming certainty that she could change and enchant his life. She was, for the moment, the only possible embodiment of his dreams. Somehow, he must kindle affection, feeling, if not love, in her, and he set about it in a clumsy, impulsive way which left Isabel in no doubt about his intentions, intentions of the most primly correct character.

No-one has recorded what manner of prince dominated Isabel's dreams as a young girl, or in what likeness she first saw H. G. Wells, but she must have needed rather more imagination than she had, to find attractive the impossibly skinny skeleton—he weighed around seven stone—upon which was draped a very shabby set of clothes, surmounted by a top-hat, the whole given a wildly improbable air by the addition of a rubber collar. It was white and rubber-covered, it could be washed overnight with soap, and it was a vital part of his everyday equipment because it did away with laundry bills. Yet Wells could and did overwhelm this gim-crack get-up by sheer power of personality, making a whole orchestra of talking until the air of Regent's Park vibrated with Malthusianism, atheism, republicanism, and in more daring moments, free-love, all turning dizzy the demure head of Isabel, nourished on far less intoxicating ideas.

Just what happened between this incongruous pair it is difficult to define. They were temperamental opposites, their brains were of a different order, but Wells undoubtedly heard the morning trumpets sound and knew the mutilating ecstasies of love. As for Isabel, she was at first as much carried along by him as convinced that she had fallen in love. But if something sparked between them at the outset, something which soon wore the fascinating hue of love, later became companionship, and never, until her death, entirely lost its colour, there was no mistaking ominous signs in the earliest days. A pitiless imagination had already torn and traversed Wells' emotional life with beautiful relationships which rarely survived the crude light of day. At twenty-two his idealized self, the man he would like to be, big, strong, handsome, but without one whit less intelligence, had found and ravished in imagination, a creature lovely beyond telling, as much in love mentally as she was physically, capable of the same superb flights as himself, and for all her delicacy, somewhere at heart a sensualist, who accepted the senses on the same level as the mind and could indulge them with equal luxuriance.

Isabel Mary Wells was far removed from this goddess. She dressed and thought prettily. She wanted a long engagement. She was very much aware of what the neighbours thought and said, and the notion of marriage in a registry office vaguely scandalized

His Mother,
Mrs. Sarah Wells

H. G. Wells
at the age of 10

When The Time Machine *was published,* 1895

*H. G. Wells'
first wife,
Isabel Mary Well.*

her. As much a virgin mentally as physically, no-one had ever come near ravishing her mind. Wells had to take her, thought by thought, to the edge of his own daring chaotic world, and looking down into the seething cauldron she was considerably frightened by what she saw. It did not stop her from becoming engaged. But neither of them knew that their engagement was to run for several murderous years, until, a blissfully frustrated couple, incorrigibly faithful and warming the cockles of every conventional heart, they sometimes wondered whether they were in heaven or hell. All went uneasily and furtively, driving them deeper into the conviction that they were inseparable, incomplete without one another. Finally, after some years, Herbert became a B.Sc., his income rose to the pitch where passion was permitted to have its way, and the deception which convention had practised on their poor innocent heads all this time, at last showed through.

They were married at Wandsworth Parish Church on October 31st, 1891. Almost at once the limitations of Isabel's personality began to take their toll. In a very few weeks the romantic haze thinned. In a few months what had once seemed glorious threatened to become gauche. Wells' starving senses ingeniously enlarged every little glimmer he found in Isabel until there sometimes emerged from the sweet, soft, simple face the spirit of a person so splendidly different that she might have claimed kinship with the creatures of his imagination, but the glimmer died and the spirit was gone before he could grasp it. Sexually it was impossible. Somewhere Wells has said that fastidiousness in sex is as primal as sex itself, and now, for all the frustrations he began to find in Isabel, he could not release his desires in casual whoring or frank, unlovely lust. It had to be beautiful. It had to have a song in it. . . . And Isabel should have come to him, her dewy loveliness brimming over, her words few, the inner graciousness of complete surrender already half-accomplished, until one personality dissolved upon another—but it never happened that way. . . .

It was hot and a little clumsy. There were dissatisfactions and tears, and as Wells wiped them away, he blamed his own inexperience and roughness, but somewhere inside him a terrible question grew which Isabel could never understand or answer. Sex was surely something more than this? It must be! He would make it so. He had looked for deep, passionate love-making and found only submission. He was capable of reaching a deep level of sexual consciousness with physical inspiration from another, but the tragic conviction grew in him that Isabel's inspiration was little more than a conventional caress. So it came about that within a few months of their marriage, something quite irresistible in Wells demanded, with growing insistence, and quickly found, an experience which left him completely reassured about sex. It went beyond that. 'After six engagement years of monogamic sincerity and essential faithfulness I embarked, as soon as I was married upon an enterprising promiscuity. . . . The old love wasn't at all dead, but I meant now to get in all the minor and incidental love adventures I could.' (4) The first took the form of a certain Miss Kingsmill who visited his home in Haldon Road, Wandsworth, to learn retouching from his wife, and quickly showed an interest in Wells. A cheerfully amoral person, from the start she appeared to know just where it would lead, and merely waited on the day when they were alone together to reveal her free and passionate nature.

It was the day his wife had gone to London, and his aunt—now living with them—was out shopping. Wells, at work upon a pile of books for the University Correspondence College, suddenly heard a tap on the door and there—with some trumped-up excuse—she stood. 'The sound of my returning aunt's latch-key separated us in a state of flushed and happy accomplishment. I sat down with quickened vitality to my blottesque red corrections again, and Ethel, upstairs, very content with herself, resumed her niggling at her negative. . . .'

But it could not save his marriage. An acknowledged mistress who gave him something his wife could never give, who came with natural passion to love-making, had a place in decadent France, but here in suburban London. . . . Half the trouble of course was that Wells had married his cousin at the age of twenty-five when he simply did not believe in marriage. Invoking his infallible gods, Shelley and Godwin, to prove that love had cast her mansions far above the mundane shores of marriage, he suddenly discovered they were easily overwhelmed by the gigantic pressures of the social sanctions and in the end he too had succumbed. That was one side of it. There were others. Their private life together produced inexplicable frictions and difficulties. Sometimes, in the mornings, a note in the newspapers would send Herbert into a viciously eloquent rage, leaving Isabel quite bewildered. It would seem to her just part of the ordinary flow of events and why he had to get so fussed about such trifles she could not make out. 'They're doing their best, dear,' she would say about the politicians of the day. He railed against the habits of the University Correspondence College, he mocked its Principal, and it pained Isabel to hear him attack the source of his bread-and-butter so flagrantly, without scruple, never sparing the most successful pupil. She stood up for the Principal of the College. She said he had always treated Herbert fairly. Why did he go on about him so ? And what was the point of wanting to write so many new and confusing things when he had his hands bursting with the University's work ? Above all she could not bear his being a Socialist, a dark and dubious creed liable to lead straight to the barricades. Dismay and bewilderment at this unmanageable husband of hers became her everyday lot. Later he rationalized it all in writing and wittily lamented the increase of gentleness, the decline in quarrelling, insisting that people should put their arms akimbo, give each other a piece of their minds, and stop the rot now threatening to overwhelm the world with an excess of mildness, an unwholesome spineless lack of rage. *The Pleasure of Quarrelling*, he wrote, is an excellent way of passing the time. 'In the first place and mainly, it is hygienic to quarrel, it disengages floods of nervous energy, the pulse quickens, the breathing is accelerated, the digestion improved. Then it sets one's stagnant brains astir and quickens the imagination. . . . And finally it is a natural function of the body. In his natural state man is always quarrelling—by instinct. Not to quarrel is indeed one of the vices of our civilization, one of the reasons why we are neurotic and anæmic and all these things. . . .' (5) Later, with a touch of irony not apparent to the public eye he added, 'Indeed the literary household is held together by paper fasteners and how other people get along without them we are at a loss to imagine. . . .' (*In a Literary Household.*)

He was more at a loss to know what to do. Quarrels threatened to bring them to sullen silence. One subject of conversation after another dwindled away fraught with too many dangers. They would set out on the simplest discussion only to have Herbert explode into another rage because Isabel seemed to defend the very things which most infuriated him. Spontaneous talk began to subside. Soon they dropped almost self-consciously into little jesting exchanges, preferring small talk to anything else, and the garden became a godsend to fill long awkward silences when something quite urgently must be said or the falsity of their marriage exposed for everyone to see.

There was yet another side to it all. Isabel was not at ease amongst people who could talk. Herself little more than normally articulate she developed an inferiority complex when garrulous intellectuals burst their banks and flooded the surrounding company. Wells too was capable of organic development, of reaching several different orders of personality where she never outran the first, and what he mistook for a satisfactory mate at the age of twenty-five could never possibly satisfy him as he ranged far beyond her interests. This was as true mentally as sexually.

But something there was in the relationship which survived constant friction and frustrations and even the final break, so that they could come together years afterwards when he was away and living with another woman, and the simple use of a nickname sent a flash between them which lit the old enchantments for more than a passing second.

*　　*　　*

Events moved with catastrophic swiftness in the winter of 1893. There had come to his tutorial classes a certain Miss Amy Catherine Robbins, an attractive intelligent young woman anxious to become a teacher. He had taught her privately as well as in class. It brought them close together. They became friends and very soon 'our friendship grew swiftly beyond the bounds of friendship and I was amazed to find that she could care for me as much as I did for her. . . .' (6) One evening in May 1893, carrying a bag of rock specimens at high speed towards Charing Cross Station, a sudden spasm shook him, he began to cough, the same dry deliberate cough from the lungs, the world swung dizzily and another haemorrhage spilt red blood into his handkerchief. It was a bad attack, worse than any that had gone before. By the time he reached home it seemed to have subsided, but then in the early morning it came on again. By candlelight he coughed more blood and in a state between dread and apprehension watched the dawn, a wild dishevelled dawn, come up. Later in life, very much later, he clearly remembered the little tickle and trickle of blood which preceded the haemorrhage. He remembered thinking—don't cough too soon, don't cough too much, let it force you first or the flow may be bigger. The horrible sweet taste of blood remained in his mind for years, and he remembered lying utterly still, hardly breathing, hands at sides, hoping it would help, until the haemorrhage came more fiercely than ever and the nightmare began that it would never stop. . . . The beautiful, brilliant red, seeping up and up. . . . The nausea and the intolerable weariness creeping through his bones. . . .

Over the next few days amongst the icepacks and the doctors and a very distraught Isabel, certain deep considerations about his way of life were borne in on him. A struggling teacher, vainly trying to write, oppressed by the sense of a mistaken marriage, he lay back in bed an invalid again and soon became aware that this spelt the end of teaching for good, the end of life in London and heaven alone knew what.

It was seven days before he could eat anything solid. As he lay there, turning over what to do, as he tried to forget the taste at the back of his throat, one person came more and more into his thoughts—Catherine Robbins. He could not see her in person now. Someone else had taken over his teaching. But she remained constantly at the back of his mind and sometimes dominated everything. Inevitably he fell to comparing her with Isabel and it soon seemed to him, as the cough quietened and the flow of blood slackened, that she was the embodiment of everything Isabel could never be. Presently the wildest notions began to cross his mind, notions which for a poor, broken-down teacher, seriously ill and living on his savings, were extravagant to the point of madness. He would run off one day with Catherine, he would escape this conventional net which was choking the very life out of him, break away, go abroad, start a brand new career somewhere.

He knew they were the fantasies of a very sick man. He knew that an invalid, penurious teacher, a person with no better prospects than destitution, could not embark on any such romantic nonsense. But by January of 1894 he had fled from Isabel to join Catherine Robbins in a guinea a week flat at Mornington Place, London. The shock was seismic. It sent reverberations to the remotest corners of Isabel's relations and produced in Mrs. Robbins all the conventional signs of emotional if not physical death, which she did indeed simulate by crying herself into a coma. That any daughter of hers should live in sin with a man, and a married man, openly, flagrantly—plainly telling her so ! If she was forced to admit that such things had been known to happen before, then surely it was the last decent rite to keep their sin secret; and why not, anyway, have just one scrap of common sense and wait until this young man was divorced from his first wife ? That seemed irrefutable logic until she learned, with complete revulsion, that they did not believe in the Institution of Marriage, and had no intention of marrying anyway. They were both arrogantly sure at the time. They were both so determined to sound their own trumpets, even though the walls of Jericho paid no heed and the ancient laws which insisted on marriage or nothing, remained intact. What recantations and disillusionment were to follow, what immense wisdom the veriest clap-trap of convention very soon seemed. But now . . . their relationship gathered a fire and life from battle which it might not have found elsewhere.

How to convey the immensely tangled skein which led to this upheaval in Wells' life at a time when he could so badly afford disturbance, let alone disturbance on a grand scale, and with his terrible illness barely over. There were so many strange confusions. Once he had escaped his cousin, the desire to hold her to him in some way returned with such violence that he did his best to persuade her not to divorce him. Isabel, too, was suddenly overtaken with remorse. She 'reproached herself for failing to understand him.' It was all unaccountable. The powerful tie between them waxed and waned for ten years, and whatever it was that drew him so dramatically to Catherine never became the passionate fixation he had for his first wife. Nor was it that Catherine had any deeper powers of sexuality, or that they could not stop their ears against some subtle emotional magic. Their affection was deep, yes, but they were not possessed by all-consuming love. They were immensely stimulated by one another, but physically at least Catherine once again was, in the beginning, an innocent. To all outward appearance made in a slight delicate mould, she was sturdy enough, but she could no more have borne the abandoned transports of mature sexuality at the outset, than she could have danced naked in Trafalgar Square, and it must have been horrifying to Wells to find that the desperately desired embraces of his deep-breasted Venus were as remote as ever with Catherine Robbins. Indeed there was a point where this lack of passion made him see the whole relationship as little more than 'an alliance for escape and development.'

But there were so many other things they seemed to have in common, the great talks, the wide reading, the biology and science, the love of literature and the determination to live their own lives whatever society might have to say. . . . Or was it Wells' determination? From the start it was he who pressed her on, and although at the time he knew his motives were mixed, he only discovered their true nature later in life. That, anyway, is how he puts it in the *Autobiography*. There is some evidence to show that he allowed the generosities always straining against the rampant egotist in him to overwhelm his story at this point, and Catherine Robbins is painted as a pawn in his game, which she never quite became: but of that in its place.

People tend to talk one way, think another and act a third. Jung, in psychology, has his own interpretation of the phenomenon. We are not one integrated personality, but many. We have a *persona*—the sort of person we want to present to other people; and an *anima*—a thrust and stir of other states of mind continuously trying to jostle the *persona* out of place. In reverie and day-dreaming, we are clothed in one of the many states of consciousness on the edge of our 'everyday selves,' and sometimes the reverie takes charge so deeply that the clergyman who sees himself as the audacious rake, puts on lay clothes and becomes it. So, now, Wells played his part, accepting one of the many states of consciousness clamouring for attention on the outskirts of his mind, but he slipped—whether by accident or design—into the wrong role, only to play it with the gusto of a born actor. For while he was playing in all good faith the part of the lover, who must at any cost win the adorable Catherine Robbins and escape from Isabel Wells, at heart the freedom he sought was from that unimaginable Venus who tormented his dreams, and not from any living person. Isabel had never been able to supplant her. Catherine perhaps might. And in a great blinding light of revelation these two rushed off together and sturdily refused to succumb to the inevitable troubles which crowded in upon them. Both were believed to have little chance of living overlong. Their emotions may or may not have been heightened by the effects of tuberculosis. Both now determined to live with the intensity which the disease so easily generates. They must squeeze the last drop from every passing second, snatch every gleam of happiness. 'We were the most desperate lovers,' Wells wrote. 'We launched ourselves upon our life together with less than £50 between us and absolute disaster. . . . And I seem to remember now that we did it with a very great deal of gaiety. . . .' (7) That they built a beautiful and lasting relationship is high tribute to their tolerance and strength of purpose, that they were able at length to laugh at themselves and the appalling discoveries they made, a measure of their final adjustment; but this was not yet. . . .

Many years later in *The New Machiavelli* Margaret wrote to Remington, 'There's this difference that has always been between us, that you like nakedness and wildness and I clothing and restraint. You are always talking of order and system and the splendid dream of the order that might replace the muddled system you hate, but by a sort of instinct you seem to want to break the law. . . . You are at once makers and rebels, you and —— too. You're bad people, criminal people, I feel, and yet full of something the world must have. You're so much better than me and so much viler. . . .' (8) Isabel might so easily have written that to the husband who had just deserted her.

Chapter Six

SCIENTIFIC ROMANCER

WELLS' attempts to write had been given a quite new twist by his illness. As a convalescent he read a book by J. M. Barrie, *When a Man's Single*, which laid bare the secrets of success in free-lance journalism. You would-be journalists, the book said, can air nothing but your views on art, life, letters, the universe, always imagining that they have the freshness of a revelation, when any editor worth his salt knows there is nothing new whatever to say about such things. Try the ordinary, the everyday, the small personal experience. Forget your opinions and messages. Put the Universe behind you. Barrie suddenly showed Wells things which—without leisure or detachment—he had been blind to for years. It was ironic that a man with such profound perceptions at one level entirely lacked them at another. He had to be shown things, people, places; he was at this stage, æsthetically illiterate, quite unaware of lesser loveliness, blind to finer shades, and before very long Catherine, like Barrie, came to play the part of dragoman in his life.

Now Barrie went home deeply with Wells. He had written *The Rediscovery of the Unique* and Frank Harris had published it in *Fortnightly Review* in 1891, the first success of any consequence heralding a glimpse of 'the white and shining city.' But this was precisely in the vein Barrie abhorred. It propounded the theory that everything susceptible of observation and scrutiny was bound to be unique. Thus two and two constantly made four, but under close examination one set of four was found to be very different from another, and all classifications were over-simplifications. Such ideas fascinated Wells and he wanted to spill them out for everyone to read until he discovered Barrie's book and wondered whether he should put away Time, Man the Universe and all the other vast abstractions. Perhaps Mr. Barrie was right. Perhaps he should release the spring of wit and mischief eternally bubbling at the back of his mind, the spring which had given him the mastery over so many despairing moments in illness; perhaps he should deign to notice the wayside daisies. In any case it was worth a trial. It would be a relief to let the lighter vein run loose, to be gay about small things, to gambol and effervesce. So began the life-long habit of emptying out his mind on the printed page with all its quirks and sparkles, explosions and wraths, brimming over as they came in an exhilarating rush; and now the first beaker-ful took the form of an essay, *On the Art of Staying at the Seaside*, which *The Pall Mall Gazette* at once accepted and printed.

They asked for more. Other papers became interested. Soon, there seemed some prospect of his being able to buy food as well as pay the rent from journalism, and given a stroke or two of luck, he might even consider clothing himself. The journalist in him was discovering his powers to the utter confusion of the scientist and teacher. Until his death he took an inverted pleasure in calling himself a journalist and kept the word Journalist as the professional label on his passport. It was one of his few affectations. But now in the early 1890's, with Isabel abandoned and Catherine the centre of his emotional life, journalism became his chief preoccupation, the one way in which he might cope with his split responsibilities and forget the lowering landscape he was trying to leave behind; journalism produced with a sort of high-pitched energy liable to lead to shrill exaggeration and great escapist flights. But —except for one supreme effort—he remained down to earth, bright, vivid, original, and so long as people like the Astors retained their taste for running periodicals at a loss, the Olympian Frank Harris volleyed and thundered on *The Saturday Review*, and Mr. Cust, blond, polished, equable, thought young Herbert one of the best things that had happened to *The Pall Mall Gazette*, all went well.

Harris found him something of a problem. Keeping his more serious vein still just alive, Wells followed up *The Rediscovery of the Unique* with *The Universe Rigid* in April 1892, a document which baffled the unorthodox mind of the Great Frank out of patience with the more meticulous laws of science. He asked to see Mr. Herbert George Wells. The invitation distressed the young author, still inclined to consider editors as gods and totally unaware what one should wear or say on such occasions. Settling, finally, for a silk hat and morning coat he gave the hat a special polish with the aid of a wet cloth, and set off.

Highly self-conscious, he arrived at *The Saturday Review* office and was further put out by having to wait half an hour before

Harris would see him. Then he was shown in and advanced across the room to a large desk where the figure of Harris sprawled with the cultivated ease of a distinguished editor. He had almost reached the desk when he became aware that the hat which he held in his hand was beginning to curl and warp from the water, and suddenly to his terrified eyes it looked oddly reminiscent of a bankrupt undertaker. He coloured and fidgeted. Harris fixed a basilisk stare on this strange buckled object. Two of his satellites also concentrated their gaze. There was a long pause which all but paralysed Wells. Then, condescending to notice the thin form behind the hat, Harris suddenly threw a manuscript across the table and demanded in a voice like Irish thunder: 'So it was *you* who sent me this Universe R-R-Rigid ? Tell me what you *think* it's about. Before Gaard what in the name of heaven is the bloody article trying to say? What's it mean? Who will read it?' (1, 2) Nobody ever did read it in the end. The type was broken down and distributed because Harris could not make head or tail of it. But Wells' relations with him improved and the possibilities of repeating his first success seemed good, until malignant fate struck swiftly and surely into his beautiful castle of words, conspiring to send the literary editor of *The Pall Mall Gazette* away for a holiday, leaving in possession a man resistant to Herbert's ramblings, killing *The Pall Mall Budget,* Astor's other child, almost overnight, and taking *The National Observer* out of W. E. Henley's hands—all at one stroke.

Herbert's income fell catastrophically. He had barely made ends meet before. Now, no amount of financial jugglery would bring them together. Gloom, deep and thickening, began to envelop his rising spirits. At the very point where the editors of Fleet Street, roused from their torpor, had detected the winkings of a new, unknown and distinctly cheeky star laughing and chuckling with a queer scientific vitality from which it sometimes threatened to explode, they were removed from office and a number of straw figures took their places. The shutters came down again. An awful sense of failure rose like a miasma. Pausing suddenly in his journalistic stride, Wells wondered—was it worth it ? Should he go on ? Shouldn't he think of reviving his connections with the University Correspondence College ? He still corrected papers by post.

One even worse trouble coloured all the rest. Now living at

Sevenoaks, by the grace of a landlady who had just discovered Catherine's unmarried state, he was suddenly subjected to showers of sly innuendo, bursts of temper, and dark impalpable threats. One day, the landlady said, she would speak her mind. One day she would tell what she knew. For the moment she was content to snipe. Bitterly, one evening, Wells turned aside from journalism and the landlady, took out the *Chronic Argonauts*—a number of papers he had written for the *Science Schools Journal*—and largely for want of something better to do, began re-writing them. Into this world at least the landlady could not follow him. There were to be six versions of *The Time Machine* written over a period of seven years, chopping and changing story and characters, but to-night the version he worked upon was a special one. Henley had told him that he might be editing a monthly magazine shortly and would like to run the *Time Traveller* articles as a serial story, if his hopes were realized. . . . It was a still, beautiful evening, with a small circle of light thrown by the paraffin lamp across the table, the moths continually dashing themselves to death against the burning glass, the window wide and the landlady, somewhere outside, explaining to a neighbour just what outrageous people sometimes took lodgings under false pretences. She reached suprising flights of invective, she flounced and gestured, and in the end stamped inside and slammed the door with all the courage which she could never muster when confronted by Mr. Wells in person. But he was half absent from this world. . . .

He was away with the Time Machine in a society of Morlocks and Eloi where graceful creatures, indescribably frail, their faces flushed as with the more lovely ravages of consumption, dallied in a world of sunshine and gentle abandon, fearing only the darkness and the pale, chinless creatures with lidless eyes who scuttled in catacombs where the sun never reached. Presently there came the moment when 'I heard an exclamation, oddly truncated at the end, and a click and a thud. A gust of air whirled round me as I opened the door, and from within came the sound of broken glass falling on the floor. . . . The Time Traveller was not there. I seemed to see a ghostly indistinct figure sitting in a whirling mass of black and brass for a moment . . . but this phantasm vanished as I rubbed my eyes . . . The Time Machine had gone.' (3) On and on he wrote, fluently, excitedly, the story unfolding with rhythmic certainty. He was completely in and of it. He became the

Time Traveller. The character enabled him to break out of his dreary limited world as he so desperately desired to do, because he was a person, young, ambitious, bubbling with frustrated ideas, who believed himself, like the Time Traveller, to be born out of his time—'A man thinking the thoughts of a wiser age, doing things and believing things that men now *cannot* understand . . . and in the years ordained to me there was nothing but silence and suffering for my soul. . . . I knew I was an Anachronic Man; my age was still to come. . . . And then *that*, the Chronic Argo, *the ship that sails through time*, and now I go to join my generation, to journey through the ages till my time has come. . . .' Already, at twenty-seven, Wells felt himself a wandering freak, a man constantly groping and bewildered in the unlovely shadows of the present world, a man whose greatest joy was to press on the pane of the next, seeing in moments of beautiful illumination, the setting for which he believed himself—and the rest of humanity when it reached maturity—made.

It is not recorded what hour he went to bed that night. It was very late. The ordinary clock anyway did not signify. At last he wrote, with the Time Machine vanished: 'I have by me for my own comfort, two strange white flowers—shrivelled now, and brown and flat and brittle—to witness that even when mind and strength had gone, gratitude and a mutual tenderness still lived on in the heart of man.' (4) If ever a writer completely surrendered to the surge of inspiration which carried him deeply into his own mind where time performed fantastic mimes at his command, it was Wells that night, who finally went to bed in a state as it were of revelation, threatened a little by the prospect of the landlady in the morning, but written out, exhausted, a new world of prophecy challenged and well on the way to being vanquished.

Somehow, in all the confusions of the next few weeks *The Time Machine* (1894) was finished, released into the blue and almost forgotten. Nothing it seemed could survive the conventional air of Sevenoaks. Half a dozen dreams came close to suffocation, articles were unexpectedly rejected, nothing he touched seemed to go right. Until suddenly, with all the rush of the heavens opening, a letter arrived from W. E. Henley saying that the magazine was all right, and his first serial story would be *The Time Machine* for which he proposed paying £100! It was untold wealth. It was salvation. It set Wells waltzing round hugging that frail delicate young woman Catherine Robbins, who had outfaced the appalling pressures of society to go and live in sin with a mad young writer, far from sure of himself, worth about £50 in capital and already guilty of deserting his first wife.

* * *

The writer with the seven-league boots who yet contrived never to be clumsy, the man of letters covering a vast acreage of print who yet found time to become a Fabian, a Socialist and—according to some—an inspired Casanova. Contradictions multiplied in the years 1895–1903 but at root it was Wells the writer, above all Wells the novelist, who flourished.

From his inexhaustible treasure house of ideas he worked at now one, now another novel, with none of the finesse of Henry James —'Oh what an artist spoilt,' James said of him—but shapelessly, with a huge exciting energy which slapped scenes down on paper and didn't gravely mind if there were ragged ends or characters lost in the scramble, so long as they were alive and conveyed his essential ideas. In the beginning it was ideas that mattered more than characters. *The Time Machine* (1894) lived by the grace of scientific gods, *The Stolen Bacillus* and *The Island of Dr. Moreau* (1896), *The Star* and *The Invisible Man* (1897) all dabbled in the scientific occult, taking the laws of science far beyond their bounds, yet never so much as to fuss broad-minded scientists, and never so little as to make dull reading. Wells knew just how to unlock the excitements, the imaginative worlds, buried beneath dull scientific data. He also knew the necessity of creating commonplace everyday people and incidents very much of this earth, alongside the great streaming fantasy world in which he placed them. 'For the writer of fantastic stories to help the reader play the game properly,' he wrote, 'he must help him, in every possible unobtrusive way, to *domesticate* the impossible hypothesis. . . .' The plausible illusion must be swiftly established with an air of ordinariness, and before incredulity overtook the reader he must be swept along by the story until he had surrendered completely to the element of magic. It was the modern mode of an old technique. A talk with the alchemist, the devil, the magician had yielded fantastic stories before. The Frankenstein monster had come out of some such primitive furnace. Wells substituted the current scientific patter of the day, skilfully turned theories of time and interstellar space to similar account. 'I simply brought the fetish stuff up to date and made it as near actual theory as possible. . . .' (5) But he also, with boundless vitality and immense humanity, created characters who saw life from their new angle with all the emotional authenticity of 'one of us,' and sometimes with an emotional magic which left a glow in the reader's mind. It did not always happen. Sometimes he became painfully sentimental and his love scenes could be embarrassing to read. 'One wonders that the picture of the awful Princess, goggling in enormous close-up, and fanning herself with half a chestnut tree (in *The Food of the Gods*) did not destroy the feminist movement,' (6) wrote V. S. Pritchett in a brilliant little essay on Wells. But the love scenes were not of very great moment yet.

How Wells worked in those early years. Between 1896 and 1897 *The War of the Worlds* and *The Invisible Man* were completed, *When the Sleeper Wakes* begun, with *Love and Mr. Lewisham* in preparation, and at least four short stories including *The Crystal Egg, A Story of the Stone Age,* and that brilliant piece of imaginative projection *The Star* finished. 'And everywhere the world was awake that night, throughout Christendom a sombre murmur hung in the keen air over the country side like the belling of bees in the heather, and this murmurous tumult grew to a clangour in the cities. . . .'(7)

Like whole chapters of Wells, the sentence read as if the outpourings of a wonderfully fertile mind were released on paper effortlessly—and sometimes it happened that way, sometimes he tilted up the cart of his mind and out rumbled stone, rubbish, and good rich beautiful soil to mount under the astonished reader's eye, into yet another chapter, if not book. There were other times when he wrote and rewrote, times when the core of meaning he sought had to be beaten out of his brain. Deeper he would go, and deeper, until the essence of what he wanted was there, and a phrase of indisputable rightness and authority rang on the page, cost him, though it might, half a morning's work. There were days when he threw over a story because it would not 'go,' only to take it up months later. There were days when he despaired of ever getting certain stories right, and words, innumerable, crowding urgent words, simply choked upon themselves, and he would see it all as clear evidence of his literary ineptitude. He wasn't really made for writing. It was an artificial business anyway. Making second-hand marks on sheets of paper and expecting them to move in the likeness of life ! Until suddenly, a cataract of words broke through all restraint and inhibition, and carried doubts, time, characters before it, so much flotsam in the tide of self expression. Yet the results of his torments in those early days were sometimes bad enough for him to say, later in life, that if anyone had brought him the first papers which were to make up *The Time Machine*, he very much doubted whether he would have advised him to go on writing. He believed, then, that the 'poetic gift, the gift of the creative and illuminating phrase,' alone justified writing.

But now, as writing revealed its hidden malignity—the hackneyed phrase always whispered its originality—his output doubled rather than declined, as if by amassing a vast array of words he could better bring them to heel. Work ran first to a pattern. A talk with the second Mrs. Wells began the morning—the impregnable champions of free love had married almost immediately after his divorce—ideas were sifted and turned and then he settled down to work them out. The development of ideas ran spontaneously enough, but there was a tendency for trouble to start once they were down on paper. *Love and Mr. Lewisham* was the one consciously conceived book at this period, a book written to a prearranged plan as an experiment, which he afterwards felt lost its pace and dash, and might have been better spilled out as it came. Later he learnt that schedules were for him a snare and a delusion, something calculated to seize up his impulsive mind which had to strike spontaneously or lose half its freshness, even if it sometimes struck into a morass.

Chapter Seven

SUCCESS COMES SWIFTLY

THEY moved to Worcester Park in 1896. There on Saturday afternoons, began the house parties for the new friends already gathering about them. To many such parties came Dorothy Richardson. A penetrating picture which Wells admitted to be authentic was drawn by Dorothy Richardson in her book *The Tunnel*, showing the two of them receiving guests with preposterously self-conscious efforts on the part of Alma (Catherine) to be bright, to say the clever thing, play the right music, while Wells—well. . . . 'The brown, tweed-covered arm of the little square figure handed a tea cup. The high, huskily hooting voice. . . . What was the overwhelming impression ? A common voice, with a cockney twang. . . . The voice was saying two things; that was it . . . it was shy and determined, and deliberate and expectant. . . .' (1)

The little man lay back in his chair, wrote Dorothy Richardson, and dropped into short sentences, directed it seemed at Alma, each with a hidden barb, each improving on the one before it, accompanied by 'subdued snortings at the back of his nose. . . .' And Miss Richardson, 'eagerly watching the curious mouthing half hidden by the drooping straggle of moustache and the strange, concentrated gleam of the grey-blue eyes staring into space, laughed outright.' But how could he speak so of Alma ? 'He met the laughter with a minatory outstretched forefinger, and raised his voice to a soft squeal, ending, as he launched with a little throw of the hand his final jest, in a rotund crackle of high hysterical open-mouthed laughter. . . .'

But there was something wrong in the room. A strange cold tide ran through the house. Host and hostess developed the bright strained duologue, with artistry enough to make it clear—so unnecessarily clear—that the public performance was merely an extension of private habit. But Miss Richardson 'averted her eyes from them, overcome by painful visions of the two at breakfast, or going home after social occasions. . . .' (2)

And then conversation broke out amongst the other clever people who had come: 'Why not write an article about a lamp-post?' 'Or a whole book?' 'I've bought a mantelpiece—I'm going to build a house around it!' 'A house? Why not a town?' 'One should buy a nation to put around a mantelpiece.' Mr. Wilson (Wells) was crimson with laughter.

To succeed amongst them one had to say something clever, and preferably the voice should be high and bright. . . . 'They were like a sort of secret society.' And what was it that sustained Mr. Wilson in his beliefs, made so exciting and vivid what he said about a man-made God, the apotheosis of love and fear? There was Man and nothing more for him, Man derived from the apes, made omnipotent by science, granted different degrees of dullness and cleverness, and Man included Woman: 'cleverly devised by nature to ensnare man for a moment and produce more men to bring scientific order out of primeval chaos. . . .'

Alma, wrote Miss Richardson, continually tried to beat things up, continually kept the brightly coloured balls in the conversational conjuring trick. If only she had stopped, relaxed for a moment, ceased being elaborately funny, something else in the room would have flowed through everyone. A presence, a softly swelling tide lifting under the feet, was there and waiting, but never came through. Alma had never yet known the something which belonged to that atmosphere, something 'she would call dull.' Mr. Wilson knew it, 'had it in him somewhere, but feared it and kept it out by trying to be bigger, by trying to be the biggest thing there was. . . .' (3) Whatever he said, he said charmingly, and even in those moments when he delivered himself of something as of the Gospel, the same sparkle broke through all defences, and in moments of utter wrong-headedness he seemed to shine with his stupidity. No—not stupidity. . . . 'It was wrong somehow; he was all wrong . . . but it caught you, it had caught Alma and all these people; and in a sense he despised them all, and was talking to something else; the thing he knew; the secret that made him so strong, even with his weak voice and weak mouth; strong and fascinating.'

*   *   *

The sketch was highly charged with all that was to happen so soon between Wells and Catherine. In a letter to me, Dorothy

Richardson added this footnote: 'At Worcester Park both Catherine and Wells remained representative of their respective classes. He, though still dependent upon his reading of her social *savoir faire,* masked his inexperience by bold informality and was jocular to the point of caricature. Both were self-conscious and shy in company. They astounded my tongue-tied self by saying that my visits were a help because I knew what to say to people to keep them at their ease. This gives you the measure of their incapacity.' (4)

*　　　*　　　*

Spring grew into the glorious summer of 1896. Articles and books continued to multiply. 'I am half way to brain fever with a damned story' became a fairly normal remark by the winter of that year. Wells was overworking outrageously. It was as if he had to demonstrate his success in a great mountain of books which he could touch and see and smell before he could believe it was not a dream; but success was real enough now as his income showed . 1893—£380 13*s.* 7*d.*; 1894—£583 17*s.* 7*d.*; 1895—£792 2*s.* 5*d.*; 1896—£1,056 7*s.* 9*d.* He could even spare money to settle his ageing mother and father in a house at Liss. Editors and publishers were clamouring for his work, people like W. E. Henley, Pett Ridge, Hind, and very soon Conrad, Henry James and Ford Madox Hueffer were becoming his friends. W. T. Stead had written when *The Time Machine* appeared: 'H. G. Wells is a man of genius,' (5) and now as fresh books and stories came streaming out, a number of critics with that happy knack of community peculiar to literary lions when the quality of the food is finally assured, agreed that this was a man to watch. Indeed Mr. Wells might become a great writer. Some of them said he was already. They spoke from a literary world still deeply embroiled in the Wessex novels, the diablerie of Beardsley and *The Yellow Book,* a world where W. E. Henley, the apostle of literary realism, the stylist and military imperialist, gave Wells all the encouragement he could spare from his own private battle with his tubercular feet, and Barrie, Yeats, Kenneth Grahame and even Mallarmé were busy trying to satisfy Henley's rugged demands in the Scots *Observer.* It was a world where aestheticism was ebbing, Kipling dominated the scene, and Shaw's audacious eloquence was beginning to alarm old-world critics apt to put more store by good taste than gusto. But they didn't seem to mind Wells' gusto. Who could ? His exuberance was so infectious. The sheer joy and rush of narrative made it seem as if he came to his desk every morning bubbling with anticipation, as readers now came to his books. It was not entirely true of course. But there was no questioning his brimming ebullience, his gifts as a born story-teller, as a novelist of original genius, characteristics which put him apart from Jules Verne. Critics drew many comparisons with Jules Verne and if the ties were there, they were not very close. Jules Verne dealt with the actual possibilities of invention, things that might in all reality come about, where Wells used scientific ideas as a pure literary vehicle, an exercise in fantasy, the most attractive and original way of saying what he wanted to say. Ivor Brown has said that Jules Verne's heroes were idealized creatures turning invention to their own private account, creatures produced by a mind steeped in the writings of Comte, highly latinized and caring not a rap for social problems. Wells' inheritance was very different. The one similarity was the scientific vehicle.

The novelist, constantly confronted with the need to find a vehicle to carry what he wants to say, so often slips into the first convenient carriage. He wants to demonstrate love between two people and the easiest way is to show their reactions when they share a common interest, so they ride horses, or listen to music, or become Socialists together. A common hate would probably reveal their love far more passionately and should demand the rejection of a common interest, but mistaking first impressions for the rush of inspiration, the novelist too often takes the easy way and travels less effectively. Not so Wells. He saw that science might run off in Frankenstein abandon, gathering more and more power over nature while the ordinary human being had less and less power over himself. Power, the concept of power, of power through scientific experiment, of the need to bring power itself under control, to constrain it for the collective happiness of mankind, dispensing in the end with the necessity for power at all; these ideas fascinated Wells and drove him into one story after another. But it was no use applying them to the average 'plot' in the hope that any one would listen. To demonstrate his message he had to choose a veritable magic carpet and if his readers were to be persuaded not only to make the journey with him, but to detect his undertones, it must be made highly exhilarating. The method of demonstration, the scientific fantasy, was supremely successful, but only because of his unique gifts, gifts far beyond Jules Verne's.

He was, at this stage, in the vein of *The Golden Ass* of Apuleius, Peter Schlemil and the *True Histories* of Lucian. The strong element of fantasy simply intensified the reader's reactions, carried him into a world of wonders, and made the message, whenever he saw it, so much more exciting. Wells understood his scientific implications to be highly romantic but each magic carpet carried a message and it was the message in the end which mattered, when the pace, the drama, the power of story-telling had exhausted itself. From the very beginning Wells' stories had this dualism entirely lacking in Jules Verne. As yet the desire to reshape the world was not imperative to him, but already this characteristic, which was to distinguish every other book from just another scientific romance, showed itself in *The Island of Dr. Moreau*, written in 1896 when he was steeped in the gall of Swift, a book which insisted that Man, deriving from the beasts, must constantly repeat the Law and suffer austere disciplines for fear he slipped back to his old animal self again. 'I make no comparison of the merits of Wells and Swift,' wrote V. S. Pritchett 'though the Beast Men of *The Island of Dr. Moreau* are derivatives of the Yahoos and are observed with Swift's care for biological detail— but in his best narratives Wells does go back to the literary traditions of the early eighteenth century. . . . We have to go back to Swift, the Swift of Lilliput and Laputa, before we find another English novelist going to science for his data and material as Wells has done. . . .' (6)

The Invisible Man (1897) showed the dangers of naked power unchecked by moral values. *When the Sleeper Wakes* (1899) was terribly aware, in its vision of the world two centuries hence, that mechanical progress could utterly outstrip and confuse ordinary individuals, that the beautiful romantic day-dreams of the Utopians might be left quite hopelessly sterile. Waking from a trance of 200 years, the Sleeper 'tried to figure the individual life. It astonished him to realize how little the common man had changed in spite of the visible change in his conditions. Life and property, indeed, were secure from violence all over the world, zymotic diseases, bacterial diseases of all sorts had practically vanished, everyone had a sufficiency of food, clothing, was warmed in the city ways and sheltered from the weather. . . . But the crowd was a crowd still, individually cowardly, individually swayed by appetite, collectively incalculable. . . .' (7)

Wells was never just the story-teller. Every book had its message. It was half the sustaining force which drove him into one story after another, into fresh and exciting explorations, until he was grossly overworking, and overwork began to take its toll. A few symptoms of his old complaint re-appeared and were ignored. He brought *When the Sleeper Wakes* right up to publishable form before he paid any heed to his health. Then he decided he must take his wife off for a holiday and they set out in the spring of 1898 for Italy, with Wells so excited on Charing Cross Station that he literally danced and talked, talked and danced. Neither had crossed the Channel before; Wells' French and Italian was negligible, Catherine's not much better. It was George Gissing who showed them Italy. He also gave H. G. his first perception of 'art.' Released from his philistine wilderness, Wells plunged in to indulge his 'finer perceptions' industriously. Dürer more than the Italians became his chief joy.

But he had already gone too far with his health. Back in England he collapsed from an abscess on the kidney, that self-same kidney trampled upon in the football match, which was to trouble him all his days. Work was abandoned, complete rest ordered all over again, and the awful fear came up at the back of his mind that he would never be free from these relapses. There was some talk, very serious talk, of an operation, until the kidney was practically starved out of existence, but over the next few weeks he for once came close to total relaxation even if *The Adventures of Tommy* had to be thrown off at the height of his sickness to amuse the doctor's daughter.

As he recovered, once more with gusts of gaiety and turning every symptom into a quip, his wife was very aware of the threat of valetudinarianism. Wells saw himself condemned to live in a bath chair, and they felt that he must anyway find somewhere high and sheltered to live. It set them searching for a house in the Sandgate-Rye area. There followed a spell at Arnold House, a semi-detached villa on the sea with an almost private beach between two breakwaters. An unbelievable sense of holiday overtook Wells. He would get up very early, do most of his work before breakfast, and then skip and gambol about the beach, wits volleying, squealing at Dorothy Richardson 'It's one long sea-side holiday. Wonderful!'

But he and Catherine still searched for a house and soon, finding nothing better than 'servant-murdering basements,' they decided to build one of their own. Spade House, when it was finished in 1900, stood between Folkestone and Sandgate, with sunken lawns, summer-houses, and a main garden which fell sharply away to the sea ninety feet below. At night the beams of Cape Gris-Nez wheeled across the sky. It was a place to encourage the writer's reverie. At night sometimes, Wells came to stand and stare at the sea and there were moments of communion with the land where the creatures of science bowed to his artistic will, the sullen ropes which held unhappy man to earth were cut, and another story began to twist and turn its way to the surface. And in the mornings he came to the desk under the mullioned window and wrote, using a fountain pen on ruled scribbling paper; wrote neatly and minutely, circling, correcting, interpolating, until sometimes the finished manuscript looked like a chart of the heavens. There were times when he wrote with the seething intensity of somebody helplessly excited by words and the story he had to tell—at any cost, and there were still times when it all moved heavily. Usually Peter his cat slept on the window-seat. Outside there was a patch of lawn, and beyond that the sea. Sometimes a boat going out might or might not be Jim Pain's, the sailorman he came to know. He could never concentrate for long spells. He worked for an hour or so and then broke off—sometimes to plunge into reverie, staring at the sea, a sea very often wrinkled and stirring under the south-west wind, sometimes to burst into boisterous games, sky-larking round the house like an unruly boy. In moments he exploded with the sheer joy of living, deliberately heightening the pleasure of the present by memories of the past. And there were times at Spade House when, looking through the window unobserved, one saw a figure tensed on the settee, hands gripped, the whole personality beside itself with its own illumination, the sea outside vacant, the great music he had just played on the pianola dead in immeasurable distances: a man possessed by visions, visions which presently became his scientific romances. The thunder of words fell away in these moods strewn with great rocks and boulders, sentences swept majestically down the page, little Bertie Wells was overwhelmed by the visionary standing serenely on the edge of the universe, granted a primitive vision and eloquence. Such exaltation could only express itself in noble language.

Spade House became enormously fecund. It remained his home for the next ten years, and book after book was conceived and sent whirling to London to bewilder the publishers with their rapidity and skill. Unceasingly a tide of words flowed into the capital, to be multiplied in their millions and released on the world again. The effect was astonishing. A man who thought a few years before that *The Time Machine* was the ultimate flower of his talent, now began to wonder, becoming as he was the literary god of a huge army of readers. But he remained modest about his writing. He was a journalist, he felt, a journalist raised to a tenth power and granted a divine gift for phrase-finding. His public thought differently. At the beginning of the twentieth century it was a wonderful thing for any young person to come upon Wells. There you were in a world full of frustrations, surrounded by stuffy conventions and stifling sexual codes, a world where half-illiterate schoolmasters preyed on their unfortunate pupils, and parents were demi-gods, and suddenly came this wonderful man to tell you about astonishing time machines and teeming protozoa, to tell you about life on other planets, to declare flatly that society would soon undergo a miraculous metamorphosis. And if you were of the brave band determined to escape the mental slums, the crushing hypocrisies of the day, there was Wells ready and eager to sustain you with beautiful words and fearless example. It brought a sparkling wind into many lives. It revealed whole new attitudes to life and it showed, as never before, the hidden secrets of science and biology and the great elemental forces of inter-stellar space, all glowing with Wells' own zest for living.

But Wells was not completely satisfied. In July of 1904 he confided to Arnold Bennett that he 'had written a humorous little novel on the lines of *The Wheels of Chance*' and offered it to Halkett of *The Pall Mall Magazine*. Halkett found it delightful but wondered whether his readers were interested in quite such 'a narrow range.' Wells instantly retorted that everyone accepted Jacobs' narrow range and Halkett gloomily came back, 'But Jacobs is a humorist.' (8) Not everyone fought for Wells' favours in the beginning. But his popularity with book publishers grew. It carried him into wild schemes for writing a play and then another play, books and then more books, until he had a capital basis of at least £20,000. That was what he needed, he said—£20,000.

* * *

The scene at Spade House was not only turbulent with writing, with finished and half-finished novels, a litter of short stories and sundry essays and satires, eventually to be read by young and old alike, and particularly by the young; his emotional life had reached another explosive impasse. He was now the father of a son, George Philip Wells, born in July 1901, but as with Isabel, things had gone awry with Catherine and the child did not help very much. Over the last few years it had steadily been borne in on two intelligent sensitive people that there were elements of estrangement in what had once seemed to them enchanting. They were, they now realized, as unlike as torrent and brook. It was not only sexually that Catherine could not satisfy Wells, or that she was no great talker amongst the highly articulate people beginning to throng his life, or that intellectually his enormous reach and grasp simply, on occasion, bewildered her. Like Isabel she was of a different temperament. Catherine moved softly, aware of the flowers, the moss and the emerald glory of a blade of grass, only to find her world suddenly invaded by a satyr dynamically alive who set the air about her quivering with great explosive words. It had been all right at first. It had carried its own impetus. It had seemed exciting, different, perpetually full of sparkle and life. In the beginning too, as they rushed their fences and defied society, the exhilaration of defiance had carried them easily over the early troubles; but where Wells could sustain himself against all comers, the innate conventionality of Catherine still reverenced the time-worn verities of politeness, modesty and reticence, and as she settled back into her true self again after the first year, she found that she was married to the very incarnation of irreverence. 'She went through life outwardly serene and dignified, one of a great company of rather fastidious, rather unenterprising women who have turned for their happiness to secondary things, to those fair inanimate things of household and garden,' (9) Wells wrote much later, and he may well have been writing about Catherine.

'Tread softly,' Catherine would quote, 'for you tread on my

dreams.' Wells was not a man to tread on anybody's dreams, and for many years he had a special consideration for the frailties of Catherine, respecting her as few others, remaining indeed—after his somewhat inconsequent fashion—devoted to her; but before their son was born, they found themselves under the compulsion of their own impetuous conduct, to evolve a way of life which sustained their undoubted need of one another, even it if bore only the likeness of love, and presently, first of all, it took the form of a fantasy world in which odd little drawings impregnated with fun, dulled the edge of reality.

'Picshuas' Wells called them. Dashed down on paper as they sat together in the evening, a burlesque diary of the day's events, they brought merriment into a world becoming claustrophobic for Wells. 'And supposing Miss Bits wants more of the table, what happens to me? . . .' he would say, using Catherine's nickname and proceeding to record the Incident of the Stolen Table, with a few ingenious lines in which Catherine swore she saw a likeness to herself. Another few strokes and there was a bald gentleman with a laurel, a pen and large nose in the unmistakable likeness of Wells, crouched like a naughty boy at the furthermost edge of the table trying to concoct Another Story. Nicknames, pet phrases, even sometimes baby talk, went hand in hand with all this. Catherine was Bits or Miss Bits or Snitch, and Wells, Binns or Mr. Binns. There were also moments when Wells, never much given to poetry, wrote doggerel for Catherine's delectation, but sometimes in mid career of a pretty jingle they suddenly became aware of a glibness in the gaiety and the smallest frown crept between Catherine's brows. She was too intelligent not to see why it all happened. Yet—'In the absence of a real passionate sexual fixation, a binding net of fantasy and affection proved in the end as effective as the very closest sexual sympathy could have been to keep them together.' (10)

Even so Catherine changed. She became two people where she had been one. Whether this was a conscious attempt to adjust herself to the so different temperament of her husband, or whether it would have happened without his intervention, lies in the lap of the psychological gods, but she now carefully preserved for her own private moments a person called Catherine, a soft, poetic, elfin spirit, and released in public someone Wells quickly christened Jane, a practical business-like soul who took charge of her husband's finances, and spun a protective web around his working day.

Jane did his typing, completed income tax forms, devised techniques for containing predatory foreign translators, advised and criticized and was forever smoothing everyday difficulties out of his path. They had a joint banking account on which either could draw without the other knowing. They had many friends in common. Streams of people descended on their house at Sandgate, and Jane remained imperturbably the perfect hostess. Still, before he launched on any new writing project, he talked it over with her; still, in trouble he turned to her; but the worlds in which they were apart grew in number. And sometimes, looking up unexpectedly from his work into her eyes, Wells found Jane had dissolved back for a moment into Catherine, and a spirit shone out of her which belonged to the world of Virginia Woolf and Proust and E. M. Forster, only to vanish again as she became aware of his appraisal. Dorothy Richardson drew the picture brilliantly in *Pilgrimage*: There were occasions when Jane 'sent forth . . . the deep magnetic radiance . . . of her inner being' which 'he (Wells) must have known while still they were lovers and it was turned only upon himself who had called it forth, and now saw only when by chance he witnessed the turning of it upon others, in payment for help given in the labours exacted by her perpetual stewardship of his well-being.' (11) Always it dissolved again. . . . 'Her sudden immortal beauty had vanished and in its place was one of the many facets of that part of her being that was turned towards outside things: the bright, brisk, active little person, selfless and strong in endurance behind her fragile austere daintiness, willing to help everyone on his way. . . .'

They still knew boisterous moments together, when Jane impersonated the fat, shining opera singer, and H. G., wholly enchanted, his face alight with pleasure, would suddenly carry her off to his study and sit eagerly talking at her: 'we'll go mad, stark staring mad. Switzerland. Your ironmongery in my rucksack, and off we'll go.' (12)

There were moments when famous women novelists came to stay for the week-end, he read their manuscripts with Jane sitting by, and recognizing incidents drawn from life, burst out 'with his wail of amusement—"This is the episode of the *greenhouse*! How do you do it, Edna? You do it. It's *shattering* that chapter end."'

And when the famous novelist, overwhelmed by his praise sat silent, he rushed on ' "I'm done in, Edna. . . . Shan't write another line." ' He would hardly notice that Jane had gone, that she had slipped away amongst the trees humming to herself. Was she 'deliberately asserting a separate existence ? Really loving her garden and enjoying the chance of being alone,' or had she slipped away because 'she knew all he had to say about *everything* ?'

They would sleep out in the open on hot summer evenings. They would listen to Wagner and Beethoven, and once he said to the assembled company when the music was done—'The thing to *do* is to go out into the world; leave everything behind, wife, and child, and things; go all over the world and come back *experienced*.' And when someone asked what would happen to the wives, which might include Jane, he answered 'The wives . . . will go to heaven when they die.'

Wells, Dorothy Richardson wrote, 'would become affectionate with reservations.' He reacted extravagantly to certain women at this time, but one side of him 'was eternally alien to women' because he was unaware that they required something more than sympathetic affection. 'He was an alien. To Alma [Jane], to any woman ever born he was an alien.' (13) Yet there were times when he needed their approval, their reassurance, sometimes badly. Woman, granted the primal function of reproduction, was not driven to ask any further sanctions from life, but man—and man raised to the tenth power in H. G. Wells—needed the reaffirmation of women's belief in some of his projects, or he fell miserably. His talk was now a blaze of brilliant self-assertion, he had 'a silencing formula which he carried about and could put his hand on at will like small change,' his walk was swift and confident, his books successful; but there remained a streak of defiance in it all and his confidence needed occasional reassurance, perhaps because what he delivered with the force and vision of a gospel sometimes turned out to be a half truth. Knowing an ultimate uncertainty, if he never admitted it, he needed a salve to set him straight with his inner self. There were moments when that salve was woman. Time and again the salve lost its sorcery. And sexually and in other ways Jane had ceased to be 'right,' and there were moments on his side of near indifference. ' "I'm going out if Hypo [Wells] won't think me unsociable," ' says Miriam in *Pilgrimage*. 'Alma [Jane] halted. . . . "Oh"—almost fiercely in a tone lower and deeper than that of her daily voice and coming from the depths of a self persisting from early days but taught by life to keep out of sight,—"*he* won't notice." '

* * *

In the year 1900, Catherine and Wells, bound by ties of law, fantasy and affection, came to an understanding about their temperamental differences so completely rational it might have seemed cold-blooded. Catherine understood and accepted 'the craving, in a body that was gathering health and strength, for a complete loveliness of bodily response. . . .' (14) Dispassionately they discussed what was to be done and there emerged an agreement so free, at first sight, from jealousy and bitterness, that it sounded slightly supernatural. This was indeed a woman. Married to a man rapidly becoming a world figure, richly endowed with creative gifts, and accumulating what promised to be wealth, she now released him from the bonds of the marriage vow, and offered him whatever freedoms he desired. It was as if she set out to become the first Rational Woman in a world where such a figure had never existed, and in the process reaffirmed her husband's flagging belief that the type of person he so often summoned to his aid in his books could, in feminine fact, respond.

Outwardly all was the same. Catherine gardened and typed and talked and received his guests. Their entertaining spread, the Picshuas grew wilder, there were elaborate games and charades, and the casual visitor would have been hard put to it to detect anything strained on the surface. Whether it was taking part in the melodrama of the Doped Race-Horse, the Gambling Duchess or the Teutonic Railway Porter, played out in one charade after another, or nursing him in illness, or criticizing his manuscripts, Catherine kept a place in Wells' affection and his life. And she continued to surprise the assembled company, whenever charades were the order of the day, with unexpected improvisations which delighted the heart of Wells. As a deeply encumbered traveller, with a string of brats represented by adults in socks and straw hats, all noisily eating buns, she stole the house one night by turning to tiny Dolly Radford (the nurse), pointing at E. S. P. Haynes, one of the huge adult children, and demanding, 'You carry Siegfried !'

Jane continued to watch over all Wells did. She comforted him in those recurring moods when terrible glooms and frustrations came down on him, helped him to slip away to France and Italy whenever escape from the everyday round became imperative, as later on it often became imperative; that 'fugitive impulse' he called it and she understood as did few others. She bore him another child, a boy Frank Richard Wells, in 1903. Famous people came to visit not Wells but *the* Wellses at week-ends. There was a glowing shell of happiness and everything ran smoothly. Nobody could mistake Wells' affection towards his wife, and when she deliberately retired into her own private world, sometimes returning with a glow in her eyes as if she had drunk from some secret spring, he did not complain. Yet the affairs had already begun, and he took no trouble to conceal them, affairs which carried him into a new emotional world, not as the promiscuous rake passing from one conquest to another, but as the romantic lover, or too highly charged sensualist, rarely capable of that self-abasement inseparable from annihilating love, but never without warmth, sympathy and immense understanding. He was indeed a lover. He fed on feeling. He knew every gradation of those magical moods when nothing could stop the tumult of the blood; but the character of love changed kaleidoscopically for him over the years.

Chapter Eight

THE FABIAN AFFRAY

WELLS came like a whirlwind into the Fabian Society one dull February day in 1903, whipped out a few revolutionary notions for improving the Fabian approach, quarrelled with the Executive, challenged Shaw and lost, made one last attempt to save the Society's soul and then vanished in an ill-tempered cloud of dust. The interval between his coming and going was longer than this may suggest, but he concentrated a great deal of fire into a very short period. As intellectual credentials he presented *The Question of Scientific Administrative Areas in Relation to Municipal Undertakings,* and it has considerable significance as the first non-fiction statement of an idea which was to haunt him for the rest of his days. The development of aeroplane and steamship were to reduce the vast wilderness of the world to toy proportions, and it meant that the earth must eventually become one administrative area variously known as the World State, Utopia, or, in the estimate of the more disillusioned, Cloud Cuckoo Land. Why not begin at the beginning, he said, and encourage this principle on the far less grandiose level of the Municipal Area, making Municipal Areas larger, more comprehensive, and placing them under one authority? In his day the lecture was listened to with polite interest. By 1940 the idea had permeated deeply enough to be on the verge of practical adoption. But the voice if not the manner of H. G. Wells in 1903, was not much different from the reedy squeak so many knew ten years later, and with Bernard Shaw throwing the spell of his soft Irish cadences about the Fabians, Wells' chances were small from the start. Oratory was no part of his equipment. He could talk, yes, like Niagara on occasion—but not orate. He read his paper in a low monotone addressed to one corner of the hall, and it was no use asking him to speak up because, as he boldly told hecklers later in life, he could not speak up. Some flaw in his vocal chords gave his voice a permanently muted squeak and he would say, with a venom he reserved for only the vilest forms of life, 'I hate my voice.' One other short-coming handicapped him severely in the eyes of the early Fabians, people who, for all their bearded thunder, grand manners and immutable belief in themselves, could not quite overwhelm him, half inaudible as he was, in the first days of their acquaintance. Wells never quite reconciled his Socialism with a formal policy which claimed exclusive rights in its own inheritance or class, or party. For him Socialism was much more a 'realization of a common and universal loyalty in mankind, the awakening of a collective consciousness of duty in humanity.'

When his prosperity took him amongst wealthy people and many a Socialist said he had fallen for the fleshpots, he retorted that most of the thinking had been done for Socialists by leisured people, and he saw nothing wrong with a little comfort, if it freed him from the treadmill of drapery to expand in a Universe of his own choosing, where he made what he took to be a far more inspired contribution to society. He did not desire this freedom alone. Everyone should be similarly free. Everyone should be able to follow their own leading, to live to the uttermost. As it was, Socialism became his 'most expensive indulgence.' Branded with proletarian birth-marks, some of his books were shunned by people who recoiled from Socialism as the devil from holy water, but it did not disturb his conviction that a sensibly reorganized social and economic system would offer a distribution of wealth and liberty undreamt-of in that feckless age, when thousands joined the ignominious scramble for money and power, and the hindmost taken by the devil turned out to be the multitude.

Edward Pease, secretary of the Fabians in Wells' day, has some vivid recollections of him. There were one or two inaccuracies in the *Autobiography*, he says. Wells appears to have put the wrong interpretation on the Pease-Bland episode. 'Bland never wished to be secretary in opposition to myself, and any coolness between us did not last,' says Pease. 'It was *Mrs*. Bland who formally opposed my appointment as half-time secretary at £50.' Pease preserves an interesting collection of letters between Guest, another Fabian, and Wells, which shows intense activity behind the scenes before his final clash with the Executive. He describes Wells at this stage as: 'A masterful person, very fond of his own way, very uncertain what that way was and quite unaware where it necessarily led. In any position except that of leader Mr. Wells was invaluable so long as he kept it.' (1) In other words a complete metamorphosis had overtaken the skinny skeleton with its rubber collar and preposterous clothes, its inferiorities and sexual stammerings, its conviction that fate and the world were against him. He had grown into a brilliantly erratic, uncompromisingly alive person, with an attitude to life fiercely embraced, he was a believer now in a brand of highly individualized Socialism, but as in his scientific student days, he still lacked any of that real consistency so dearly beloved of the British, and quickly annoyed such Fabian goddesses as Beatrice Webb: 'We have seen something lately of H. G. Wells and his wife,' she wrote in her diary. 'Wells is an interesting though somewhat unattractive personality except for his agreeable disposition and intellectual vivacity. . . . But he is totally ignorant of the manual worker, on the one hand, and of the big adminis-trator and aristocrat on the other . . . he ignores the necessity for maintaining the standard of life of the manual worker, he does not appreciate the need for a wide experience of men and affairs in administration. . . . But he is extraordinarily quick in his appre-hensions, and took in all the points we gave him in our 48 hours' talk with him, first at his own house and then here. . . .' (2)

Beatrice shifted her position in 1904: 'We have had a couple of days with H. G. Wells and his wife at Sandgate, and they are returning the visit here. We like him much—he is absolutely genuine and full of inventiveness—a "speculator" in ideas—somewhat of a gambler, but perfectly aware that his hypotheses are not verified. In one sense, he is a romancer spoilt by romancing —but, in the present stage of sociology, he is useful to gradgrinds like ourselves.' (3)

She pumped Wells about her Fabian troubles. He might have troubles himself but so had she and Sidney: 'I asked him to tell me frankly why Wallas and some others were so intensely suspicious of us and seemed bent on obstructing every proposal of Sidney's. He threw out two suggestions: first, that Sidney (and no doubt I) was too fond of "displaying" his capacity for "tactics," that he gave a "foxy" impression—that he had better fall back on being an enthusiast; secondly, that we were always regarded as a "com-bination," working into each other's hands but not impelled by *quite* the same motives. . . .'

Wells' challenge to the Fabians came to a head in 1906. He wrote to Mr. Guest, a member of the Fabian Executive, 'Dear ill-treated Guest, I am having a go at the Fabians on January 12th. . . .' A paper, *Faults of the Fabians,* intended to shake their complacent gradualism, was already prepared. Shake it, it did, but where Shaw could have read the same paper and added song to the slaughter, Wells brought the full wrath of the Society—Olympian when the joint thunderbolts of Shaw, Webb, Bland and Olivier were released at one stroke—down on his head. Who was this audacious little man so impudently tilting at their established gods ? What evidence had he for saying that they were ineffective, that propaganda, loud, prolonged and all-embracing, was better than permeation, that the Society was too small, too poor, too sluggish, that it needed ten thousand members . . . ten thousand members. . .! Scientific romance had gone to his head. He must control his imagination before it devoured him. 'This is still half a drawing room society,' Wells told them, 'lodged in an underground apartment or cellar. . . . The first fault of the Fabian Society is its smallness, the second that even for its smallness it is needlessly poor. . . .' The task undertaken 'is nothing less than the alteration of the economic basis of society. Measure with your eye this little meeting, this little hall; look at that little stall of not very powerful tracts; think of the scattered members, one here, one there. Then go out into the Strand. Note the size of the buildings and business places, note the glare of the advertisements, note the abundance of traffic and the multitude of people. That is the world whose very foundations you are attempting to change. How does this little dribble of activities look then ?' 'It is a fantastic idea' that 'the world may be manœuvred into Socialism without knowing it' that 'society is to keep like it is . . . and yet Socialism will be soaking through it all, changing without a sign. . . .' (4)

Written before the 1906 election, *Faults of the Fabians* may or may not have anticipated the astonishing outbreak of interest in Socialism and remarkable successes for the Labour Party. It can be read in two ways. But the election showed, past any doubt, that the great tide of Toryism was on the turn. Without any striking leader or programme of popular appeal, the Labour candidates defeated many Conservatives as they had not been defeated for three-quarters of a century.

Wells' battle with the Fabians quickly narrowed to highly personal issues. Geoffrey West has told more fully how Wells asked for a committee to examine his scheme, how he tried to nominate all the members himself, how a 16 page report from the

Committee was circulated to be answered by a 27 page document from the Executive, how the Executive's reply simply brushed aside the Committee's work with a Shavian sparkle and briskness. Wells worked hard to get the report signed by the right people. So-and-So's 'ratting off and doesn't want to sign. . . . Go and tame him for God's sake!' he wrote to Guest—one of many letters—on September 15th, 1906. But it was all of no avail. At the crucial meeting it became in effect the Executive versus Wells, the old against the new, and Shaw—it appears, on his own initiative—said the Executive would resign if the rank and file followed Wells, clothing the statement in such magnificent language that it was hard to resist. Wells, for his part, pledged himself not to resign, and Shaw answered, 'That is a great relief to my mind. I can now pitch into Mr. Wells without fear of the consequences.' Pitch in he did and with devastating effect, but not entirely without scruple. 'I forced myself on the committee as its spokesman to save him from being slaughtered by sterner hands,' he said later. 'That I easily and utterly defeated him was nothing; it was like boxing with a novice who knocked himself out in every exchange; but the Society, though it did not give him a single vote, reproached me for my forensic ruthlessness and gave all its sympathy to H. G. . . .' (5) Shaw had in fact been chosen to deal with Wells because he liked him and would probably let him down easily, but it was characteristic of Shaw that the people he most liked bristled with every vice and shortcoming his ingenious mind could find, or if not find, invent. 'Take all the sins he ascribes to his colleagues,' Shaw wrote of Wells on May 19th, 1909, 'the touchiness of Hyndman, the dogmatism of Quelch, Blatchford's preoccupation with his own methods, Grayson's irresponsibility; add every other petulance of which a spoiled child or a successful operatic tenor is capable; multiply the total by ten; square the result; cube it; raise it to the millionth power and square it again; and you will still fall short of the truth about Wells—Yet the worse he behaved the more he was indulged; and the more he was indulged the worse he behaved. . . .' (6)

According to Shaw, Wells insulted the Fabian Society freely, and demanded that the Society should pass a vote not merely of censure but of contempt on its Executive, which would force the leaders to resign and leave Emperor Wells in sole charge. 'At this point any other man would have been hurled out of the society by bodily violence with heated objurgation. Wells was humbly requested to withdraw his demand, as it was not convenient just then to serve him up Sidney Webb's head on a charger.' (7)

And oh the utter impossibility of working with him. With the exception of himself, Shaw said, no other member of the Fabian executive was perfect, but even with him, the shining, blameless knight of Fabian thinking, Wells could not work. He admires, said Shaw, 'Keir Hardie, Ramsay MacDonald and Philip Snowden. This is a proud day for the three; . . .' But let them try working with him; just let them try. . . . 'When they do try the verdict of the coroner's jury will be justifiable homicide, or else Keir and Mac will be hanged and Snowden will see nothing but Wells' ghost, with two dirks sticking in it, for the rest of his life. . . .' (8) The Fabian episode cost Shaw 'personally over a thousand pounds hard cash,' wasting his time trying to undo the mischief which Wells religiously repeated each and every day the Fabians met. But at length, for the moment, they brought Wells down. Considering his defeat more honourable than Shaw's victory, Wells presently retired with the words, 'I am reluctantly taking up a secondary position for a time in the campaign for an effectual reform of the Society's constitution because of the perverse and partially successful efforts to represent this as my personal campaign. . . .' (9)

It forced him to shift his line of attack. If the Executive refused to endorse his reform, he must create an Executive with different ideas. Deep plots were laid to find the right candidates for the next Executive election, considerable guile and ingenuity employed by his fellow-conspirators to pile up votes, until Wells was driven to write to Guest: 'I suggest . . . that we should do no fancy work in the way of rigging votes . . .' and later: 'I've left things very much in your hands and so far you've done nothing except get up a difficult vote-losing row. . . . And then underline the trouble by losing your temper last Friday. Do pull things together now and get the tickets and the circular envelopes ready.' Across one corner: 'Keep calm.' And across another: 'Warmest affection. Whom he loveth he abuseth.'

If the elections in the following March put Wells on the Executive Committee nearly at the top of the poll (fourth) and several friends along with him, it was still an Executive dominated by the old-timers, and reform in the widest sense of the word remained a dream. From then on Wells refused 'to attend committees or do any routine work whatever, and presently resigned, writing a letter for publication at the same time to explain that he had done so because we were a parcel of sweeps.' (G. B. Shaw: *Pen Portraits and Reviews*.)

What did it all amount to ? Did Wells leave an indelible mark on the Fabian Society or radically alter its constitution ? Certainly membership increased enormously under his splenetic spell and great new questions surged through its hardening arteries. But we have the evidence of Edward Pease, Fabian Secretary and a man of invincible integrity, that when the tumult subsided 'the chief change made in the Fabian policy was one which Wells did not initiate, and which as soon as it was actually adopted he virtually repudiated. . . .'

But Wells was not done with politics. Certainly three new novels were kicking unborn in his mind, and literary parturition with its own immutable laws could not be delayed much longer, but the first seeds of the sociologist had now been sown and the first disturbing symptoms of the tremendous clash between the scientist and the artist in him, were beginning to appear. Over the next ten years it was to go very deep.

Chapter Nine

AND NOW UTOPIA

Nov. 19th 1905.
Lamb House, Rye.

M^{Y DEAR WELLS,}

MY DEAR WELLS,

If I take up time and space with telling you why I have not sooner written to thank you for your magnificent bounty, I shall have, properly to steal it from my letter, my letter itself; a much more important matter. And yet I *must* say in three words, that my course has been inevitable and natural. I found your first munificence here on returning from upwards of eleven months in America, toward the end of July . . . I recognized even from afar (I had already done so) that the *Utopia* was a book I should desire to read only in the right conditions of coming to it, coming with luxurious freedom of mind, rapt surrender of attention, adequate honours, for it of every sort. So, not bolting it like the morning paper and sundry, many, other vulgarly importunate things, and knowing moreover, I had already shown you that though I was slow I was safe, and even certain, I 'came to it' only a short time since, and surrendered myself to it absolutely . . . And it was while I was at the bottom of the crystal well that Kipps suddenly appeared, thrusting his honest and inimitable head over the edge and calling down to me, with his note of wondrous truth, that he had business with me above. I took my time however, there below (though 'below' be a most improper figure for your sublime and vertiginous heights) and achieved a complete saturation; after which re-ascending and making out things again, little by little in the dingy air of the actual, I found Kipps, in his place awaiting me—and from his so different but still so utterly coercive embrace I have just emerged. It was really very well he was there, for I found (and it's even a little strange) that I could read *you* only—*after you*—and don't at all see whom else I could have read. But now that this is so I don't see either, my dear Wells, how I can 'write' you about these things—they make me want so infernally to talk with you, to see you at length. . . . Let me tell you, however, simply, that they have left me prostrate with admiration, and that you are for me, more than ever, the most interesting 'literary man' of your generation—in fact the only interesting one. These things do you, to my sense, the highest honour, and I am lost in amazement at the diversity of your genius. As in everything you do it is the quality of your intellect that primarily (in the Utopia) obsesses me and reduces me—to that degree that even the colossal dimensions of your cheek (pardon the term that I don't in the least invidiously apply) fails to break the spell. Indeed your cheek is positively the very sign and stamp of your genius, valuable today as you possess it beyond any other instrument or vehicle, so that when I say it doesn't break the charm, I probably mean that it largely constitutes it, or constitutes the force; which is the force of an irony that no-one else among us begins to have—so that we are starving, in our enormities and fatuities, for a sacred satirist (the satirist *with* irony as poor dear old Thackeray was the satirist without it) and you come, admirably to save us. There are too many things to say, which is so exactly why I can't write. Cheeky, cheeky, cheeky is any young-man-at-Sandgate's offered plan for the Life of Man—but so far from thinking that a disqualification of your book, I think it is positively what makes the performance heroic. I hold with you that it is only by our each contributing Utopias (the cheekier the better) that anything will come, and I think there is nothing in the book truer and happier than your speaking of this struggle of the rare yearning individual toward that suggestion as one of the certain assistances of the future. . . . Meantime you set a magnificent example—of *caring*, of feeling, of seeing, above all, and of suffering from and with the shockingly sick actuality of things. Your epilogue tag in italics strikes me as of the highest, of an irresistible and touching beauty. Bravo, bravo, my dear Wells ! . . .

And now coming to Kipps, what am I to say about Kipps, but that I am ready, that I am compelled, utterly to *drivel* about him ? He is not so much a masterpiece as a mere born gem—you having I know not how, taken a header straight down into the mysterious depths of observation and knowledge, I know not which and where, and come up again with this rounded pearl of the diver. . . . But of course you know yourself how immitigably the thing is done—it is of such a brilliancy of *true* truth . . .'

That Henry James with his inbred awareness of every nuance, his love of intricate counterpoint, should be swept, vulgarly, from the world of undertones into anything so flagrant as admiration, was some measure of the impact Wells had on his generation. It was to be expected that a person of James' breeding would release a well-appointed murmur of approval, for nobody could deny the primal vitality in everything this man Wells did, but that he should wantonly and with scarcely a reservation give himself up to admiration, was as if the god of literature suddenly unbent and revealed himself in the likeness of common clay. James did not succumb alone. Many distinguished writers, critics and thinkers now made public obeisance, fell into open admiration, on the appearance of *A Modern Utopia* and *Kipps*.

William James, brother of Henry, and a man Wells considered as deep an influence in his middle age as Huxley was in his youth, wrote:

MY DEAR WELLS,

I have just read your *Utopia* (given me by F. C. S. Schiller on the one day that I spent in Oxford on my way back to Cambridge Mass. after a few weeks on the Continent) and *Anticipations* and *Mankind in the Making* having duly proceeded together with numerous other lighter volumes of yours, the 'summation of the stimuli' reaches the threshold of discharge and I can't help overflowing in a note of gratitude. You 'have your faults, as who has not ?' but your virtues are unparalleled and transcendant, and I believe that you will prove to have given a shove to the practical thought of the next generation that will be amongst the greatest of its influences for good. All in the line of English genius too, no wire-drawn French doctrines, and no German shop technicalities inflicted in an unerbittlich consequent manner, but everywhere the sense of the full, concrete, and the air of freedom playing through all the joints of your argument. . . .

It would be ungenerous to carp at this highly discriminate orchestra from the safe distance of another generation, almost another world, but the simple fact is that the cachet of *Kipps* and *A Modern Utopia* does not survive intact to-day. *A Modern Utopia* was the biggest of the World State evocations, the most sustained moment of revelation in the darkening human scene, and though it never had a wide popular sale, Wells considered it a most vital and successful work, a book he would set against any other. It derived from two or three earlier books, and its origins need some examination to see it in perspective. *A Modern Utopia* (1905) really began with the New Republic conceived in the rolling clouds of *Anticipations* (1901) a sane enough book for two-thirds of the way, true to the shining optimism of the late nineteenth century, and in parts most persuasively written, but skilfully vague and woolly when the solution had to be found. Liberal democracy it seemed was beginning to crumble, and the governments of the day just would not do, but the New Republic to arise from the ashes would consist of 'all those people throughout the world whose minds were adapted to the demands of the big scale conditions of the new time . . . a naturally and informally organized educated class, an unprecedented sort of people. . . .' It would be a 'conscious organisation of intelligent and quite possibly in some cases wealthy men. . . .' It would be a movement with 'distinct social and political aims, confessedly ignoring most of the existing apparatus of political control, or using it only as an incidental implement in the attainment of these aims.' It would become 'a confluent system of trust-owned business organisms, and of universities and re-organised military and naval services' presently discovering 'an essential unity of purpose, presently thinking a literature, and behaving like a State.'

Precisely *how* is never explained. The unprecedented sort of people are expected to materialize—despite the resistance of the active-dull—by an inevitable permeation of the social process, until a new race is born before even its own members are fully aware of the change; but this is no explanation at all. The optimism of nineteenth-century England, the lack of any need for fact granted the reality of faith, the power of wordy evangelism to replace revolution, sustained a whole world of beautiful illusions for many people before the turn of the century. Summon up your visions, oh ye writers, and garland the world in beautiful words, for by words alone shall the way be opened, it seemed to say. But the way remained obstinately closed. *Anticipations* hazarded some astonishingly accurate mechanical prophecies and was to that extent a brilliant book. There is a picture of aerial battle not far removed from the 1914–18 truth. *Anticipations* said some eminently sane and sensible things, swept sparkling through a dozen hypocritical places but it had a terrifying tendency to carry half humanity away in its sweep. 'And for the rest, these swarms of black and brown and dingy white and yellow people who do not come into the new needs of efficiency ? . . . I take it they will have to go. . . .' 'This thing, this euthanasia of the weak and sensual is possible. I have little or no doubt that in the future it will be planned and achieved.' Wells wrote to Sidney Dark, 'My biggest thing, my most intimate thing, my first line of battleships is *Anticipations*. . . .' And to Miss Healey, '*Anticipations* is designed to undermine and destroy the monarch monogamy and respectability. One has to go quietly in the earlier papers, but the last will be a buster.' Alas it wasn't. Or at least it bust very little. Everything continued to march its measured timeless course.

Mankind in the Making (1903) came closer to earth. It saw the imperative need for a new education alongside the New Republic, it saw the illusion of the eugenic society, but presently it too wandered off into richly rhetorical gardens where the larval souls of the world laboratory would soon become 'boys and girls and youths and maidens, full of the zest of new life, full of an abundant joyful receptivity . . . helpers beside us in the struggle.' Struggle to what precise end was frequently enveloped in a cloud of language, rather too rococo for modern taste, still groping in self-created mists, and open to have the biggest coach and horses driven through it in almost every other chapter. 'They will in their own time take this world as a sculptor takes his marble and shape it better than our dreams. . . .' But the marble remained implacable.

Caution now overtook Wells. He had rubbed the lamp and muttered the incantation without 'one unprecedented sort of person' materializing, unless his own erratic person qualified. Perhaps it might be necessary—unnaturally and against his best persuasions—to *assist* the emergence. But one more effort yet before anything so artificial as forceps were used, one more effort on the grand scale. The effort took the form of *A Modern Utopia*.

*   *   *

Disarmingly *A Modern Utopia* (1905) adopts the widest possible hypothesis, the complete, unstained vacuum of a community totally emancipated from tradition and habit. It matters not that Wells has described most Utopias as 'comprehensively jejune,' as lacking blood and warmth, as having 'no individualities but only generalized people'; he now accepts a wider generalization still. Only within the sweeping ambit of a society completely free from the debris of the past, can he work with any real zest. He must begin with a *new* world.

From it grows a fascinating society, so unreal in some aspects as to read like romance, but beautiful, inspiring, lifting the leaden dullness of everyday life into gracious gaiety, breathing an air incomprehensible to half humanity and as difficult of realization as it is desirable. It is a world where people are divided into five temperamental classes, the Samurai, the Poietic, the Kinetic, the Dull and the Base. The Samurai, the voluntary nobility, are the ruling class, distinguished by that disinterested feeling for people and beliefs of which Wells thought many men capable, even if it amounted to nothing more than enthusiasm for sport or industrial work well done. The Poietic were the creative class with well-developed mental individuality, capable of constantly exploring new ground; the Kinetic the very intelligent people, able to work within accepted formulas. They lived while the Poietic experimented with life. 'A primary problem of government was to vest all the administrative and executive work in the Kinetic class, while leaving the Poietic an adequate share in suggestion, criticism and legislation, controlling the base and giving the dull an incentive to kinetic effort. . . .' Only the base were forbidden entry into the ranks of the Samurai and by base Wells meant 'people who had given evidence of a strong anti-social disposition'—how dangerous a phrase! Otherwise the flow from one class to another was largely self-determined and was certainly irrespective of the circumstances to which a child had been born, his accent, dress or manners.

These were the broad divisions of his Utopia, a green pleasant sunny land where the weather smiled in summer calm, men were gay with a gaiety out of the heart, and a sense of spacious ease, of beautifully healthy organisms stretching in the sun, pervaded everything. Whenever he is dealing with these sweeping generalities the picture unfolds in rhythmic beauty, but once slip down from the heights, move into the streets, into the crevices of everyday life in his Utopia. . . .

Work appears to finish for some of the inhabitants around midday or shortly afterwards, they use the duodecimal system of counting, they have gold coins stamped with Newton's head—each denomination celebrates a centenary—but there is some debate about substituting force or energy units for the common currency. The buildings are beautiful. Even the factory where one of the protagonists works is set high in hills open to the summer sun, with a water slide carrying down from the forests the logs to be carved into lovely shapes by the wood carvers, a resinous arcadia quite untroubled by economic strife. Prosperity is the automatic order of the day. Eccentrics are encouraged just enough to be picturesque. Sir Thomas More insisted upon absolute community of goods in his Utopia, but here there are many relaxations. Payment is made by one section of the community to another for light services carefully rendered in somewhat indeterminate form. Everyone gets a job.

As for houses and the rooms in these houses—there are no sharp corners to harbour dirt, floor meeting wall with a gentle curve, and each apartment can be cleaned by 'a few strokes of a mechanical sweeper.' The bed disappears into the wall at the touch of a lever and the bedclothes automatically hang airing. 'A little notice tells you the price of your room and you gather the price is doubled if you do not leave the toilette as you found it. . . .' It is when Wells breaks into these practical details, when he abandons the spirit of the thing and tries to show the machinery at work, that the Utopia becomes naive, with moments of near farce inviting derision. He can dash in the towers and pinnacles with a few scrawls of his coloured chalks, invoke vaguely beautiful cities, reveal noble boulevards, stumble accidently on vistas he no more knew were there than we did, and go glinting on, exciting the eye and mind, forcing them to take part in the writing because these flashes of line and colour are always incomplete: but when he attempts the details . . . He can write of a marriage system totally different from ours and make it sound convincing. The parties to a projected marriage would 'have to communicate their joint intention to a public office after their personal licences were granted and each would be supplied with a copy of the index card of the projected mate, on which would be recorded his or her age, previous marriages, legally important diseases, criminal convictions. . . . Possibly it might be advisable to have a little ceremony for each party, for each in the absence of the other, in which this record could be read over and discussed in the presence of witnesses. . . . There would then be a reasonable interval for consideration and withdrawal.' He can explain the way in which mothers would be paid by the State, until a career in wholesome motherhood—where a woman with seven or eight children becomes a prosperous, well set up person, quite independent of her husband's income—seems real enough. He can write 'In the sense that the State guarantees care and support for all properly born children, our entire Utopia is to be regarded as a comprehensive marriage group,' and we do not gasp, or openly resist.

But once let him loose describing the clothes of the Utopians, the transport system, the civil service, the everyday minutiæ, and unreality enters in, even though he never reaches deeply enough into detail to disturb the general picture. It is comparatively easy in an unrestricted vacuum to conjure to life a broad vision of the perfect society. Men have been at the game for generations. Plato, More, Campanella and Butler were merely the figureheads of a whole race highly skilled as professional Utopians. Clothing it in detail is less easy. Giving life to the small streets, the shops, the clothes and speech, breathing in the laughter, language, scents and sounds, begins to hamper the free imaginative sweep and is liable to land the writer in a morass of intricate doubt. But there is another trouble far and away more difficult than detail, a trouble to which Wells—like all his Utopian ancestors from the mists of Plato—failed to face up. No one has yet contrived to combine the surge of prophetic vision with the practical machinery of change-over from one way of life to another. It is utterly false to sweep away society as it exists, and start out as though the human race were freshly born without one preconceived prejudice to ensnare the new society; it is easy: it is—almost—cheating. The marriage of the old to the new is the major problem, reconciling deep-embedded tradition with rabid revolution.

Looked at in one way, Wells' Utopia amounted, in the end, to a world where beautiful people played gently in their gardens, some indulging a lofty polygamy, some cerebrating with the State's connivance, some having children rather inconsequently, most working and making gay in a fashion sometimes a little too deliberate, and all accepting the decisions of the spartan Samurai, while remaining invincibly unaware of the joys of sin or unrestrained selfish indulgence. But it was much more than that. It was much more than a scented, emasculated Paradise given over to a sort of superannuated happiness. The sweep of its conception, the inspiration of its Samurai dedicated to disinterested service, were undeniable and carried their own noble message. Perhaps in the Samurai lay the highest achievement of all. A hardy, bare-limbed race who followed the Common Rule—an austere system of self-disciplinary renunciations—they were forbidden wine, meat and tobacco, and lived together in group marriage, free-lovers amongst themselves, but serving, before anything else, the State. 'On the principle that the bow need not always be strung [membership of the Samurai], could be abandoned and resumed, under proper safeguards, according to the way of living desired by the individual at any time.' And once every year for seven consecutive days they must, under the Common Rule, retire into the wilderness, go right out of life, alone, holding no communication with any living person, seeking spiritual refreshment for the high purposes to which they had been called. They epitomize the finer spirits, half saint, half scientist, with room yet for the poet, whom Wells dreamt would one day inherit the earth as Plato hoped philosophers might become kings.

Indeed the whole book was impregnated with the Platonic approach and if, sexually, it overlooked those appalling fixations which tend to confound the most emancipated spirits, if it ignored the complications of a completely voluntary ruling class, and if it would, as it stood, have availed the practical world-makers little or nothing, nevertheless once more it stirred the dullest imaginations, summoned an artist's vision in place of dull data and statistics. The fabric had never glowed like this before. Here was a community freed from all the sordid little drives of our own generation, instinct with a quite different purpose. It so very nearly came alive that people were persuaded to hope that perhaps one day these beautiful dummies would confound everyone and step down into life; perhaps the lights were not altogether the lights of fairyland, even if for the moment it was all a glorious illusion to the planner and the politician who could not detect one practical point in the whole romantic medley.

They were very sceptical about Mr. Wells' qualifications to dabble in Utopias. Mr. Wells didn't understand that specialized faculties and knowledge were as necessary for administration as any other job. He assumed anyone could fall into it. He had too much faith in the physical scientists straight from the laboratory, and so far as the economic machinery of his Utopia was explained at all, he didn't seem to know how economics worked. Worse still, he was ill-equipped with any detailed knowledge of social organization or machinery. By all means congratulate him on such a colourful feat. Bravo, Mr. Wells! Bravo again! But pass the book to the music-makers, the dreamers of dreams.

A Modern Utopia was widely read among university students. It released hundreds of young people into sexual adventure, only to find the fierce net of jealousy and fixation closing tightly around them, it made a sudden music amongst the squalid attempts at government and administration. A hand moved across the deeper strings and for a moment the echo did not die. This was beautiful if slightly impractical. This was worth reading aloud to the not completely lost. This was inspiring. But the total effect of

A Modern Utopia on its limited reading public was to change for
all time Wells' romantic belief that the Samurai and the New Republic would emerge of their own accord. Many years afterwards
he wrote, 'I realised that an Order of the Samurai was not a thing
that comes about of itself, and that if ever it were to exist it must
be realised as the result of very deliberate effort. . . .' (1)

A tremendous *volte face*. Not natural selection but deliberate
interference, a continuous sustained effort, must now set in motion
the delicate mechanism which would finally change the old order
irrevocably. Nothing if not audacious, Wells himself proceeded to
make the effort. All unaware, the little Fabian Society—how he
loved to denigrate its size—was to be converted into the spearhead
of the Samurai, the beginnings of a new order of human beings,
who, if they did not live according to the Common Rule, bore
resemblance enough to his voluntary nobility to inspire their
fellows. It would skilfully employ all the arts of propaganda to
win over and consolidate the rising generation into a self-contained group, impregnated with Samuraian beliefs and devoted to
disinterested service. It would aim at the complete reorganization
of the Socialist Party and many another dangerous feat. How fine
and futile and lit with tremendous verbal lightnings it all turned
out to be. What a courageous, imbecile attempt Wells made to
quicken and transfigure the immutable flow of Fabian logic. For
this was the real issue underneath his battle with the Fabians. It
was not only the character and constitution of the Society he
wanted to change, not only the widening and deepening of its
reach; he wanted to draw off its blood into the veins of his Samurai.
'On various occasions in my life,' he wrote many years later, 'it
has been borne in on me, in spite of a stout internal defence, that
I can be quite remarkably silly and inept; but no part of my career
rankles so acutely in my memory with the conviction of bad judgment, gusty impulse and real inexcusable vanity as that storm in
the Fabian teacup.' (2)

It had to fail. The whole notion was preposterous to the plod-
ding, certain world of Sidney Webb, steeped in statistical analysis
and capable of darkening the vision of any social artist, and this
vision, this dramatic sword-and-cloak, Wellsian fantasy! Were the
Fabians to drag themselves into the world of the theatre? Did he
expect them to take his melodrama seriously? Better get the Old
Vic to try it out. They were social scientists, not character actors.

That was the view of one faction of the Fabians. And the immaculate Hubert Bland, frock-coated, monocled and with a magnificently resonant voice, went to the Fabian platform as though to the front bench of the House of Commons, and spoke in a perfect parliamentary manner, 'debating, yes actually debating, Sir,' this infernal romanticist into the dust. Fie upon you, Mr. Wells. To hope to tamper with society in such a fashion! A grown writer should know better. The grown writer went melancholy away. He was baffled. He did not know where to turn next. He could talk and write and the words echoed back at him, while everything remained much the same. The English were disposed to dally with his theories and enjoy self-consciously a little flexing of the mental muscles, playfully aping the international impulse, but the grim realities which were driving Lenin along a parallel, if far cruder path, had no substance for them, nor bothered them in the least. Wells soon came to believe that Lenin was succeeding where he had failed. The reconstructed Communist Party allowed members periodic withdrawal from its ranks as the Samurai could drop out of the voluntary nobility, its members, too, underwent training in directive ideas, suffered special disciplines, and the Communist Party proceeded on the assumption that large numbers of sensible, very worthwhile citizens, were far happier outside the administrative circle than in it. This superficial similarity did not stand very close examination, but Wells in melancholy reaction against the resistant English, did not for the moment stress the differences, differences which later brought his hackles up most viciously.

Chapter Ten

THE NOVELIST

NOBODY is going to get peevish about *Kipps*. It was a great comic rumbustious feat and as a sheer piece of story-telling came close to Dickens, but Dickens unfolded his stories with greater technical skill, if they moved heavily beside the swiftness of Wells. One must make one's choice. Wells wrote for a more urgent age. Where Dickens was prepared to work patiently away at all those details which breathe verisimilitude into the very pores of a book, or slow it to a snail's crawl missing nothing which the snail might see, Wells, bored by minutiae, pressed on with a few impressionistic strokes. It was swift, stream-lined, beside Dickens. It brought Kipps alive in a few easy episodes. There were intensive references to Dickens on the appearance of *Kipps* in 1905, as earlier there had been to Jules Verne. Wells, to his discomfiture, constantly resembled some one or other. It was the literary tradition. But once again, Dickens in outlook at least was half a world away. Sometimes he drew the grossest caricatures of people, labelled them with little tricks and habits meticulously reiterated on every other page, the easiest way of establishing character, and insisted that if only the Gradgrinds and the Bounderbys were better people all would be well with the world. It was human nature he attacked, not society. It was moral not economic values which concerned him. What his people did for a living was of trivial moment unless they happened to do something easily turned to spectacular account—burglars, money-lenders or convicts. Trade Unionism in *Hard Times* was a regrettable incident susceptible only to benevolent paternalism on the part of the employers. In a word, workers and society would be all right if only people behaved decently.

All this was anathema to Wells. What people did for a living became vital in his books, the *organization* of society its greatest evil, the future more important than past or present, and the people he intensely disliked—kings, soldiers, landowners, priests and peasants—belonged to a dying age, the age of Dickens. Dickens loved them all, fell into open admiration of the quaintness in things which Wells found sentimental. Dickens lost himself interminably in warm hostelries reeking of punch and good fellowship, where Wells craved the clean swift air of the future.⌐

And if *Kipps*, when it was finished, became a study of one struggling shop assistant—a universal figure in the likeness of all shop-assistants—it was far more realistic than anything Dickens would have permitted to escape his pen. He would have over-drawn, overstated Kipps and left out half his life—his work. He would have made his illiteracy immutable, something to be pre-served for its quaintness, made Kipps a lovable buffoon licensed to the sort of society in which he believed, a society capable of awe at the imbecility of the lower orders. Wells did it quite dif-ferently, and *Kipps* had, what was for Wells, one shining quality. It avoided the disease which overtook and disfigured much of his later work. He rarely achieved complete transference in his later novels. He was half in, half out of his character's shoes all the time, his enormous egotism could, by then, never quite tolerate a character living in its own right, and he constantly pushed his way back into his own people. It happens with William Clissold and half a dozen others. There are universal moments, and there are moments of pure Wells, with Wells blustering into the book to overwhelm his characters with his own by no means dull talk, but Kipps was almost completely Kipps, running off to say things of his own, sustained by a vitality independent of Wells, a man people assumed to have living counterparts. Yet what Dickens would have overstated, Wells now underestimated. For where, where in the whole conception of *Kipps* is there that depth of awareness which must emerge from books with any pretensions to probing the heart of life, or reaching the full range of emotional understanding ? The question would be invalid if *Kipps* were not considered an important novel. It cannot apply to second-rate fiction. But ask it of Kipps the man and it soon becomes apparent that he moves very much on the surface. He comes alive in warm comic reality, unfailingly entertains in his smallest moment of embarrassment, sets off ripple after ripple of homespun humour touched with its own irony, plays havoc ever and again with the emotions, and does all this without ever reaching those profound elemental reactions which can so suddenly and disturbingly spring from the simplest situation under the touch of a great writer. It is not that Kipps was without them. Wells ignored them. He never really explored the riches of his humble shop assistant. He was too hasty, too overwhelmed by surface gusto to see the wealth he had created. It needed deep patient delving, and perhaps the use of that delicate literary dynamite peculiar to E. M. Forster, before the inner Kipps would erupt. But that was asking for the moon. It just was not in Wells' nature. He simply could not contrive the small aesthetic explosion which leaves a sudden stillness in eye and mind, as one waits for the exquisite convulsion to subside and the dark and beautiful under-belly of life to be—for a second—revealed. *Kipps* is four-square, unsubtle without depth. It is done with a literary harrow.

But how successfully in all his *surface* reality the stumbling word-bound Kipps comes to life, to endear his pathetic little soul to our heart, a figure in the likeness of all human beings blinded through lack of education, humiliated by snobberies and sick at heart for a few homely reassurances, for a little warmth and affection, and a sense—no matter how illusory—of security. *Kipps* will survive so long as young people undergo the ordeals of adjustment to adult life, and one class covets the graces of another. *Kipps* was good, very good indeed. But it wasn't great and it might have been.

* * *

A Modern Utopia and *Kipps* marked the beginning of a new phase in Wells' life. Two strains were now running deep in his development, and if there were moments when they appeared to follow an indistinguishable course, when together they made a mighty chorus, one was the self-conscious attempt to find the right solution, the right attitudes—the scientist; the other of the very *id* itself—the artist. As a scientific romancer Wells' first pre-occupation had been with the mass of mankind, and in the early books he could achieve a serene isolation which was occasionally terrifying. 'At times I suffer from the strangest sense of detachment from myself and the world about me. I seem to watch it all from outside, from somewhere inconceivably remote, out of time, out of space, out of the stress and tragedy of it all,' (1) he had written in 1898. Then the individual began to get more attention again, and 'the personalities thwarted and crippled by the defects of our contemporary civilization' came under analysis with a second wave of novels where the artist held undisputed sway: *Love and Mr. Lewisham, The Sea Lady* and *Kipps.* By temperament an artist and by training a scientist, Wells had constantly set the dogs of science on to his romantic self and watched them fight it out, but now in the years from 1903 to 1906 there was a disturbing tendency for the self-contained spectator to become involved in the *mêlée.* Intuitive man prowling deep in the subconscious constantly waylaid and overwhelmed intellectual man, and Wells could no longer stand outside the struggle. With *Kipps* and the *Utopia* it burst into the open. The scientist, trying to escape from the artist into pure sociology, into world-making stripped of its fictional glamour (the *Utopia*), found the artist clamouring ever more loudly for comedy, simplicity, love of the ordinary, untroubled by any vestige of science at all (*Kipps*).

The clash became acute. Something had to be done about it. So it was that an uneasy understanding took place between the two, his scientific self insisting that if he must have these extravagantly human indulgences with men so lovable as Kipps, then for heaven's sake let him make the man rational, and test the world we knew against him—which brought him to *Tono-Bungay* (1908) where many divergent streams suddenly met to produce a magnificently unexpected answer. Wells' conflict was not his alone. It epitomized in highly intensified form the dilemma of his age, an age nurtured on the romanticisms of Victorian England, but lately recovered from Oscar Wilde's extreme æstheticism, and desperately trying not to shudder as it felt the first cold brush from the cheek of science.

As a novelist, it was not in *Kipps* or *Mr. Polly* that Wells put his inspiration to the final test. In the same year as *A Modern Utopia* and *Kipps* appeared, he was at work on *Tono-Bungay*. the second of what were to be the three most important novels he ever wrote. In many ways it is Wells at his best. Intermittently it took him three years to write and when he had finished he admitted to a friend that this was his highest creative moment beyond which he could not go. Later he changed his mind, but then it was the final touchstone.

On the surface *Tono-Bungay* moves simply enough. It brings to life an odd ignorant little man who seems to be a combination of Whittaker Wright, the financial fraud who committed suicide, a certain daily newspaper proprietor, and someone in the likeness of all ambitious shopkeepers. From the suffocating calm and near poverty of a small country town, Uncle Ponderevo, by inspiration an inventor, by profession a chemist, suddenly emerges into the breathtaking world of finance, carried thither on the effervescing wave of his own patent medicine. Along with him goes his nephew George. A simple enough formula: the dull, rather stupid, completely mediocre chemist makes good and carries other people along with him to fame and fortune. But how much more this story turns out to be. The bottles of slightly injurious coloured water foisted on an unsuspecting world under the magic formula 'Tono-Bungay' become a national drug. Uncle Ponderevo, awed by his own unthinking audacity, says before the story is half spent—perhaps it does 'em good because they think it does 'em good—and then abruptly the whole colossal towering sham of the patent medicine world, shining forth one night in brassy glory, has disappeared in dust the next.

But *Tono-Bungay* not only dissolves the patent medicine towers about the head of Uncle Ponderevo, with a poetic insight into his sordid soul which makes his death lyrically moving; it not only gives his struggles to understand forces which reduced him to a weeping cringing shambles, incongruous beauty. As Geoffrey West has said, it is Wells, now the fully fledged rationalist, in the likeness of George Ponderevo, testing one experience after another with his intellectual consciousness, and finding all wanting. Here is George Ponderevo given a childhood so close to Wells' that it is almost duplicity to call it fiction. Here is George Ponderevo finding Bladesovery, class distinctions and 'her leddyship,' anachronisms too baffling to understand, but demanding some protest, even though it meant blacking the eye of an aristocratic brat born to the ways of luxury. This way of life, where the big house and the squire dominated everything, was already sapped, and some intuitive perception in this very avid little boy all but knew it. And then the exquisite Beatrice, aged ten and full of cunning adoration, deceives and grossly maligns him: 'I have regretfully to admit that the Honourable Beatrice Normandy did, at the age of ten, betray me, abandon me and lie most abominably about me.' Calf love has let him down disgracefully. So does justice when he is brought to book for being the sole instigator of a fight he never sought. There follow some glimpses of the ramshackle shortcomings of modern capitalism built on feudal foundations, until the sordid stratagems it forces on so many people in the struggle for existence, become, for the rapidly growing George Ponderevo, unendurable.

So the first third of the book runs on. It is largely reminiscence. Puppets in the likeness of Wells play out his early days, occasionally admitting his more mature self to protest—in case you mistake this for a novel—'I've read an average share of novels and made some starts before this beginning, and I've found the restraints and rules of the art (as I made them out) impossible for me. . . .' A man who invented games for the diversion of the elderly had now found the supreme game which could be applied to his work with endless variation. Noisily stepping in and out of his characters' shoes, he insists with straight face and laughing mind that this humble pedlar of words known as Herbert George Wells must not be mistaken for an artist or even a novelist, and this book is not in any circumstances to be taken for a novel.

But he has hardly finished saying it before spontaneous combustion intervenes, the characters come alive in their own right, the pace begins to mount, and one after another the remainder of the great experiences which exalt and degrade our days are put to the rationalist sword, and nothing it seems can survive. After justice and capitalism, religion: ' "There's no hell," I said, "and no eternal punishment. No God would be such a fool as that." ' With those few thrusts, revealed religion seems to die. Adult love next, with the trumpets sounding, the morning stars singing together, and George Ponderevo driven by continual frustration to demand marriage at any price. When the price turns out to be £500 a year, the lovely creature bought reveals stultifying limitations, and the whole dreary suburban business can no longer sustain itself with romantic illusions, there is a moment of parting, a fraternity of pain when two human souls almost create the thing they have so long craved—deep, deep affection—but Ponderevo goes out of the house down the road for ever, and marriage and conventional love have failed him too. Systems capitalist and otherwise are now burst open afresh to reveal the monsters feeding on their own evil, offering frustrated lives a nostrum, a Tono-Bungay, and making, in the process, a profit from the very misery they create. Omniscient in the background lies the great, dirty, glittering face of London, brought alive in all its fecundity, a stupid giantess breeding sniffling Ponderevos who take advantage of laws they do not understand and are flung into fame or the gutter. Men practise petty deception. Enormous energy is devoted to slaying paper dragons. The rich insist on keeping their ignorance of the poor intact. Until a red blaze comes out of George's nature and he will have none of it. Nor will he tolerate the gathering of the great where they fawned on his zzzzzz-ing uncle because accident had made him rich, nor Ewart and his cold-blooded cynicism, nor all the discarded heap of human hopes and aspirations which blotted out the sky above London and left little room for George's scientific gods who might perhaps survive, against all hope, the rationalist test.

His uncle's final collapse is beautifully done. Some special alchemy finds music in the defeat of this now paunchy old man. Or is there beauty in ignorance and clumsiness and sordid self-deception feeling it has but to reach out a hand and it will touch the stars and find redemption ? Their meeting at the moment of bankruptcy remains in the mind long after the book is finished. 'I discovered that his face was wet with tears, that his wet glasses blinded him. He put up his little fat hand and clawed them off clumsily, felt inefficiently for his pocket handkerchief, and then to my horror, as he clung to me, he began to weep aloud, this little, old, world-worn swindler. It wasn't just sobbing or shedding tears, it was crying as a child cries—It was—oh ! terrible ! "It's cruel," he blubbered at last. "They asked me questions. They kep' asking me questions George." '

The whole crazy castle of high finance which set Uncle Ponderevo on the cloud-capped pinnacles, a fumbling old man, trying to convince himself it was his own skill and not black magic which had carried him there, has dissolved like a cloud, and a pathetic, tear-stained wonder stares at the last fading wrack, as little aware of the forces which broke him as those that made him. A balloon, the invention of George, finally carries him away across the Channel out of the clutching hands of his creditors, only to die an ignominious death in a forgotten French village. To the end George Ponderevo goes on testing events in the light of rational thinking, and it is the peculiar distinction of these last scenes that they destroy one set of values after another not with the cold grin of the iconoclast, or the acid of Huxley, but warm-bloodedly and with regret, as a great humanist might. Amongst the strange band of people gathered about Uncle Ponderevo's death-bed is one who is suspected of asking the dying man where he can get a safe 6 per cent. A little clergyman, falling on his knees to murmur Low Church piety in French, finds so many people stumbling over him he all but gives up. Nothing is sacred to the end. Even the life hereafter, which the rationalist George could not countenance at any price, he tells his uncle may be true—a sentimental sop because the old man craved it. So the great events exhaust themselves. Presently there is nothing left in the common pool of experience to test, and the rationalist must turn his sword upon himself or abandon it altogether. Abandon it he does, and with it the whole magnificent box of intellectual tricks. Childhood passes, marriage passes, love, religion, immortality pass, our own society crumbles, and then in a blinding flash of revelation the rationalist too goes down over the horizon and the intuitive self surges up once more to take complete command. It is a moving moment of near exaltation, of lyrical triumph.

'Something comes out of it. . . . How can I express the values of a thing at once so essential and so immaterial ? It is something that calls upon such men as I with an irresistible appeal. . . .

'I have figured it in my last section by the symbol of my destroyer, stark and swift, irrelevant to most human interests. Sometimes I call this reality Science, sometimes I call it Truth. But it is something we draw by pain and effort out of the heart of life, that we disentangle and make clear. Other men serve it, I know, in art, in literature, in social invention, and see it in a thousand different figures, under a hundred names. I see it always as austerity, as beauty. This thing we make clear is the heart of life. It is the one enduring thing. Men and nations, epochs and civilizations pass, each making its contribution. I do not know what it is, this something, except that it is supreme. It is a something, a quality, an element, one may find now in colours, now in forms, now in sounds, now in thoughts. It emerges from life with each year one lives and feels, and generation by generation and age by age, but the how and why of it are all beyond the compass of my mind. . . .'

Rational man in despair has turned to—is it mysticism ? How many times, in book after book from now on, this battle is refought, the issues restated, Wells' own enormous conflict, never entirely resolved in his lifetime, projected on to the printed page, with somewhere at the heart a baffled cry as once again the inner secret, the final resolution of earthly woe, escapes him, or evaporates—or was it ever really there?

Tono-Bungay contrives one hallmark of a great mind in its concluding chapters—compassion, unselfconscious spontaneous compassion, not deliberately written into the situation, but welling out of the very nature of the book itself. These chapters make you feel for some stinking bundle of humanity, which by all the laws of god and nature should be carried away in the tumbrils, an inexplicable warmth and sympathy. The pitiful, the weak, the silly, glow under Wells' magnanimity until what might so easily become merciless satire turns into a benediction, and oh the light which shines through sordid acts when that supreme rationality sees how little people may be to blame for what they are and do. Uncle Ponderevo is a weak self-seeking swindler, the epitome of one way of business life, but venom is as out of place with him as the whip to the untaught child, and time and again comes this feeling of Olympian tolerance as Wells watches his character drive to his own perdition, melancholy that he is so immutably his own executioner.

Tono-Bungay came fresh and vivid to men and women of Wells' generation. These great questionings, the challenge to one eternal verity after another, shook their world and their way of life, and it was all tremendously exciting. Already they were dimly aware of the changes he wrote about—the shift in the social scene, the gradual decay of the aristocracy, the working-class movements coming into the ascendant, the millions of men and women pouring into factories and offices, the savage farce of advertising and patent medicine, the trumpery of obscurantist marriage and mating. All this they apprehended, but without an artist to make it articulate—and such an artist as Wells—imagination would have remained unlit, the blinkers in place for another generation. Wells brought the Modern Word from the Rational Mountain with noble language and enormous creative fire. He spoke for the multitude with their voice because his life had been a microcosm of the whole social process and he had suffered each one of these changes, upheavals and questionings in his own personal and super-sensitive way. There lay half the secret of his appeal. He was his world in miniature. There lay his difference from Bernard Shaw, a man always outside the experiences he described, a man implacably debonair and detached.

Perhaps because of its wellsprings, *Tono-Bungay* did not admit any compromise with the novelist's technique. Wells was making coherent the mutterings of the early twentieth-century tide, and literary frills of any kind would have been false. It wasn't entirely true of course. Shape and form have a sincerity of their own and should illumine the truth which they contain. But if words were not weighed and flavoured with care in *Tono-Bungay*, if there were no subtle unfoldings of the story, the book—conceived in the vein of Balzac—had more shape and form than some of Wells' novels, and gained enormously by it. There is nothing very new to say about the threadbare argument of matter versus manner in the art of novel writing, and Wells, as everyone knows, as much suspected form as Henry James considered it imperative. Both were wrong. The novel was never a happy hunting ground for purists like James. Too often the accidental, lopsided, slap-dash effort came off very well without any concession to shape and design, and novel writing revealed itself as an impure art, but the precise balance between form and matter could create an impact greater than too much emphasis on either. The novel sought to communicate life, to assess values, to explore character and to entertain. At its highest it was granted spiritual insight and placed its characters in the dynamic web of the universe. Wells seldom achieved spiritual insight, but he achieved many other things which belonged to good novel writing, with very little use of its higher techniques. Yet how much better *Tono-Bungay* might have been, granted the technical skill of E. M. Forster; how awesome to imagine Wells' boundless vitality and creative fire married to the art of Forster. For whatever else is said on these matters, life as lived in the flesh can be a damnably dull business, and what we talk about excruciatingly mediocre, yet communicate these self-same lives and words to paper, with the literary skill of a Forster, and they emit a quite new glow. The monotonous folds of every-day experience are smoothed flat, the self-same stretch of life refolded in a fresh and vital way. So treated, events may, like a fan, make new patterns as we unfold them again, revealing unsuspected relationships between one episode and another. A year is made to pass in a page of a novel. Climaxes are seen from afar off, where they were unsuspected in everyday life, or released on the reader with the exquisite devastation of an æsthetic explosion which life so rarely contrives. The whole of a man's career

crowded into two hours' reading, quickly makes apparent its
purpose and direction in a novel where, lost in the everyday maze
which drags itself out unendingly in real life, the individual drifts
aimlessly, unaware where he is going. The sense of purpose and
direction in a novel transfigures everyday events. Life unaware of
it can be very dull. Form, in a word, takes the monotony out of
life. Even in his worst novels Wells used form in his own loose,
gay, carefree manner, but he wrote 'I was disposed to regard a
novel as about as much an art form as a market place or a boule-
vard. It had not even necessarily to get anywhere. You went by it
on your various occasions.'

*   *   *

Close on the heels of *Tono-Bungay* came *The History of Mr. Polly*,
(1910) written it appears in reaction from the tensions of George
Ponderevo and his rational inquisition. Eternal damnation seize
this cerebration ! To laughter now, to gusto and good sound
British sense, and all those clumsy, simple, endearing characteristics which give Mr. Polly, under the alchemy of Wells, moments
of immortality and phrases of incomprehensible enchantment.
'Beastly, silly, wheeze of a hole. . . . Sesquippledan verboojuice.'
No bitterness, the whole thing of a piece, no great knockings on
the door, but compassion and humanity and rollicking fun. Oh the
excellence of the ordinary ! This is a fair-ground of a novel with
roundabouts and slapstick, an interminable roar of words and
irrepressible life. Like *Kipps* it shows the same Cockney spirit
arising in the midst of hopeless inadequacies—Wells rarely went
outside the Home or Southern Counties for his characters. In
Kipps it uncovered the matador hidden inside the stumbling shop
assistant, a matador quite capable of facing a charging bull with
no better weapons than a ludicrous phrase. 'He told her [Helen
Walsingham] to walk quietly towards the stile, and made an
oblique advance towards the bull. "You be orf," he said, "You
be orf." ' It is the sublime Cockney moment, the epitome of in-
articulate, ill-bred audacity. 'You be orf!' No bull could face it.
Kipps and Mr. Polly are wonderful incarnations of what might
have happened to Wells without education, a Wells driven to use
the words bubbling in him and getting them all so delightfully
muddled, a Wells who was, in fact, quite afraid of cows. In *Kipps*
it is also Wells telling all those people who had once thought

themselves superior to him, to be orf. In some novels—and part of his private life—he drew his inspiration from a deep, inexhaustible sense of inferiority. He had been made to feel inferior, he had inherited many hurts, humiliations and snobberies and his very physical appearance put him on the defensive. He was never, in himself, a complete and satisfying spectacle, like Bernard Shaw, tall and broad, equipped with beautiful voice and magnificent head. He carried a dumpy, inept little body from success to success with a venomous dislike of half its attributes. Physically and socially, there were moments when his sense of inferiority released floods of energy and anger in him. He was frequently in a state of violent reaction. He lived every moment passionately, sprang unnecessarily to defend himself, became shrilly enraged at the buzz of a gnat, but where the ordinary man demeaned himself by making such a fuss, Wells' special alchemy transmuted indignations into novels. . . . *Kipps*, *Mr. Polly* and *Tono-Bungay*. Sometimes his inferiority became his inspiration, an inferiority fused in the fire of imagination which produced tremendous encounters with bulls and sublime effronteries like—You be orf.

There is unmistakable evidence that in *Kipps* and *The History of Mr. Polly*, Wells the artist was untroubled by Wells the scientist. It is, again, a considerable token of what might have been if the unfettered artist had surrendered completely to his own genie and let it take possession. How many great, warm crowded canvases we shall never get now, how many people whose deaths might have moved us were never born. In *Mr. Polly*, Wells was back for the moment in the full-blooded Dickens tradition, rebelling against the frustrations of the human personality in the petty bourgeois world, kicking hard at the dumb elephant of education, but possessed more than anything with the essence of Polly, the man as a man.

*   *   *

Kipps, *Tono-Bungay* and *Mr. Polly* were harmless enough. With *Ann Veronica* and *The New Machiavelli*, written in the 1905–11 period, it was dangerously different. Ann Veronica came like an angel of freedom, a very determined audacious angel, into the lives of endless young women. These were the days of chaperons, when father was infallibly right, the days when it was vaguely indecent for a girl to earn a living, when to have political opinions if you were female and under thirty was to invite ridicule, and to play any part in the barbaric antics of the suffragettes ostracized you from all decent society.

People, especially young people, had lived too long among these stifling conventions, and taken refuge too often in a dream world where all went boldly free of inhibition, free of tyrannical parents and dusty, outdated taboos. And now suddenly, their favourite prophet came along to make the dream-world real. Here was a middle-class daughter, Ann Veronica, who defied and out-raged her father, ran off and lived apart, became a fiercely zealous suffragette and threw herself into the arms of the man she loved. She behaved like an independent woman when everyone knew no woman was independent, and she talked about biology and even sex as though they were everyday occurrences. Leaving the iron circle of filial devotion was heresy enough, but to leave it for the company of a lover, unredeemed by any ring or law or statute—this was the final ecstasy! Fiction offers the perfect device for experience at one remove where all the emotions are stirred to the same unbearable pitch but danger does not in fact exist. It is one half the reason why people read novels. If it stopped there, novels would remain a vastly entertaining medium with very little sig-nificance for society, but the novel with convincing characters, good dialogue and new valuations, may set a sanction on the type of behaviour it describes. People behave that way in books; why not in real life? And if those types of behaviour resemble a code which has been struggling against the conventions for years . . .

So it was now. How many daughters left their mothers because of Ann Veronica can never be told, but if few dared the final out-rage which they so happily endorsed on the printed page, Ann was to pioneer modern attitudes to sex in a quite startling way. She came right out of the book to breathe and disturb and ravish. The correspondence which mounted about her ears in newspapers and periodicals took it for granted that such a person moved in their midst. She was, she must be, alive. Ann Veronica was in fact a portrait drawn from life. There might be an emotional queasi-ness about certain passages towards the end of the book, the exit remark of Capes—'Blood of my heart I know, I understand'—might curl something inside one, and Ann herself lack the finer lines of any deeply interesting character; she might prove that Wells could never 'successfully draw the portrait of a really culti-vated woman,' and show him as 'no profound connoisseur of the human heart'; (2) but there was a pace about the book, the writing had enormous movement, and for the ordinary reader Ann lived and that was enough.

The freedom of the sexes in the twentieth century, the rational attitude towards sexuality, was first made articulate by Wells, laughingly reaffirmed by Shaw, developed in lyrical unrestraint by Lawrence, and given a cynical sanction—if not smear—by Aldous Huxley. In Wells' day it came as a dangerous breath of fresh air in the stuffy Victorian streets. Ann was a fast woman, a hussy. She couldn't be countenanced if you were over thirty. But she stimulated and excited, and all went well until *The Spectator* 'in a fit of apoplexy, unhappily not fatal,' suddenly described *Ann Veronica* as 'capable of poisoning the minds of those who read it' and rose to this tremendous crescendo . . . 'a community of scuffling stoats and ferrets, unenlightened by a ray of duty or abnegation. . . .' There were other views: 'Whether one accepts Mr. Wells' reading of the feminine riddle or not' said *The Globe*, 'one gladly concedes he has written a novel which in its frank sincerity and its bold grappling with a social question of compelling force, stands out as one of the best things he has given us. . . .' (3) But now the pack released itself in full cry. The Church gathered up its skirts and plunged into the chase. Unknown preachers enjoyed belabouring someone they had never met. This book was anti-social, dangerous to young and old alike, a vile blot on English literature. It was a dirty book. Correspondence flowed. There was no doubt that *Ann Veronica* had taken an audacious step in the development of the modern English novel, bringing alive the contemporary circumstances of physical love, but it seems laughably innocent when read to-day and needs no defence.

Worse was to follow. An author is expected to propitiate his gods rather more often than an ancient Aztec; to outrage them rarely; but to produce the first chapters of *The New Machiavelli*, serially in *The English Review*, barely more than a year after Ann Veronica had brazenly outfaced the worst slanders heaped upon her, was to behave according to no known code. For *The New Machiavelli* unmistakably travestied living people, made mock of men and women who were fixed stars in the social courses, and, was even charged with exchanging Ann's immorality for sheer eroticism. There was an attempt to stop the story appearing in book form. Three publishers turned it down. When it did appear, each review copy carried a booklet *Select Conversations*, a dialogue between Ralph Straus and Wells about the book. Either this or good plain sense on the part of the newspapers produced a batch of quite reasonable reviews where the charges of eroticism were refuted and the suggestions of caricature. . . ? Well, there was no mistaking a searing portrait of Beatrice Webb in Altiora Bailey, one which a far less fine spirit than hers might have found cruel, and coming dangerously close on the heels of her refusal to recommend Wells for a certain job because his public manners weren't good enough. But Beatrice Webb, whether from intellectual conceit or plain broadmindedness, recommended all her friends, and whoever went so far as to call themselves her enemies, to read the book. She openly admired it. After all, she was not the only one to suffer. Graham Wallas and McTaggart lurked somewhere in its pages and Evesham was so obviously a sketch or caricature of Balfour.

That this book marked the beginning of the retreat of Wells the story-teller, a moment not to be regarded lightly, was entirely lost in the tumult. The story as such had dominated *Ann Veronica*, *Mr. Polly* and *Tono-Bungay*, and social criticism emerged more from character than by direct comment, but with *The New Machiavelli* whole pages, indeed chapters, broke out of the story to indict the dog-fight of politics which should have been a great constructive process, and Remington was swamped again and again by the force of Wells' own opinions, as though he could no longer contain them in character but must burst into the book himself. It was the first ominous eruption of those magnificent moments of self-assertion which were to disintegrate the novelist in him. It was the first moving moment of retreat, of surrender to the huge *alter ego*; but for the present the morals of the book were the talk of the day and on one score, a question of taste rather than morals, there was some reason for the outcry.

The sting of retaliation gives many chapters in *The New Machiavelli*—for all its lovely passages of nostalgia, of a man abandoning the fascinations of public life for the far-off shores of Italy because he loved the wrong woman, and its noble passages of writing and reflection—an astringent quality. There are moments when it becomes the cutting edge . . . is it of revenge? Wells had suffered at the hands of many people and society still could not altogether stomach him. In *The New Machiavelli* he hit back. There is no doubt that Herbert Wells was capable of becoming a magnificently irascible, if not vengeful person, when the mood really seized him. It was on him now.

It led to an organized attempt to suppress Wells once and for all, to put him finally in his place. 'I have had the apparent bad fortune to get myself disliked by a group of eminent and influential persons. They are going, I am told, to obliterate me. My luck is out at last and I am doomed. My annihilation began with a virulent review of *Ann Veronica* in *The Spectator* . . . and a noisy boycott of that entirely decent and harmless story followed. . . . It was written and spoken about as though it were the ultimate thing in vileness. . . . But indeed the only dirt about the book was thrown at it. . . .

'There has been in the last two years an organized attempt to suppress Wells, and it is still, I understand, going on. . . . The disapproval of influential persons was to kill my best work unborn. It was to appear in an awful silence and freeze and die. Then I should freeze and die, and people like Mr. — would be almost happy. . . .' (*My Lucky Moment*). (4)

It wasn't bravado. Wells was an immensely courageous person. He valued courage in his friends above many other qualities. Right up to those days when he sat, a defenceless old man, the last person left in Hanover Terrace while the war raged about him and his servants severally put out the incendiary bombs, he continually outfaced dangers which might have shaken a far less sedentary, more robust person.

'In the last resort I do not care whether I am seated on a throne or drunk or dying in the gutter. I follow my leading,' he had said, and now it led him into a withering fire of rumour. He led a reckless sexual life. He was the gay, careless, successful writer who plundered the hearts of young women and never recked the consequence, he behaved on occasion like a cad, not a gentleman. And for all he protested—'I never was a gentleman'—people continued to hurl the word like a javelin at his head and the rumours grew. He was the avowed champion of free-love against marriage, he wanted votes for women and encouraged young people to dash parental authority to pieces under the eyes of their weeping mothers, he incited the Suffragettes, and he believed that mothers should be paid—paid ! Gossip about his private life was the easiest form of attack, since so many quotations torn out of context had a habit of looking much less poisonous when replaced and read in perspective. So gossip was given its head. The veriest strangers soon knew more about his private life than his closest friends. They whispered a story about a girl in her teens swept off to Paris and there wantonly seduced, they multiplied his conquests until Casanova became a clumsy innocent beside him, granting him at least irresistible charms. Some people were far more crude. One described him as the greatest stallion of his day. The melancholy remorse which is usually the rumour-monger's lot did not deter the people hellbent to reduce Wells' power over the minds of the young. They were quite without remorse. They forgot anything sane he had ever said about sex.

Whether he did in fact seduce a row of young women, father an illegitimate child, find with his feminine mind romance where it did not exist, or make exotic play with half the dark practices rumour put into his hands, may presently appear. It was inevitable that a person so emotionally rich should be the centre of a whole vortex of relationships, some deep, some dubious, but all imbued with that *élan* inseparable from the torrential vitality which sometimes consumed him and led him into heaven knew what complications. For himself, at the moment, one shred of truth behind the furtive whisperings consisted in the fact that he had not conformed to conventional behaviour, but had used his own judgment, and felt that judgment produced far more civilized reactions than the ready-made reasoning of the multitude who now fought so self-righteously to condemn him. They were jealous! That was at least half the matter. They would have liked to live the same way. But their courage failed them. The social sanctions were too frightening. . . . Frightening? Pshaw! Wells would show them! He did not in fact show them. He wrote an acid word or two on the matter and left it at that. For the rest their attempts to drag him through the dirt only exaggerated, in the end, his eminence in the eyes of the young and very soon he wrote: 'I have become a symbol against the authoritative, the dull, the presumptuously established, against all that is hateful and hostile to youth and tomorrow. . . .' (5)

*　　　*　　　*

He had become much more than that. Four great waves of novels were now exhausted, three of his many selves tried and found wanting in one degree or another. First the young scientist, burning with the drama of science, desiring to re-order the world by scientific means, had written *The Time Machine*, *War in the Air*,

In the Days of the Comet, The Island of Dr. Moreau and, at his peak, *A Modern Utopia*. If only, he seemed to say, we could get scientific order into the world, there would be no wars, no distress, no hunger, and life would become infallibly gracious and satisfying. The second wave gave the artist a short-lived triumph over the scientist and singled out the individual from the multitude as of overwhelming importance. Here were the great, down-to-earth, comic pieces of autobiography, untroubled by science, where Mr. Polly, Mr. Kipps and Mr. Lewisham held undisputed sway, playing out again Wells' early life as shop-assistant, schoolmaster and lover. The third wave repeated the first in another field. Now it was the anachronistic confusions of the relations of the sexes which appalled him, not the disorder of the social system, and as from a magic pouch came another row of novels like *Ann Veronica*, designed to do nothing less than reweave the warp and woof of human relations, stretching convention to breaking point in the process. Then the fourth. These were idea novels, *The New Machiavelli*, *The Research Magnificent*—to be joined by *The World of William Clissold*. In each, a member of his Samurai, his own élite ruling class, told half-biographically what was wrong with the world, and how he strained at the bonds which prevented him from putting it right. They were all richly intelligent, if they lost some of their emotional drive for the simple reason that doctrines do not make good heroes. . . .

One after another the waves had rolled out to excite the young and dismay the old. Established institutions had been rocked, the inevitability of marriage, religion, rich and poor, so deeply questioned that they would never be quite the same again. A great throng of readers now hung upon his words as they once hung upon Dickens', and immense excitements overtook the young as each fresh book or pronunciamento rolled down from Olympus. But here was the extraordinary thing about the first three phases of Wells' work. He came as the Messiah of Rationalism sustained by scientific gods, yet the message he brought was almost as moving as revealed religion, and for every one person who soberly settled to the new way of thought, there was another raised to the ecstasy of deliverance as if an angel of freedom had appeared among them. If for nothing else Wells will be remembered as the man who liberated the mind of a whole generation with the passion of the artist.

Chapter Eleven

THE LOVER

IT wasn't easy to penetrate his masks. The public knew him in the early nineteen hundreds as a successful author, a warm friendly soul full of Cockney impudence, immense intelligence and a wonderful gift for interpreting what they took to be their innermost yearnings. They knew two dimensions. There was a third. The inner Wells did not erupt easily. His rages and indignations were just another *alter ego*, his quarrels and even, in one way, his books, part of his public life. Before one glimpsed the depths beyond the eddies it was necessary for the brilliant conversationalist, so terribly aware of an audience, so capable of dazzling any company, to abandon the comedic sprite enthroned in his conscious self. It was necessary for the novelist to step down, for the world-maker to retire, for half-a-dozen selves to dissolve into thin air. It happened sometimes when he was alone with intimate friends. Add more than one to the company and the spell would be broken, but alone with someone that mattered, and particularly a woman, extraordinary intimations of a very different Wells were liable to come through.

Dorothy Richardson was one such person. We have already seen one glimpse through her eyes which Wells acknowledged to be authentic. There are many others he never acknowledged. It is clear now that in her series of novels *Pilgrimage*, there emerges a three-dimensional portrait of Wells which it would be difficult to match. It reveals the inner Wells as no letter, book or talk ever could, because it is a fusion of many years' friendship with the intuitive eye of the artist; it is Wells, stripped of his many masks, spiritually naked under the solvent of a woman with uncanny powers of penetration, aware of profound levels of consciousness which he could reach but perhaps found too disturbing to hold. So much which fiction recreates the factual world would never dare, so many shifting thresholds forbidden to documented evidence lead into the secret places of personality. And if occasionally, the times and places are different and the incidents open to minor adjustment, the spirit, character and talk in these novels are brilliantly true to Wells' unseen life. Silently, with a dark rush of narrative, the other Wells materializes and it is a disturbing experience.

See him first, rounded, whole, as Dorothy Richardson saw him in his middle years. He came round the corner from the terrace 'his arms threshing the air, to the beat of his swift walk . . . casting kind radiance as he came. . . .' 'The luminous clouded grey, clear-ringed eyes, the voice husky and clear, the strange repellent mouth below the scraggy moustache, kept from weakness only by the perpetually hovering, disclaiming, ironic smile. . . .' He brought . . . 'a fascination that could not be defined; that drove its way through all the evidence against it. . . . Married yet always seeming nearer and more sympathetic than other men. . . .'

They talked. ' "We don't know what life is," he said. "You don't know what life is. You think too much. Life's got to be lived. The difference between you and me is that you think to live and I live to think. . . . You've made a jolly good start—Done things—Come out and got economic independence. But you're stuck. . . ."

' "Now *there's* somebody who is writing about life. Who's shewn what has been going on from the beginning. Mrs. Stetson. It was the happiest day of my life when I read *Women and Economics*. . . . I don't want comfort. I want truth."

' "Oh you don't," he said, "One gives you facts and you slide away from them." '

The moods varied kaleidoscopically. There were romantic moments when a rose, thrown through an open window, fell at Dorothy Richardson's feet and a voice said, 'Come out and play.' Wells understood those enchanting gestures which send a spark to the very heart of woman. There were moments when his rush of words carried along on a 'high squeal of laughter,' 'reducing everything to absurdity,' would falter and stop because at last they were alone together, and he no longer needed to counter opposition with spirals of wit. There were moments when suddenly, behind the certainties, the gusto and the irrepressible vitality which seemed to render him immune to normal doubts and fears, she suddenly glimpsed 'the single, simple, lonely helplessness of the human soul.' And 'robbed of the subtle curves drawn about them by his watchful readiness for witty improvisation or facetious retort, robbed of the authoritative complacency they wore during the ceaseless social occupation of definition and commentary . . . his features were homely, reverted to his very homely type, the raw material of his personal appearance.' She had to turn 'her eyes away from the strange spectacle of him abdicated and docile. . . .'

She had known him on the tennis court when he rushed wrangling to the net, filling the summer air with witty shoutings, she had seen him glory in just rushing about the house, shouting incoherent nothings, with nobody taking the slightest notice, 'shouting and laughing for the sake of a jolly noise, . . . saying more than could be said in talk.' She knew every facet of the animated gnome who presented a sparkling face to the world, seized every other minute with paroxysms of talk and vitality. She knew him at the opera, listening to Wagner, when the 'tremendous ado, by its sheer size and strength,' emphasized for her 'all that it left unsaid, all that is said by the music of Bach . . . the quiet, blissful insight whose price is composure. The deep quiet sense of *being*. . . .' And she had heard him call it, this composure, 'turnip emotion' and she had heard him, as she drank her lager in the bar after the concert, remark—so hopelessly in or out of key —'Bravo—Ain't she splendid. . .? Tossing off her beer like a man. . . .'

His social self was deified in bars and restaurants. He sat with his small plump hands 'clasped before him on the table and his sightless, entertaining-seeking, and for the moment, entirely blue eyes . . . moving from point to point, searchlights, operated from a centre whose range . . . was restricted by the sacred, unquestioned dogmas ruling his intelligence.' He sat and directed swift glances towards the next table revealing 'his everlasting awareness of neighbours-as-audience.'

He fell in love with many women after his fashion. Miriam or 'Miretta' as Dorothy Richardson calls her chief character, received one morning a thin grey envelope from Hypo [Wells]. 'Welcome to your London my dear. I'm more in love with you than ever.' And by the same post came another letter to Miretta from Alma [Jane]. 'And my very dear, tremendous doings. We're invading your London; next week. We'll do a Wagner you and me and Hypo.'

In love ? What did it mean for Wells in middle age ? His affair with 'Miretta' gave at least half the game away if any such collo-quialism can apply to the complicated processes which led him into one *passade* after another. Miretta told him how she knew, one morning, with a wildly beating heart, what waited for her down there in the letter box, knew more plainly than speech could ever tell, what his letter would say.

' "Yes," ' Hypo said, ' " One has these curious premonitions, in certain moods. Certain states of heightened perception. One is exalted and luminous." '

So he knew, experienced it, was aware of something he could never define and perhaps because he could not define it 'remained incurious.' He was like that as a lover; part of him forever absent or without those finer sensibilities which made intimacy more absolute than any total surrender.

A moment of insight, a sudden flash of awareness told Miretta how 'very slight, how restricted and perpetually baffled must always be the communication between him and anything that bore the name of woman.' They paid a price for love or friendship, the women who knew him, the price of excluding half their deeper preoccu-pations to become a sounding board for his ideas, to meet him 'in his world, his shaped world, rationalized according to whatever scheme of thought was appealing to him at the moment. . . .' He needed disciples, 'vitalizing relationships,' but the 'intelligent, emancipated creatures for whom he expressed so much admira-tion' he fought shy of, because 'a rush of brains to the head usually made them rather plain in the face.' (1) He expected women to adapt themselves to him, not he to them. They were to play up, to permit themselves to be transmuted into the women he saw in them, the women he needed whenever they were with him. They were to trot 'briskly about on his maps and diagrams' living 'for the rest of their time in their own deep world.' And physical beauty for him had none of the abstract qualities 'Miretta' found in it. She had become deeply aware of the 'lines and curves of her limbs, their balance and harmony.' She saw 'the long honey-coloured ropes of hair framing the face . . . beautiful in its Flemish Madonna type . . . against the rose-tinted velvety gleaming of her flesh.' She read in it something dispassionately inspiring. There was abstract beauty within the sensuousness. He saw it as something desirable and in many ways pretty. 'You are a pretty creature Miretta,' he said, 'I wish you could see yourself.'

Was this all ? Did the man whose vision unlocked the secret beauties of science so hopelessly fail to see them in human beings, in women, in the rich, deep pools they inhabited as fish, waiting eternally on the surface for him who could dive effortlessly to the depths ? Not quite. He knew the depths. But his own body was unlovely, the breath he drew belonged to the rational upper air, and he suffocated all too soon, rushing back to the surface.

It was true even in the final intimacies. When she 'leaned forward and clasped him, the warm contact drove away the idea that she might be both humiliating and annoying him and brought a flood of solicitude and suggested a strange action. And as gently she rocked him to and fro the words that came to her lips were so unsuitable that even while she murmured "My little babe, just born" she blushed for them, and steeled herself for his comment.

'. . . She found his arms about her in their turn and herself surprised and not able with sufficient swiftness to contract her expanded being that still seemed to encompass him, rocked unsatisfactorily to and fro while his voice, low and shy and with inappropriate unwelcome charm in it and the ineffectual gestures of a child learning a game, echoed the unsuitable words.'

It was warm and beautiful. It revealed him as a simple, lonely soul, aware of his own limitations, but marred in the end, as he was so often, so inevitably marred, by self-consciousness. It left something in 'Miretta' still unpossessed. 'From far away below the colloquy, from where still it sheltered in the void . . . whence it had set forth alone upon its strange journeying, her spirit was making its own statement, profanely asserting the unattained being that was promising, however faintly, to be presently the surer for this survival. . . .'

Thus it was with several women in Wells' life. They became part of him, moulded in the likeness of his own desires, abdicating momentarily something of their true selves, and so often feeling in the end a sense of uninvaded beauty waiting on the last surrender.

'Miretta' was a lovely warning. Beautifully frustrated, she had found the secret Wells aware as she was of other dimensions, found and walked with him awhile, only to discover him at the deepest moment admitting the falsity of charm, not entirely with her, still intact. 'A mass of obstructive clay from which the spirit had departed on its way to its own bourne. . . .'

She tried to tell him about it once and he wrote 'Dear Miretta, I don't perhaps catch your drift. But I think you're mistaken and I don't share your opinion of yourself. The real difference between us is that while you think in order to live, I live in order to think.'

*　　*　　*

That was one view of him, a very personal private view. There were other views and other women. Gossip in fact ran riot until many a Babylonian orgy was conjured from careless words and chance meetings. He saw it all so differently. He found nothing intrinsically evil in promiscuity, but was more concerned with the *passade*—a stroke of mutual attraction, as different from love as light from fire, and of the very texture of everyday life. Too many ravishing impulses, he felt, were choked in the net of convention until the stillborn children of desire darkened the air, too many lovely faces encountered in the dusk were lost for all eternity. Not for Wells this deformed emotional world. Incurably romantic to the last where women were concerned, he never let the glancing spark die on the air without some effort to pursue and blow upon it, until he kindled that light in which he loved to live, becoming so often under its radiance quite irresistible. It did not necessarily lead to the passionate love affair, it was a *passade*, a relationship of doubtful duration, but none the less rich in those delights which tend to become more exquisite as they belong to the morning and die under the accomplished day. Persuasions of this kind would have raised little more than a casual eyebrow among the emancipated English had they remained in the nature of an intellectual exercise, but Wells was of the breed who carry their beliefs over into their behaviour. It was a dangerous creed. At various stages in his life gossip took every advantage of him, and if he survived the first conspiracy against him with ease, that was not by any means the end of it. Regularly, at least once every few years or so, some new rush of rumours set people in one circle or another talking again. These were still the decorous days of the early 1900's when matrimonial faithfulness was considered by the masses an inviolable law of nature. To behave as Wells now behaved and take no trouble to conceal it, excited the imagination of the least lascivious until every charge had been hurled at his quite unheeding head. . . . No girl is safe with Mr. Wells. Mr. Wells is a seducer. Mr. Wells is a wolf. Plainly Mr. Wells is vicious. All culminating in an excited series of calculations designed to establish the precise number of his illegitimate children, but failing rather badly when it came to identifying mothers. In the more esoteric cliques the game was played with great deductive skill and no small learning, until people who could barely stand the sight of H. G. were implicated on the flimsiest evidence. Hyperbole feeds on alleged promiscuity. It now ran riot.

Any examination of these accusations must suffer certain inhibitions. The story of 'Miretta' had its living counterpart. There were several others, but they must be seen in perspective. True the toiling millions of Britain paid lip service to a code of conduct which only permitted *passades* of the most clandestine and rare character, and everything moved to a conventionally correct measure. But young Fabian and middle-class women seething on the edge of a revolutionary cauldron, wanted to go out into the world, wanted independence, and in the case of some of the Fabians they flouted Mrs. Grundy on principle and even considered 'having babies and going on the rates.' It was all epitomized in *Ann Veronica*. The middle-class crust of society was strained by the pressure of a number of independent young women. Some of them tended to concentrate in the circles in which Wells moved. It had all sprung from a distortion of Darwin and Huxley. Scientific materialism as a basis of belief and experience did not yield any great importance to personality. It could be surrendered easily—if it existed. It did not gravely matter what you did with the body. In this peculiar climate Wells, dependent to some extent on the creative stimuli of sympathetic affairs, flourished. He was not alone in this. Generations of artists before him had the same characteristic. But it would be wrong to imagine that 'love' came lightly to Wells for the rest of his life. Over the years his 'affairs' varied kaleidoscopically. Some were flirtations, some *passades*, some bursts of sheer sensuous enjoyment, but there were others involving feeling of a different order. His passion was as protean as his intellect. He came to know many forms of love.

*　　*　　*

It has to be recorded of H. G. Wells that in his thirties and forties he recaptured with some skill, profound capacity and complete determination the full free romantic love which had so tragically eluded him as a young man. The unimaginable goddesses now came to earth in all their loveliness. Most striking amongst them was the 'student from the U.S.A.' barely twenty-one, but splendidly emancipated and oh so enraptured by the dazzling gnome who had suddenly discovered amongst his own friends— was it the young lady he had conjured to life in *Mr. Polly*, sitting on the old lichened wall talking nonsense, only to vanish with a swirl of skirts and legs into the forbidden garden? No. This time she was flesh and blood. This time she came down from the wall out of the garden and they went off together, Wells the writer approaching middle age, Miss X. the young modern woman, and some subtle emotional magic enwrapped them in just such a cloud as they desired. There are many versions of what followed. The more romantic would have them fly to Paris where unbelievable risks were taken and disaster inevitably came down on them, but the evidence is not only scant: it points in another direction. It seems likely that they were in love, and when Herbert George Wells fell in love now it was no mere grocery of love within which presently appeared a tumult of kisses and moonlight wanderings beside the Thames. For them the enchantment of mutual response was said to be something out of this world, touched with a strange sun-light, but Wells no longer believed in half measures or artificial restraints, and Miss X. presently became aware that she was pregnant. Conventionally, Wells should have been overwhelmed by the news. He should have offered everything to Miss X. and the mere matter of divorcing his wife would seem the simple and obvious expedient. Whether they talked of this or not I do not know, but it soon became clear that he did not intend doing any such thing. Marrying Miss X. was out of the question. To the average mind there was something appalling in Wells' reaction. He was middle-aged and had lately written another successful book, she was still not twenty-two and a member of a highly re-spected family. Now it seemed the student daughter had fled with the infatuated author to play the part of Samuraian free-lovers rather more recklessly than anyone expected. It should have brought remorse, bewilderment, even disaster, in a world so violently opposed to anything resembling the freedom of the Modern Utopia. Instead, quite quietly, they went their separate ways. The story too divides once more into a maze of rumour. None of the evidence of what followed seems particularly reliable, even from those who witnessed it at first hand. Whatever decorative detail may have crept into it all, the fact that a young woman became pregnant by Wells is undeniable: so also is the final episode when a young man, of equal social standing, announced his intention of marrying Miss X.

No breath of this reached the outside world. Millions of readers continued to worship the prophet, the liberator Wells, quite unaware that a cyclone had blown loose and was trying to sweep him away while Wells himself ecstatically rode its crest. For he was now very sure of himself and his creed, would brook no interference from mawkish prudes and did not very much mind what people said about him. He had loved and made love and the natural consequences had overtaken him. Something magical and inevitable had come into his life and remorse as much belonged to it as it might to an earthquake.

There were some who never forgave Wells for the consequences of this affair. Acknowledging that he and Miss X. might be 'in love,' they still could not find it in their hearts to excuse him. It was ungentlemanly. He had taken advantage of her love. He should have respected it. He had deliberately exploited the most beautiful thing in the world. It was for him, the mature balanced personality to show restraint; not for her. There was another school of thought which placed the blame elsewhere. A third considered the word 'blame' out of place, and added a quite different, far more material slant to the whole story. Indeed, Wells himself, re-telling the episode to a well-known writer later in life, rendered one side of it richly hilarious and materialistic. Whichever way it went, echoes of the affair still hung about the high places of literature ten years later. Any woolliness which may be apparent in this sparse account is inevitable. To-day H. G. Wells and his wife are dead, but other people involved in the story are still alive, and have no desire to revive the cloud of scandal which disappeared long ago when the child of this affair married and settled back into normal life again. So there the story must rest for the moment. But the fiery particle had shown its mettle again. . . .

Many other sparks flew between Wells' first successful years, between the realization that Catherine could never emotionally or sexually satisfy him, and the early days of his decline. He had several mistresses and a number of *passades* and there was one other child by a famous women: a son born in 1914 who also became a writer. Wells would talk freely about these illegitimate children. Ask after the health of his family, and according to mood, he might answer: 'My legitimate or illegitimate family ?' Neither the children nor the mistresses were in any sense superficial accidents. He found some women irresistible. There was an occasion when—at an I.L.P. dance—he clapped his hands above his head in time to Sir Roger de Coverley, chanting irreverently and with a fervour quite unmatched by the music, 'That's a pretty girl ! That's a pretty girl !' He once abandoned a weekend jaunt at the very point where it was due to begin because a friend unexpectedly called with a beautiful girl and the sight of her was too much for him.

Young women made music for him. They were all that he had missed in his youth. Satiation could never occur because—if one psychological mechanism ran true to pattern—he was either looking for the likeness of the mother he never knew, or wreaking his vengeance on the mother he had known. At the same profound level of emotional consciousness he was probably trying to reassure himself that he need never again undergo the emotional malnutrition which was said to have haunted his early manhood, leaving him permanently maimed and hungry for something he could not clearly define because it was the ghost of a distorted appetite, constantly driving him on. By this reckoning he was doomed to become the prey of a passion he could never satisfy and women were for him a constantly renewed, ecstatic hell. Somewhere eternally round the bend lay that full, beautiful promised land where the *passades* would cease and this dreadful demon riding him confront an unpremeditated passion, capable of assuaging every fresh pang it produced—only he was doomed never to reach it.

But no. Psychology can in unskilled hands find a pattern where none exists. The evidence for early emotional malnutrition is not very convincing, and something there was in these affairs of Wells, a sense of poetry and song, which must have yielded as sustained a satisfaction as any highly imaginative person can expect in a world where feelings tend to fluctuate so tragically. Certainly some of his mistresses were considerable emotional experiences which left their mark on him, and if one ocasionally overlapped another, there were deeply twined spirits who survived and grew richer for twenty years. And each one of them held an element of that slave-goddess who haunted his imagination to the end of his days, and perhaps it was the incarnation of this being he still so hopelessly pursued.

His idea of love changed as his experience deepened. He had begun by believing that one all-consuming fixation, one great passion, was too often merely a distortion. One man one woman, was not written into the laws of nature. 'People do not, I think, fall naturally into agreement with these assumptions; they train themselves to agreement.' (2) Later this changed. Later he ceased to ignore fixations, possessiveness. As he observed his own reactions and the reactions of others, he knew complete freedom was a more harrowing, painful illusion than many other forms of emotional self-deception. 'In theory I was now to have *passades*. . . . But life and Latin logic have always been at variance and it did not work out like that.' (3)

Soon he came to see two forms of love. First the mystical merging of personality where one person was incomplete without another, two people were prepared to 'live and die' for 'the sacred symbol' they had created, and each rescued the other from the terrifying isolation of individuality; the other 'the happy worship of Venus, the goddess of human loveliness, the graceful mutual compliment of two free bodies and spirits' brought together in beautiful intimacy without trace of obligation. Many people knew both experiences. Some succumbed to an annihilating fixation only to have it dissolve in distractions. There were periods of possessiveness and periods of promiscuous impulse, of being in love and loving, and love was a different thing for men and women. At its highest love 'broke down the boundaries of self' and people once lonely within their race were at one with it, raised to a tenth power of living—'Suddenly the metal fuses, the dry bones live ! One loves.' (4)

It was these divisions which played such havoc with any attempt to find a single all-embracing solution of sex. Bertrand Russell remarked that in peasant societies, where women were not so highly differentiated, distraction did not easily arise, since other women had too much in common with one's wife. And Wells said, 'The more marked the individuality the more difficult is it to discover a complete reciprocity. The more difficult therefore is it to establish an exclusive fixation.' (5)

It helped him to support the sense of guilt as his own 'fixations' broke in beautiful variety. There were many cynical stories. The man who warned him: 'It's easy enough, H. G., to accumulate a row of blondes—getting rid of them's the trouble'; the rejected lady who quoted Rochefoucauld at him, 'We can forgive those who bore us, but we cannot forgive those whom we bore'; H. G. shrilly stamping about his home, Easton Glebe, kicking the furniture, tumbling books, braying at nobody in particular, 'Get that woman out of my sight.'

And the woman who scintillated in any company, who brought a clever, intuitive brain to any and every problem, who spoke a passionate English capable of stirring the dullest listener, who sometimes enjoyed shocking people and once shocked—or was it enthralled—Wells himself. She was a person with an uncomfortable habit of total, outright frankness, and when she and Wells went one day to have tea with a neighbour, he warned her that her more abandoned habits of speech and gesture might prove alarming to the quiet of this Victorian household. There are many versions of what followed. According to one, all would probably have gone smoothly if they had not met, on the way to the house, a friend of Wells, a friend he had romantically nicknamed Casanova. Arriving for tea, Wells first introduced Miss Z. then turned to his friend and said, 'And this by the way is Casanova. . . .' Whereupon their hostess smiled pensively and said, 'Now what was it Casanova did . . .?' Swift as a falling star that impossible, Anglo-Saxon, one-syllabled word struck from Miss Z.'s lips '——' and the air slowly froze about them. The word lay there on the table the whole afternoon palpitating while they all went, stiffly smiling, through their tea-table mime, until the ordeal was over and Wells and Miss Z. were outside alone together again.

There was another woman discovered saying one evening, when he was in his late fifties, 'fancy a man of his age coming to me twice in one night,' and Wells quickly breaking the breathless pause, his eyes brilliant with venomous good humour—'You know there are times when —— makes me feel as if I were wearing glass trousers!'

He could be deliberately down to earth whenever he chose. There were moments when his language was not the most delicate. Frank Horrabin, the artist, and his wife, went to stay with Wells one week, and walking on the terrace one afternoon, Mrs. Horrabin remarked on the great oil jars standing around the garden.

'Yes,' said Wells, 'and if in the very early morning you happen to be about and see our gardener sitting on one of them, don't be too inquisitive—we badly need manure !'

Gaiety, coarseness, craziness, all had a place, but it would be absurd to judge his life, emotional or otherwise by these episodes alone, or by the great dramatic climaxes of which there were now several. At least one woman threatened to shoot him.

*   *   *

There could, it seemed, be no further complication in an emotional pattern as complex as this; for behind it all still stood the blurred figure of Catherine his wife, the charming, self-effacing hostess sometimes confronted with one of the mistresses amongst her guests, but never revealing a glimmer of jealousy or bad temper or even distress—to the public eye. Yet there was another extraordinary strand. Incredibly, amongst all the other women, Wells was not entirely done with his first wife yet. Down the years she had come and gone in the background of his life, a shadow figure he could not entirely forget. He ran away from her and, after divorce, married Catherine and became involved with many other women, but one beautiful summer day the desire to see her again became irresistible and he went, on one pretext or another, to visit Isabel at Twyford where she ran, with not too much success, a poultry farm. They spent the day together at Virginia Water and Wells, very much aware of the enchantment of the scene, suddenly felt the old magic stirring on the air again, slipped unconsciously into nicknames, the old tricks of speech, and presently felt a quite fantastic urge growing at the back of his mind. It was an urge, utterly irrational, to recover Isabel. Torn and perplexed he sensed himself on the verge of an appalling emotional storm and then, involuntarily, he was pleading with her, pleading for her to come back to him. She had only to weaken slightly and he would have swept her away, heaven alone knows where, or into what fresh entanglements. But Isabel refused. As perplexed as he was, she tried to understand this fresh, amazing sidelight on his character, but she would not leave the farm to go with him, even for a day.

He did not sleep that night. Before dawn the house became unbearable to him. He rose, went softly downstairs out into the hushed, scented air, took his bicycle and was on the point of going when Isabel came hurrying after him. He could not rush off like that she said. He could not disappear without something to eat. He must wait for her to make breakfast. There were tears in his eyes and he slipped into her arms. Deeply distressed she held him close and said in utter bewilderment 'How can things like this be, now ?' He wept uncontrollably. Isabel was suddenly, once again, more desirable, more important, than all things in heaven and earth. But as they stood together in the dawn he suddenly knew that it was all a fantastic dream, that it just could not be, and abruptly he drew back, recovered himself and rode away on his bicycle 'into a sunlit intensity of perplexity and frustration, unable to understand the peculiar keenness of my unhappiness. I felt like an automaton. I felt as though all purpose had been drained out of me, and nothing remained worth-while. The world was dead and I was dead and I had only just discovered it.' (6)

There was an interval of six years. They were crowded, brilliant, successful years in which other women took the place of the first wife he could not recover and at last, it seemed, she was successfully blotted from his memory. Then he heard by chance that she had married again. At once a wild resentment arose in him. Jealousy, fierce and unbridled, seized him and drove him to smash her photographs, burn her letters, forbid any mention of her name in his presence, search out and ruthlessly exorcise all remnants of the grip she once had on his life until he had finally—as it were—destroyed her and she could never live for him again. There was nothing unusual in this. He never expected a woman who had played a serious part in his life to have anything to do with anyone else. The same fury overtook him when one of his mistresses went off and married, even though they had quarrelled, parted and he had not seen her for months.

Another five years passed. The possessiveness, the jealousy for Isabel waned again and presently died. This time the other women successfully overwhelmed her memory. She sank back once more into the recesses of the past. By the time he met her again in 1909 it was 'in a mood of limitless friendliness, free from all the glittering black magic of sex. . . .'

Their friendship lasted until her death. But the paradoxes were not entirely done on the day of her second marriage. Ceasing to receive his alimony Isabel found herself less well off, so Wells decided to settle an income on her. Then she wanted to set up in business on her own account and he bought her a laundry. It was hardly started when she fell ill, and Wells was told that she needed careful nursing, close attention. Thoughtfully he put a plan—extraordinary in conventional eyes—to Jane. He wanted Jane to take Isabel into their home where she would get the nursing she needed and be quite free from other worries. If Jane had remained the same sweet, smiling, outwardly content person, to whom nothing which her husband did came amiss, all might have been well; but Jane had changed. The strain of her shadow life had begun to tell. It had been easy enough to sustain the sham with some conviction when the outer world knew nothing of her husband's eccentricities and everyone accepted her as the unchallenged Mrs. Wells—indeed the sham had long periods of intense satisfaction—but soon there was an unpleasant tendency for the literary people who crowded like moths around Wells' incandescence, to indulge cruel frivolities. 'Have I met Mrs. Wells ? But madam *which* Mrs. Wells ?' 'Do I know Mrs. Wells— but *who* is Mrs. Wells ?' 'No, no, my dear, not the Wells *family* the Wells *concubines*. . . .' In one melancholy mood—and his moods could change very swiftly—Wells said to a close friend, 'Home ! Home ! What is home ? A good place sometimes to escape from ?' It was a burst of gloomy irritation and it did not last long, but it had its significance.

Jane hardened under all these strains. A person of iron control and great strength of character gradually grew over the sweet simple Catherine, but there were intimate friends who knew her when the mask was off and then, in very rare moments, the deep unhappiness which had come and gone for years appeared. She hated these complications. She loathed losing her husband to other women. She yearned for those first glorious days when she had his undivided attention. They had always been together then, and adversity made any extravagant adventures difficult. The Rational Woman who had so generously given Wells his freedom rarely lost control, but sometimes the part proved too much for her, and jealousy, possessiveness broke in. And Wells, believing that the wife 'should never be let down' wanted only freedom for excursions, not another wife, and for this and other reasons never broke away.

There was a time when other difficulties arose, a change of residence to Hampstead was called for, and Jane had to make some modifications of their way of life. She put her foot down then, and extracted a promise which was kept for a time. Then another lover appeared.

Somewhere intertwined with all the rest there ran a streak of guilt in Jane which did not make matters any easier. Wells may have protested in his autobiography that he was the ringleader who had urged Catherine Robbins to go and live in sin with him, but there is evidence to show that she also felt some responsibility for what had happened, for the trouble they were now in.

So when Wells, still absorbed in Isabel's fate, asked Jane to take his first wife—even in sickness—back into his household, it must have put the whole relationship to a new and dangerous test. But Jane at once agreed and there followed the odd spectacle of Wells living in the same house with his first and second wife, while his emotions were involved with yet a third very different woman. Apart from Jane, no one knew that the invalid lady Isabel was his first wife. He had several cousins and this they took to be —with an unassailable innocence—one of them. As Isabel grew better she took long walks with Herbert about the beautiful garden of Easton Glebe and the countryside, untroubled by the old emotional upheavals, admiring at ease the golden pheasants, and the lilies in the lily pond. They were happy, content, even sometimes gay in each other's company.

Years after, Isabel wanted to build a house of her own and Wells agreed to help her. They chose the site together. The foundations were being laid when she again fell ill. Quite well on Saturday she dropped into a diabetic coma on Sunday, and on the Monday she died. He remembered very clearly on the day of her death, the last walk they had taken together to admire the lilies and the golden pheasants.

Chapter Twelve

SEX CREDO

WHERE practice led him into private trouble, Wells' writings on sex over the same period, suddenly trapped him in a net of political cunning from which he escaped in the end by a somewhat awkward compromise. The trouble began in the Fabian Society when he said, 'I no more regard the institution of marriage as a permanent thing than I regard a state of competitive industrialism as a permanent thing. . . .' The meeting was crowded. Some new members agreed with him and had already taken action on their beliefs. Beatrice Webb went away from the meeting to read *In the Days of the Comet* where, in the last chapters, 'promiscuity' was given full and—for Wells—beautiful play. His gift for making outrageous ideas palatable with emotional magic was delightfully used in this book. He could also state his case bluntly and fearlessly: 'In the old days love was a cruel proprietary thing. But now Anna could let Nettie live in the world of my mind. . . . If I could hear notes that were not in her compass, she was glad because she loved me, that I should listen to other music than hers. And she too could see the beauty of Nettie. Life is so rich and generous now, giving friendship and a thousand tender interests and helps and comforts, that no-one stints another of the full realisation of all possibilities of beauty. . . . I loved Nettie, I loved all who were like her.' (1) Beatrice read this with the warmly sceptical eye of the wife of Sidney Webb, a person considered the very epitome of emotional correctness. In her diary for October 18th, 1906, she wrote: 'The argument is one that is familiar to most intellectuals—it has often cropped up in my own mind and has seemed to have some validity. Friendship between particular men and women has an enormous educational value to both (especially to the woman). Such a friendship is practically impossible (or, at any rate, impossible between persons who are attractive to each other—and, therefore, most remunerative as friends) without physical intimacy; you do not as a matter of fact, get to know any man thoroughly except as his beloved and his lover.' (2) The diary then breaks into this aside: 'If you could have been the beloved of the dozen ablest men you have known it would have greatly extended your knowledge of human nature and human affairs. . . . But there remains the question whether, with all the perturbation caused by such intimacies, you would have any brain left to think with ?' (3)

Beatrice did not of course agree with Wells. She speaks of him with great restraint and sympathy throughout the diary, but she could not bring herself to defend his heresies after witnessing some of the results of his own behaviour. She rejected very firmly free love—as appears in later paragraphs of the diary—but she came to the question with the cool detachment of the emancipated woman who had to examine every idea on its merits and not allow isolated disturbances to distort her point of view. It did not help Wells very much. As his writings on love and the family were more widely read, certain Fabians, reviewers and many quavering literary hacks of the day fought back at him and he fell into public as well as private bad odour.

In the same year (1906) as his pronouncements to the Fabians, he was advocating 'the repudiation of private ownership of women and children and the payment of mothers. . . .' 'The state will pay for children born legitimately in the marriage it will sanction. A woman with healthy and successful offspring will draw for each one of them a wage from the state.' (4) In his usual impatient, large-handed way, Wells, at the Fabian stage, knew just what should be done to infuse new freedoms into the prison of marriage, but how to reconcile it with the demands of a stable society, with social responsibilities and the jungle of jealousy as inseparable from love as hate from war, either did not bother or did not occur to him. 'I thought it preposterous,' Wells wrote, 'that any young people should be distressed by unexplained desires, thwarted by arbitrary prohibitions and blunder into sexual experiences blindfold. . . . But a propaganda of more and franker and healthier love-making was not, I found—as Plato found before me—a simple proposition.' (5)

Indeed not. In her diary Mrs. Webb, wrote 'H. G. Wells is I believe merely gambling with the idea of free love—throwing it out to see what sort of reception it gets—without responsibility for its effect on the character of hearers. It is this recklessness which makes Sidney dislike him. I think it is important *not* to dislike him . . .; he is going through an ugly time and we must stand by him for his own sake and for the good of the cause of collectivism.' (6)

In November of the same year Wells went to stay with the Webbs for two days and they took him to task over the last chapters of *In the Days of the Comet*. Wells simply said that it was a work of art and no normal moral measure could be applied—'When Michael Angelo displayed groups of nude figures in stone or colour, it does not follow that he desired to see all his acquaintances sprawling about without clothes.' He admitted to the Webbs, even so, that he felt a 'free-er love' between the sexes was more or less inevitable. 'At present,' he told them, 'any attempt to realize this free-er love means a network of low intrigue, assumes and therefore creates, an atmosphere of gross physical desire—but this is only an incident of a morality based on the notion of private property in women. No decent person has a chance of experimenting with a free-er love today—the relations between men and women are so hemmed in by law and convention. To experiment you must be base; hence to experiment starts with being damned.' (7)

The Webbs were not shocked. Mental emancipation did not permit any such violent reaction against *opinion*, even if what Wells himself *did* was a very different thing. But Beatrice saw it all as entirely negative and clung to the conviction that 'man will only evolve upwards by the subordination of his physical desires and appetites to the intellectual and spiritual side of his nature,' (8) while Sidney . . . well Sidney just did not like Wells, and plainly said so.

But it wasn't the Webbs, the Fabians, or strictures on his private habits or even his friends and enemies in the literary world, which eventually forced him to compromise. The politicians had long ago pricked up their ears at Mr. Wells' pronouncements. They realized that fate had brought them a most usefully indiscreet dupe. He should be encouraged down this showy, sinful, emancipated path, until presently perhaps. . . . And presently it happened. Unwittingly he put a devastating weapon into the hands of the Conservative Party and the subtleties of conduct recognized by the literary world—where you threw your vitriol in private —being anathema to politics, Mr. Joynson-Hicks quickly took full advantage of it. Campaigning at Altrincham in 1908 Joynson-Hicks declared that the Socialists threatened to invade the sacred rights of the family, part husband and wife, and reduce women to a sort of graceless concubinage in a society where, if one read Mr. Wells aright, every infant would be taken away from its mother and father and placed in a state nursery.

Challenged to justify this, Mr. Joynson-Hicks simply referred to Mr. Wells' book where it was clearly stated that 'wives no less than goods were to be held in common.' (9)

The Labour Party threw up its hands in horror. What had Mr. Wells done ! The sanity of people who spent their days shut away from their fellows, writing, was necessarily suspect, but H. G. Wells had in some mysterious way become a great man, and they credited him with rather less imbecility than normally went with authorship. If Wells carried no official sanction that they would recognize, his Left Wing alignments were unmistakable and it was easy to use him to discredit a whole party, as the Labour Party now clearly and too late, saw. Later in life their embarrassment wouldn't have troubled him in the least, but now it produced in him a sense of remorse to which he was quite unaccustomed, and for the first time in several years he faltered in his stride. Mr. Bottomley, seizing the psychological moment, at once brought his own special gifts to bear and produced a pamphlet calculated to make Wells' words sound far worse. 'Essentially the Socialist position,' wrote Bottomley, 'is a denial of property in human beings; not only must land and the means of production be liberated, but women and children just as men and things must cease to be owned. . . . So in future it will not be *my wife* or *your wife*, but *our wife.*'

The last sentence merely carried to its logical conclusion what had gone before, but the words were not Wells'. He had never said anything of the kind. The catchpenny phrase was unscrupulous hyperbole, but once coined it caught on. 'Our wife' opened up huge promiscuous perspectives where all women became common property to be indulged as cows on a collective farm. The words performed the complementary function of inflaming the suppressed impulses of half the electorate and heaping their own sense of guilt at such wicked and abandoned joy upon someone else's head. It was calculated to delight and dismay in the same breath, with poor H. G. left to bear the collective remorse of half the community. It set the wits of the town at work upon its more ironic implications. . . . Our wife ! Our children ! Cows and collective farms ! But of course. There had always been too much private enterprise in marriage. The laws of emotional copyright flatly contradicted instinctive impulse, and monopoly practice must be stopped in marriage as in industry, but what insulting pittance would the Socialist state offer as compensation to the present owner-husband of flaxen-haired Mrs. Smith when it took her over, or how convince her that she was worth a whole lot less than the smoky-eyed ladies who haunted the studios of Hampstead ?

Nothing could have been more remote from the emotional world in which Wells now lived, or his attitude to women. Love for him took many forms but whenever it deserved the word love it was something very different from the mere acquisition of female property or faithful intercourse repeated at mutually approved intervals over the years, and certainly it was something in which no state could ever trade. Where he asked for relaxation of the sexual codes and greater responsibility by the state they offered to socialize love and told him that was what he was really after. He did not stand alone in his beliefs. 'I think,' Bertrand Russell had said, 'that where a marriage is fruitful and both partners to it are reasonable and decent, the expectation ought to be that it will be lifelong, but not that it will exclude other sex relations.' (10) It did not help very much. Russell could not smooth away Wells' troubles with the Labour Party, or hold off the mob clamouring for his blood. '. . . The comical attempt made recently . . . to suggest that Mr. Keir Hardie and the Party he leads was mysteriously involved with my unfortunate self in teaching free love to respectable working men,' Wells wrote, but he could not escape by irony. He outfaced his critics alone for a time, and then found himself forced, for once in his life, to change his mind as publicly as possible. Change his mind is rather an exaggeration. It was a compromise, a climb down, at most a contradiction. Fabian back-benchers, certain sections of the Labour Party, a mob of priests and teachers and writers, hounded and misquoted him until at last, largely to relieve his Left Wing associates from his damning company, he unsaid half of his dearest illusions and went sorrowfully away to forget the whole business. In 1908 he wrote, 'Socialism has not even worked out what are the reasonable conditions of a state marriage . . . contract and it would be ridiculous to pretend it had. . . . Socialism offers no theory whatever as to the duration of marriage. In these matters Socialism doesn't decide and it is quite reasonable to argue that Socialism need not decide. Socialism maintains an attitude of neutrality.' (11)

He had compromised if not climbed down, but there was a big element of self-sacrifice in the surrender. In any case he could never be mistaken for the cool, unbiassed intellectual preserving detachment in the face of all solicitations to surrender, and his convictions—if not his intellectual principles—were not at this stage inviolable. Later in life he found the whole episode of self-repudiation so distressing that he swung round once again and came out with an even more vigorous reiteration of his original ideas. There was no mistaking their meaning this time: 'The family can remain only as a biological fact. Its economic and educational autonomy are inevitably doomed. The modern State is bound to be the ultimate guardian of all children, and it must assist, replace or subordinate the parent as supporter, guardian, educator; it must release all human beings from the obligation of mutual proprietorship and it must refuse absolutely to recognise and enforce any kind of sexual ownership.' (12)

*   *   *

There was to be a very unpoetic justice in that last romantic moment so much later in his life, when Wells, after the death of Catherine, proposed marriage to a mistress who had held his deepest affections—only to be rejected. Wells the unbeliever, Wells who wanted no kind of sexual ownership, did not play the unrequited lover, the rebuffed writer, quite as he should have done. He was ill at ease. He simply did not understand the part. Ageing, worried, unhappy, he strode about his study muttering 'Why ? Why ? Why ?'

*   *   *

First and Last Things appeared in 1908. It said everything his sexual writings had omitted. It filled in many other sides of his character and quite fantastically revealed a streak in him, a mystical streak, which none of his detractors admitted or wanted to know about. *First and Last Things* came as near to explaining the 'philosophy' of his middle years as any book he wrote. If the word 'philosophy' meant an organized system of thought which explained the universe, it was not this or anything like it which Wells now offered the world. If it meant an attempt to see things *whole* for the sake of wise action, he came closer to it. As in his novels he had brought fresh, invigorating valuations into many a mental slum, so in *First and Last Things* he brought an exhilarating attitude of mind into the stuffy philosophic towers. It was an attitude of mind which believed men to be rational beings capable of envisaging their destiny as World Citizens, possessed by inexplicable yearnings for Beauty, Love and Higher Purpose. He did not stand for Kant, Berkeley, Britain, Empire, Peace or Prosperity; he stood for Man, Rational Man, granted unimaginable possibilities; but he never brought it within anything resembling a system of thought.

First and Last Things railed derisively against the universities for enthroning philosophy in temples inviolate to any but the finer spirits. Philosophical study he held was 'the common material for every type of sound adolescent education,' and yet under the farcical name of Greats it languished in the less frequented places of our universities. 'A general need was treated as a precious luxury.' With this complaint he swept on to bring together the diffuse clouds of philosophical, metaphysical and scientific thinking, audaciously reducing immense tracts of learning to a few easily understood and very stirring pages, as though the divine simpleton, the untutored genius in him was bewildered that anyone should find it difficult, obscure, or in any sense over their heads. Here it all was clear enough. Read and enjoy it.

How well he could do this whenever he wanted. How pompous and aloof and unnecessarily learned he made half the philosophers and professors seem, how easily his brain, so instantaneously receptive, moved among the clouds, rushing to earth with something which, if it did not encompass the heavens, was as refreshing as rain. There followed a deep incursion into his own beliefs which still did not amount to a philosophy within the narrow meaning of the word, but made a confession of faith, carried him away in a moving rush of self-revelation. Try as he would he could not quite contain it all in the vessel of commonsense. There were moments in the book when he approached what, for Wells, can only be described as a state of mental grace. Ever and again something bubbled up in him, ever and again a nearly mystical fervour emerged against all rational restraint, the writing became rough, unpremeditated, and at its worst, most moving. The academics might be amused. There was much here to offer a great deal of innocent fun amongst professors of philosophy, and well-mannered smiles were the only possible answer if you were a classical scholar, scientist or pedagogue; but for Wells and his readers it meant a great deal and carried them along passionately.

At the outset he admitted a scientific bias in favour of predestination, a universe to be seen as fixed, determined and orderly, but there was something so utterly barren in determinism that it could never for him yield deep enough satisfactions. He needed something more. He needed a personal belief in his own free will. He wanted to know that for him and his conduct there was 'much wide practical margin of freedom. I am free and freely and responsibly making the future—so far as I am concerned. You others are equally free. On that theory I find my life will work, and on a theory of mechanical predestination nothing works.' (13)

He did not see his individual self as immortal. He saw it as part of a greater immortality. He believed he was a temporary device of skin, bones, arteries and ganglia, a mysterious encasement of flesh and blood, involving consciousness, and with certain things to do which no-one else could do, but when they were done he would dissolve into dust, finished beyond any hope of resurrection. If there was an unknown scheme of things, he felt it must be so profound, so utterly outside the reach of brains of our order it would never suffer the perpetual encumbrance of his egotism. 'I shall serve my purpose and pass under the wheel and end. That distresses me not at all.' (14)

But it remained a working hypothesis. He admitted the lack of satisfying evidence, until he came to the life of the race, and there began the streak of near mysticism which recurs throughout *First and Last Things*. Individual immortality there might not be, the ordinary personality could so easily remain imprisoned within its own sensibilities, but when one came to the life of the race. . . . Some deep primal flow had grown and deepened in one form or another since the first amoeba stirred in the mud, and we were immutably part of that flow, mightily possessed by its purposes if we so chose, or frustrated in a futile search for absolute individuality. Yet even in the innermost caverns of individuality the voice of the race still echoed. That was inevitable. We were all blood relations. We sprang from a common stock. 'Disregarding the chances of intermarriage, each one of us had two parents, four grandparents, eight great-grandparents and so on backward, until very soon, in less than fifty generations, we should find that, but for the qualification introduced, we should have all the earth's inhabitants of that time as our progenitors. For a hundred generations it must hold absolutely true that everyone of that time who has issue living now is ancestral to all of us.' (15) The future reiterated the past. The same mesh of relationships would unravel, to marry in the end children of the worst enemy to children of the best friend, to bring the Celt into the Saxon fold, to merge and make one, now impossible opposites, until 'in less than fifty generations . . . all the population of the world will have my blood.' (16)

This essential oneness of the race was his touchstone, his sole hope of immortality; and a sustaining challenge in his life when he wrote *First and Last Things* was to awaken everyone from the delusions of individual emancipation. He had known despair and sin and remorse, he said, he had suffered engulfing experience, and through it all he had come to a sort of salvation. 'I see myself in life as part of a great physical being that strains and I believe grows towards beauty, and of a great mental being that strains and I believe grows towards knowledge and power. In this persuasion . . . I find both concentration of myself and escape from myself; in a word I find salvation.'

An extraordinary cry from the lips of Wells. But that was not the end of it. A mesmeric power ran through the race which permitted us to go about our shabby little searches for individual satisfactions unaware that we were serving a common end. Biologically, we were sleep-walking. But what a transformation if the sleeper woke and from his own free will determined to serve the spirit of man, for then blind destiny became beautiful, then by the very act of awareness and decision, we became as gods.

Power and Beauty. These were the twin forces inspiring the universe of Wells in 1908. One was form and the other light. One appealed to his rational, the other to his mystical self. 'The first places me as it were in a scheme, the latter illuminates and inspires me.' Rationally, he knew that the frustrated human being, wrought upon by so many conflicting stresses, victim of black despairs and rages, ill-balanced, easily given to misery and craving some strength beyond his own, desired above all things—

invulnerability. By losing his own petty troubles in oneness with the race he might not achieve invulnerability. But he achieved something we all needed of steadfastness, of pattern in life, of order which affords escape from personal fluctuations. The unchanging certainty of the lifestream steadied and reassured the wavering individual, and in proportion as the stresses were shared, we became less vulnerable, as the mutual reassurance of love gave greater strength.

Irrationally, Wells' other self desired something more. Repeatedly, in *First and Last Things*, he swung away from the earth and surrendered to mystically inexact statement: 'I believe in the great and growing Being of the Species from which I rise, to which I return, and which it may be, will ultimately even transcend the limitation of the species and grow into the Conscious Being, the undying Conscious Being of all things.' And then, at last, it comes. 'What the scheme as a whole is I do not clearly know; with my limited mind I cannot know. There I become a Mystic.'

The mood ran strongly in the period when he wrote *First and Last Things* and persisted far longer than his one relapse into religious thinking, but it was rarely, in any exact sense of the word, 'mystical'. It was a glow thrown off by the senses. He found intense joy in living things, but had little regard for the beauty of inanimate objects, he entered sensuously into the burning beauty of a fire, he felt the exaltation of emotional excitements, he felt purified, holy, in the presence of great elemental mysteries, and it led him into a heightened awareness which he sought to communicate in phrase after phrase, but the refinements of spiritual experience were not for him. The finer shades in most things eluded him or were deliberately avoided. The sheer force of vitality too often carried subtlety away in a rush of reckless experience, and refinement seemed to him a poor thing beside it. Whenever he did surrender to the otherness in him, it was a catharsis of the senses carrying him into a singing cloud of words. It was rarely the attenuated awareness of spiritual mysticism. He could never have written with T. S. Eliot

> 'When the evening is spread out against the sky
> Like a patient etherised upon a table' . . .

That was too complete a spiritual triumph over the forces of nature, too deep an imposition of personal vision on inanimate matter. He was closer to D. H. Lawrence's dark gods in his moments of emotional ecstasy. Stephen Spender has said that 'the point of comprehension where the senses are aware of an otherness in objects which extends beyond the senses, and the possibility of a relationship between the human individual and forces outside himself . . . is capable of creating in him a new state of mind.' (17) It sometimes created one in Wells.

Chapter Thirteen

CRY HAVOC

HE was now 46. A tubby, ebullient little man given to fero-
cious quarrels, he bore no resemblance to the gawky beginner
who, twenty years before, had presented a scarecrow frame to the
world insolent with frustration. The face glowed with health, the
gleam in the eye had become a twinkle, the personality grown into
wholesome prosperity; but rather than diminish his fires, middle
age and success gave them a licence they had never found before.
He was indeed inflammatory. In the years 1912–18 he took on all
comers and he didn't mind who or what they were. Some said he
grew inordinately vain. Some said he succumbed to snobberies
and must have a title at his dinner parties, and there were signs
they said of the conversationalist receding, the enchanting companion turning into a high priest who pontificated at table and
held forth to the exclusion of normal conversation. It wasn't quite
true. In later years he became some of these things. In later years
he could be quite intolerable. But although Shaw had made a good
thing from cultivating vanity and self-display, Wells was not yet
at heart vain, and his exhibitionism seemed a poor thing beside
the Irishman's. On the surface he would often play the part and
there were unbelievable moments when he pompously announced
'God Wells believes the human race must die.' Later in life, to the
amazement of close friends, he sometimes spoke of 'God Wells,'
and then would watch to see what effect this had, and suddenly
—if he thought they were taking it too seriously—burst into
laughter. The surface Wells who played such tricks was very often
mistaken for the real Wells. There were fine performances in many
roles. As the 'snob' he sometimes enjoyed people who carried a
title and loved to have a countess for a neighbour, but the next
week would find him entertaining with Dickensian zest men once
his friends in the early days, drapery shop-assistants, still very bad
at talking and of the worst possible social origins. His friends
included butchers, newsagents and people who seemed to spend
their lives solving crossword puzzles. He sometimes relaxed in the
company of fools. He wasn't a very effective snob.

Another affair developed in 1912. His wildly changing views of women now included one which said they should be soberly clad and carry the dishes while men did the Scientific Work. But women were still sounding boards, rejuvenators, creatures who rescued him from unutterable deserts of flatness and sent him spiralling to his creative towers. And Jane—'If there was no love and delight between them there was a real habitual affection and much mutual help,' (1) he wrote, some time later, of a character who could easily be mistaken for her.

He moved to his new house, Easton Glebe, in 1910, and there, any summer afternoon one was liable to witness the ludicrous episode of G. K. Chesterton, hugely overtopping Herbert, saying with great supplication in his voice: 'We don't go for a walk today do we?' (2) Wells liked exercise as much as Chesterton loathed it. Wells constantly berated him for habits calculated to add another acre to the side of the hill, and habitually insisted: 'I cannot allow you to use the word "jolly" more than forty times a day.' But they played wonderful games together in their own toy theatre, and successfully dramatized such high-lights of public affairs as the Poor Law Commission. The play opened with the Commissioners taking to pieces Bumble the Beadle, stewing him in a huge cauldron, only to have a bigger and more robust Beadle leap from the pot before the ceremony was over. Wells and Chesterton enjoyed one another's company enormously. They made immense fun of living. And when Chesterton complained of his own inadequacy as a lecturer, of his vocal inefficiency, Wells— notorious for squeaky inaudibility—suggested that they should tour America together, lecturing simultaneously, one at each end of the hall.

In those middle years Wells didn't mind who or what he tackled, or—sometimes—what he said. Even the swollen figure of Chesterton, enormous in its eloquence, could not deter him. G. K. C. looked upon Wells as a 'sportive but spiritual child of Huxley' and said of him: 'I have always thought that he reacted too swiftly to everything; possibly as part of the swiftness of his natural genius. . . . I have never ceased to admire and sympathise. . . . Whenever I met him he seemed to be coming from somewhere rather than going anywhere. . . . And he was so often nearly right that his movements irritated me like the sight of somebody's hat being perpetually washed up by the sea. . . . But I think he thought the object of opening the mind was simply opening the mind. Whereas I am incurably convinced that the object of opening the mind as of opening the mouth, is to shut it again on something solid.' (3)

It was penetrating enough to provoke the most tolerant writer, but it wasn't so much Chesterton's opinions of Wells which bothered him as the incalculable habits of a group of reviewers somehow inseparable from the enormous, overhanging presence, steamily seen behind *The New Witness*. In some way Wells held Gilbert Chesterton responsible for everything *The New Witness* (Cecil Chesterton's paper) said or did, and one day, infuriated by the treatment F. M. Hueffer received at its hands, he plunged in, words flying—

My dear G. K. C.,

Haven't I on the whole behaved decently to you ? Haven't I always shown a reasonable civility to you and to your brother and Belloc ? Haven't I betrayed at times a certain affection for you ? Very well, then you will understand that I don't start out to pick a needless quarrel with *The New Witness* crowd.

But this business of the Hueffer book in *The New Witness* makes me sick. Some disgusting little greaser named —— has been allowed to insult old F. M. H. in a series of letters that make me ashamed of my species. Hueffer has many faults no doubt but firstly he's poor, secondly he's notoriously unhappy and in a most miserable position, thirdly he's a better writer than any of your little crowd. . . .

The letter finished by saying that he, Wells, had no intention of letting *The New Witness* into his house again, it all reminded him so much of 'the cat-in-the-gutter-spitting-at-the-passer-by.' (4)

To which G. K. C. replied:

My dear Wells,

. . . Any quarrel between us will not come from me; and I confess I am puzzled as to why it should come from you, merely because somebody else who is not I dislikes a book by somebody else who is not you, and says so in an article for which neither of us is even remotely responsible. I very often disagree with the criticisms of ——; I do not know anything about the book or the circumstances of Hueffer. I cannot help being entertained by your vision of ——, who is not a priest, but a poor journalist, and I believe a Free-Thinker. But whoever he may be (and I hardly think the problem worth a row between you and me) he has a right to justice: and you must surely see that even if it were my paper, I could not either tell a man to find a book good when he found it bad, or sack him for a point of taste which has nothing in the world to do with the principles of the paper. For the rest, Haynes represents *The New Witness* much more than a reviewer does, being both on the board and the staff; and he has put your view in the paper—I cannot help thinking with a more convincing logic. Don't you sometimes find it convenient, even in my case, that your friends are less touchy than you are ?

By all means drop any paper you dislike, though if you do it for every book review you think unfair, I fear your admirable range of modern knowledge will be narrowed. Of the paper in question I will merely say this. My brother, and in some degree the few who have worked with him, have undertaken a task of public criticism for the sake of which they stand in permanent danger of imprisonment and personal ruin. We are incessantly reminded of this danger; and no one has ever dared to suggest that we have any motive but the best. If you should ever think it right to undertake such a venture, you will find that the number of those who will commit their journalistic fortunes to it, is singularly small: and includes some who have more courage and honesty than acquaintance with the hierarchy of art. It is even likely that you will come to think the latter less important.

Yours, sans rancune,
G. K. Chesterton. . . . (5)

Wells wrote back:

Dear G. K. C.,

Also I can't quarrel with you. But the Hueffer business aroused my long dormant moral indignation and I let fly at the most sensitive part of *The New Witness* constellation, the only part about whose soul I care. I hate these attacks on rather miserable exceptional people like Hueffer and Masterman. I know these aren't perfect men, but their defects make quite sufficient hells for them without these public peltings. I suppose I ought to have written to C. C. instead of to you. One of these days I will go and have a heart-to-heart talk to him. Only I always get so amiable when I meet a man. He, C. C., needs it—I mean the talking to.

Yours ever
H. G.

*   *   *

Easton Glebe became the scene of the famous week-ends in the shadow of Dunmow when the Olympian figures of literature biked, rode and walked to H. G.'s house to have him tear their personal illusions to shreds and suddenly convert academic debate into momentary quarrels in between the talk, the games and a great deal of affection. There was a varying ritual to the three-day Saturnalia. Bed perhaps by ten-thirty or eleven on Friday night to prepare for the rigours of the week-end, with H. G. climbing into his specially designed sleeping suit which made it possible to rise at any hour of the night without feeling cold; sometimes he did not sleep very well, sometimes he browsed over books half the night with the aid of his special reading table—but the fountain of high spirits rose in the morning again if it were a fine day. Much of his work was done in his bedroom at a very small table. He had a primus stove to make tea whenever he wanted. Sometimes he worked in the middle of the night, sometimes he was still writing as the dawn came up.

Then came the ball game in the barn where the long, lean Shaw might stand one side of the net beside Sullivan the mathematician, and Wells and someone else stood on the other, to whack and pursue a rubber ball with energy enough to win a war, and yells characteristic of the more abandoned Red Indians. It was Wells' way of keeping fit, of having fun, of knocking the stuffing out of decorum, and everybody had to serve the cult. In the household of Wells there were moments when pomposity had to be ejected with the intensity of a ritual and sometimes commonplace sobriety vanished in the scrum. He would play lawn tennis with bare feet just for the hell of it. As J. W. N. Sullivan remarked 'Wells was an old man in his youth and a schoolboy at 50.' It was Sullivan who arrived at Easton Glebe one week-end—having carefully carried an empty attache-case all the way down from London—and sitting in the sun beside the lily pond, considered the house and fine prospect and said, 'Think of it. . . . all this for writing what you want to write, not for pot-boilers.' And Arnold Bennett wrote in his journal of Easton Glebe: 'A lovely, a heavenly morning: very clear and sunshiny . . . I breakfasted with Jane Wells at 9.15 and then others came down. . . . H. G. and I changed and all six of us (without the Nevinsons) played ball games for 50 mts. Fine lunch with 3 ducks and a hot apple pie. After which sleep which enabled me to miss the tennis. There was some tennis and some bridge and some Schubert trio on the gramophone and some yacht talk and some tea—with rose leaf jam. . . . H. G. disappeared for about 90 mts. after tea. We thought he was reading or asleep. But at midnight he told us that he had suddenly had the ideas for continuing a novel that he hadn't touched for a month and so had gone on with it. . . .' (6)

Long hours of work sometimes began at nine o'clock behind sound-proof doors, with Wells writing, and the household suitably hushed in respect for the great man's creative moments. It might continue till one. Luncheon, then, of varied duration. The afternoons might mean a walk in the country, with tea and work again until dinner, and very often games after dinner, for Wells without games was the sea without a tide. How he loved to get a bunch of children riotously engaged in some outrageous game while he stood, whistle in hand, squeakily excited, the worst of referees, liable to burst into the fray and break all the rules himself, commenting, shouting, arguing, the biggest child of the lot. And the children were very often no less personages than Lord Olivier, Bernard Shaw, Bertrand Russell and even that impossibly gargantuan infant, Chesterton. Sometimes 50 people came to a trestle tea in the garden. Once Wells sat like a child on Lady Warwick's knees, holding her hand, trying to wheedle a favour out of her for someone, and deliberately making a show of it.

These were the days elsewhere, of the 'great parties.' There were elaborate suppers in vast tents, wild chorusing would wreck the Chelsea night, and the colour of the guest's behaviour tended to become more violent as the state of intoxication advanced, until there were times when it all bore comparison with the glories of feasting in ancient Babylon. Maurice Baring celebrated his fiftieth birthday by performing an incredible Dervish-cum-Russian dance and then plunging into the sea fully clothed in evening dress; Chesterton was challenged and fought a spectacular duel with real swords, reflecting later on that it was fortunate his opponent had drunk more than he had; and Wells . . . ? We have the uncorroborated evidence of a French journalist who retired from one of these parties and began an article in his paper: ' "I denounce Shaw: he's sober." Who said these words ? These were the words of Herbert George Wells. . . .' (7)

* * *

The 1914–18 war broke into the life at Easton Glebe with explosive results and carried Wells away on a wave of excitement. If he adopted what was called the average liberal view, he also became squeakily certain that this was a huge watershed in the affairs of the human race, which would carry us over into a quite new way of life where war was unknown. He talked rather more than usual. He flung newspapers, in a rage, into the fire. He wrote many letters to friends in high and low places, seething letters which made Chesterton's words seem even more apt: 'I have always thought that he reacted too swiftly to everything. . . . I think he has always been too much in a state of reaction. . . .' (8)

His state of reaction now carried him—with almost schoolboy impetuosity and a brand of patriotism few had suspected in him—to nail his own highly distinctive colours to a mast whose existence was becoming a little doubtful under so many flags. There followed a series of patriotic cartwheels which set Chesterton bombinating about the dangers of hurrahs too hastily delivered. It went beyond hurrahs. It ran over in an emotional surge which left many of his disciples in a state of bewildered dismay, and took him, breathless and fierce, into half a dozen new quarrels. For it has to be said that the spirit of the times seized Wells and reduced him, on occasion, to a noisy propagandist mouthing all the familiar cries of the day, with the one difference that he carried them to their logical conclusion in a blaze of verbal valour. In *The Passionate Friends* he had written a year before the war, with magnificent effect, 'I know that a growing multitude of men and women outwear the ancient ways. The blood-stained organized jealousies of religious intolerance, the delusions of nationality and cult and race, that black hatred which simple people and young people and common people cherish against all that is not in the likeness of themselves, cease to be the undisputed ruling forces of our collective life. We want to emancipate our lives from this slavery to these stupidities, from dull hatreds and suspicions. . . . A spirit . . . arises and increases in human affairs, a spirit that demands freedom and gracious living as our inheritance too long deferred.' The words rang oddly now as his disciples listened to bursts of something which could easily have been mistaken for jingoism, distinguished more by the way he said it than anything else.

Once upon a time it seemed very clear that Wells hated jingling spurs, thundering guns, uniforms, hussars, and even the poor innocent horse which he so savagely attacked. And although August 1914 saw him discriminating between the German people and its leaders, found him talking of a war without revenge, of honour amongst democratic nations, and a peace without passion, suddenly, overnight, by the autumn of the same year his head was stuffed with the most astounding nonsense about Germans, Germany, pacifism and war. The shrilling bugles went to his head. The deep drums sounded and he was drunk. The British flag fluttered before his eyes so coloured with righteousness that it might have had divine sanction. How else explain his announced intention of looting Berlin when our armies overran Germany, his desire to leave a stigma on the German people by the childish device of stamping railway tickets 'Extra for Louvain Outrages— Two Marks,' (9) and his sudden belief that whatever was good in German literature had been written by the Jews ? True, German ruthlessness and revelations of a long and thorough preparation for war were calculated to chill many generous minds once constrained to suspend judgment, but Wells seemed to enjoy his own metamorphosis and plunged in, phrases flying.

When Shaw came out with one of the few sound documents of the day, *Common-Sense about War*, Wells immediately described him as 'like an idiot child screaming in a hospital,' (10) and Bertrand Russell, the avowed disciple of pacifism, cool, dispassionate, preserving his own principles in the face of all mass persuasions to surrender them, became a man who 'objected to Euclid upon grounds no-one could possibly understand, in books no-one could possibly read.' (11) Wells did not seem to care how much of Germany we annexed, what happened to the German colonies, what horrors the tank brought into modern warfare, so long as we gathered all our forces into one mighty mailed fist capable of crushing the German aggressor in a few months. In the early days of the war, he talked as if the Germans had shot their bolt, and believed the French would storm their way across the Rhine into Germany, yet remained apprehensive of landings in Britain and called on the War Office to accept volunteers for what would then have been the Home Guard, only to be met with bland War Office smiles and an assurance that they too knew a little about the business. Several times he sought active service in one form or another.

As the first subdued murmurings against the war from the intellectuals and pacifists came into the open, he felt they had to be answered with all the weapons at his disposal, and setting aside whatever of his own work he had not already dropped, stopping books and stories in mid-career, he plunged into print in *The Nation*, *The Labour Leader*, *The Daily Chronicle* and *The Daily News*, rolling back the pacifist arguments, trying to illumine the essentials of the war. So far as one can make them out, the essentials began with the broad belief that this was a war to end war, and led him quickly into the conviction that under war conditions the World State 'ceased to be a subject for discussion and exalted resolution and became as a matter of course the general form of life for a reasonable man of goodwill.' (12) There was at this time a naive conviction that by pouring the world into the melting pot something better would emerge, granted a modicum of goodwill and the acceptance of universal Government. Once the horror of the Hohenzollern had been swept away—something which he repeated could be accomplished in a matter of months—neutral statesmen would determine the fate of the world, without bitterness or rancour, at an international peace conference, and the inevitable outcome would be a starry-eyed World State dedicated to the disinterested service of man. Lofty commotions of this kind did not ring so doubtfully in those days, and there was no questioning the high inspiration which drove Wells to abandon his own private work for what he thought to be the public good; but there were many confusions in the scene, confusions which became, at their worst, shrill and strident.

The World Set Free, published in 1914, foresaw the atomic bomb, a weapon so powerful, so utterly cataclysmic that after one abandoned use of it, war involved genocide and became impossible. It was in many ways a brilliant book. It drew a picture fearfully possible to-day. . . .' From nearly two hundred centres and every week added to their number, roared the unquenchable crimson conflagrations of the atomic bombs: the flimsy fabric of the world's credit had vanished, industry was completely disorganized and every city and every thickly populated area was starving or trembled on the verge of starvation. Most of the capital cities were burning; millions of people had already perished. . . .' But *The World Set Free* foresaw in the end a World Parliament (by 1950), atomic energy sanely liberated, and everyone belonging to a comparatively leisured class free to devote himself to gardening, artistic decoration and research.

There were many other prophecies in the early days of the war but they were a small part of the torrent of words which poured away from him. Granted the journalist's gift for creating an easily grasped idea with a single evocative phrase even if some of the details refused to fit, Wells often spoke as for the people of Britain rather than in his own right, and that comes near to explaining some of his war-time utterance. The eye and mind get a little bewildered surveying the general scene. As the war advanced his views changed considerably. At one point it seemed Britain was to emerge from it all a magnanimous victor quite free from any trace of venom, and at another—if Wells' opinions meant anything— we were to consider looting Berlin. There was somehow to be compassion and justice and never a sign of revenge, not so very far removed from stigmatized railway tickets, annexed colonies and a dreadful military reckoning. It was confusing if not be-wildering. It was a rag-bag of Jingoism and justice and good healthy English rage.

But confusions were inevitable in those days. Wells so clearly aligned Germany with the rampant war machine which had to be crushed before peace could be established, irrespective of any other deep, underlying cause, and Britain with all the ideals of World Government, that contradictions were of the very essence of his attitude. These were the days of over-simplification. It is difficult to see straight in the middle of a tornado. Over-simplifi-cation now became more dangerous than over-elaboration. It led into a row of labels which people were determined to apply with imperishable gum, a row of labels sometimes smothering real identities. All Germans became Huns, acts of violence atrocities, German minelayers monsters, German colonists trampling bullies, pioneering pimps, and many another horrible travesty.

People were aware of being used for great purposes, of immense cravings for something they could not clearly define, of violent waves of emotional reaction, and when Wells, charged with similar emotions, released them on the printed page transmuted by his power of writing, they let out a cry of recognition. This was what they meant—this was what they felt—this man was indeed a writer.

It happened in *Mr. Britling Sees it Through*. The book, written in 1915, recorded the day-to-day reaction of one Englishman to the war, and what might have read like racy journalism, touched with all the appropriate emotions, became a moving document trans-figured by his own powers of writing and the impact of the muddy meaningless tragedy of war. Perhaps that goes too far. It wasn't in any sense a great book. It told an elaborate story redundantly and whenever it did plunge beneath the surfaces the depth of the plunge was never great. Whatever his writing did to it, the book remained a popular novel. It was an entertainment but in its day it moved many people deeply. The same delight in drawing his characters half from life animated *Mr. Britling*. Wells had been personal before but now he excelled himself. Sidney Dark wrote: 'Colonel Rendezvous is the highly competent soldier who for some time commanded the Canadian Army in France and is now known as Lord Byng. The journalist is Ralph Blumenfeld, American-born editor of *The Daily Express*; Lawrence Carmine is Cranmer Byng, the oriental scholar and poet.'

Mr. Britling's son enlists for service and tragically dies. The change of fashion in emotional climates becomes painfully clear when we read the death scene again to-day, a death which deeply moved readers in the first World War with its 'masterful and beautiful compassion—unequalled in Wells' writing.' (13) What came unbearably close to the heart then, hovers on the edge of sentimentality to-day, and the sophisticated modern mind finds an emotional immodesty about the last sentences—'The door had hardly shut upon her before he forgot her. Instantly he was alone again, utterly alone. . . . Across the dark he went and suddenly his boy was all about him, playing, climbing the cedars, twisting miraculously about the lawn on a bicycle, discoursing gravely upon his future, lying on the grass breathing very hard and drawing preposterous caricatures. Once again they walked side by side up and down—it was almost this very spot—talking gravely and rather shyly. . . . And here they had stood a little awkwardly before the boy went in to say goodbye to his stepmother and go off with his father to the station.

' "I will work to-morrow again," whispered Mr. Britling, "but to-night—to-night. . . . To-night is yours. Can you hear me? Can you hear? Your father . . . who had counted on you. . . ." '

Mr. Britling was a best seller. The Americans paid £20,000 for it. They were starved of real news in the emaciated British newspapers, restrained from half they wanted to know by their own censorship, and *Mr. Britling* filled out the story in all its moving humanity, brought Hugh's tragedy to the American door, a tragedy cast for them in heroic mould.

The book became a household word in Britain and people wrote long letters to Wells, sympathising with him on the loss of his imaginary eldest son. Enthusiastic strangers even asked to see the place where he wept when he heard the news. 'I have no sons in the war,' he replied to one letter. 'My eldest boy is 15. But I have seen the tragedy of my friends' sons. . . . I do feel we owe a kind of altar to all these splendid youths.'

God suddenly and flamingly took possession of Wells after *Mr. Britling Sees it Through*. Some transcendental spark lit his mind and away he raced with the same creative effervescence to burst into two more books: *God, the Invisible King* and *The Soul of a Bishop*, from which it was clear that he had little communion with the Christian Christ, a person he considered too refined, too unblemished and idealized. He needed a 'more blundering finite leader' (Ivor Brown). There were to be two Gods for him. One a struggling God, close to each one of us, capable of revelation, an immanent God, the other a Creator, a Veiled Being, at the very wellsprings of the Universe, inscrutable, unknowable, because all things sprang from him. After a time one of these deities bore a distinct likeness to a 'personified five-year plan.' Wells had turned his New Republic 'into a divine monarchy.' Unable to bear any longer the clap-trap of King and Country he called on people to live and die for a Higher Purpose or Person. The idea of God exercised his mind deeply at this period, but within a few years, his natural streak of Voltairian anti-clericalism had re-asserted itself with all its old vigour. Later in life he was a little uneasy about the lapse.

*　　*　　*

Mr. Britling Sees it Through harmed nobody. With *War and the Future* and *Joan and Peter*, it was different. *Joan and Peter* went out of its way to savage the pacifists. In *War and the Future* Wells turned on the conscientious objectors and said some unforgivable things which twenty years later he deeply regretted. It was all of a piece with his passionate surrender to the easy persuasions of the day, but 'my pro-war zeal was inconsistent with my pre-war utterances and against my profounder convictions,' he said, many years afterwards. *What is Coming*, a collection of the 1915 newspaper articles, published in 1916, does not make very impressive reading to-day. Even some of the sackcloth and ashes he later

wore in self-abasement at such behaviour smelt a little of rationalisation. 'The anti-war people made me the more impatient
because of the rightness of much of their criticism of the prevailing
war motives. I was perhaps afraid, if I yielded to them, of being
carried back too far towards the futility of a merely negative
attitude. What they said was so true and what they did was so
merely sabotage, I lost my temper with them.' (14)

He also won an immense popularity with the people of Britain,
but at bottom Wells did not go out of his way to enjoy his
oneness with the herd, or sell his convictions for a mess of popularity. Indeed in 1917 he said that his day was over. He met Arnold
Bennett one October afternoon in the National Liberal Club,
and fell to slanging the Webbs. Then suddenly 'My boom is over.
I've had my boom. I'm yesterday.' (15) Air raids were bothering
him at the time. He had been through several at Southend.
Afraid of going to pieces under bombardment, whenever he could
he chose a balcony to stand on, but still became 'very huffy and
cross.'

In the end he wrote of the war in his *Autobiography*: 'The thing
that occupied most of my mind was the problem of getting whatever was to be got for constructive world revolution out of the
confusion of war, and being pro-German and non-combatant,
finding endless excuses for the enemy and detracting from the
fighting energy of the Allies, seemed to me of no use at all towards
my end.'

There were many other war-time battles. One with censorship,
showed the rationalist returning to power, resuming his 'habitual
criticism of government and the social order' as the propagandist
ceased to plunge and proclaim. He had written a series of articles,
disagreeable to the military mind, and when he wanted to publish
them in book form, the Censor remonstrated with him and returned the galley proofs richly blue-pencilled. The book, *War and
the Future*, expressed Wells' belief that Britain's military machine
was in a sad state of muddle, and for obvious reasons, the man
'now mentor to the mind of England' felt that criticism of this
kind was slightly heretical if not traitorous. Wells read, absorbed
his corrections, and fell into deep meditation. Were these blue
pencillings intended to shield military mistakes, and if men like
himself could so easily be muffled, where was England to find its
free critics capable of assailing all and every shortcoming ? If he

did not speak now 'these soldiers would go on with their bloody muddle, muddle until disaster was assured.' Wells quietly burnt the Censor's elaborately corrected galleys. Taking a second set of galleys he sent them to his publishers with a note to say that the Censor had read one set. The book duly appeared. After a brief interval the Censor wrote an inordinately polite letter asking whether he might see the original corrected proofs, if it was not troubling Mr. Wells too much and Wells, with even greater courtesy, replied that it was no trouble at all but unfortunately the galleys had been mislaid. On which note the correspondence ended.

There was also a brief incursion into the Ministry of Propaganda. With the connivance of Lord Northcliffe, in the last stages of the war, Wells took over propaganda against Germany for the new Ministry of Propaganda, an organization designed, he believed, to keep the inquisitive noses of Lords Northcliffe and Beaverbrook from prying too deeply into the mysterious activities of the Foreign Office, and quietly and ruthlessly the bureaucratic machine proceeded to have its revenge on him. His appointment almost coincided with the publication of yet another book, *In the Fourth Year* (1918), a book which laid down some very sane, sensible and for once highly practical plans for a League of Nations, although the idea, in its original conception, was not his.

'The plain truth is that the League of Free Nations, if it is to be a reality, if it is to effect a real pacification of the world, must do no less than supersede Empire; it must end not only this new German imperialism which is struggling so savagely and powerfully to possess the earth, but it must also wind up British imperialism and French imperialism. . . . Both countries (Germany and France) have been slaves to Kruppism and Zabernism—*because they were sovereign and free* ! So it will always be. So long as patriotic cant can keep the common man jealous of international controls over his belligerent possibilities, so long will he be the helpless slave of the foreign threat.'

It made his position, when he arrived at the Ministry of Propaganda, very clear. There was no equivocation on either side. Almost at once he wanted to answer the war propaganda pouring out of Germany in a way which not only said it was desirable to end the war—victoriously for the Allies—but stated, publicly, to the whole world, for the first time, Britain's War Aims. He

persuaded the Propaganda Ministry that it was imperative to state
these aims with the official blessing of the Foreign Office, and in
conjunction with Dr. Headlam Morley, he produced a mem-
randum which eventually penetrated the outer Foreign Office
defences and arrived one day on the desk of Sir William Tyrrell.
Sir William was quite put out when he read it. This was most
unorthodox. Ministries of Propaganda really should not meddle
with diplomacy in this cavalier fashion. He summoned the joint
authors to his presence. This would not do, he said in effect, this
just would not do, and proceeded to analyse all those deep-rooted
traditional prejudices born of the metaphysical urge which distinguished the German peoples from any other. 'Tyrrell was a
compact, self-assured little man who . . . delivered a discourse
on our relations to France and Germany' which 'would have
done credit to a bright but patriotic schoolboy of eight,' Wells
wrote in *An Experiment in Autobiography*. Wells did not then
know that British diplomatists had already committed themselves
to tacit agreements abroad, in complete secrecy, which rendered
his memorandum ridiculous, and revealed the terrifying powers
possessed by 'little undeveloped brains such as Tyrrell's' pro-
tected from criticism and privately arranging the world according to their own traditional lights. But Wells went away and
behaved as though the spirit of the memorandum had implicit
acceptance. It was a rash, audacious move, and he could scarcely
complain at what followed. But, of course, he did. For now, while
the Ministry of Propaganda blithely pursued the policy laid down
in his memorandum, the Foreign Office withdrew into its fast-
nesses and made no protest, reassured that it could repudiate these
idealistic undertakings whenever the need became too pressing.
Presently Wells believed himself led into the position of T. E.
Lawrence. He was the dupe used to lure Germany into false opti-
misms about any Armistice that might be arranged as Lawrence
had, all unaware, played the decoy to the Arabs. Censorship he
might outwit. But not the Foreign Office. 'Plainly I had not learnt
the A.B.C. of diplomacy. . . .' (*Experiment in Autobiography*.) No,
Wells was never in any sense of the word a diplomat, and he
retired at last, routed, angry, self-righteously splenetic, and suspect
to the Foreign Office for the rest of his days. Even Northcliffe he
quarrelled with before he resigned. *The Evening News* had developed
an anti-German line completely opposed to the Memoranda and

Wells told Northcliffe that he must 'control his own newspapers and stop this mischievous foolery' (*What is Success?*) only to be met with a blunt refusal.

*   *   *

There was another war-time battle, which had little to do with the war. It was a literary battle which took a very different turn, and had quite different origins. From the early days of the war, and indeed long before the war, the James-Conrad-Hueffer group had insisted that Wells' attitude towards creative writing was philistine, and now with the war in full cry, they tried to persuade him that if he permitted the trampling feet of the journalist to overwhelm the artist in him, with these public brawls and propagandings, he would be guilty of personal treason. Personal treason! What did they mean? It revived, with far more force, the once restrained skirmishes which had taken place between Wells, the journeyman of letters prepared to defend his faith with a pike, Henry James, the self-conscious artist, overwhelmed by the 'luxuriance of his own evolution,' and Arnold Bennett, determinedly the novelist, self-consciously equipped with all the writer's ritual. Bennett had said at one point that Wells was without a scrap of the artist in him and did not conceive books in the æsthetic vein. He was a little put out when Wells, momentarily a journalist at heart and mightily pleased with the part, welcomed the description, adding that he hadn't the remotest notion what fellows like Dostoievsky, Turgenev or Henry James were trying to do. Remarks like this infuriated Conrad as much as Bennett. Conrad owed Wells a great deal—'It strikes me, my dear Wells, that in your quiet almost stealthy way, you are doing a lot for me,' he had written some years before—but he could not stomach his sturdy, homespun disregard for the subtleties of novel-writing any more than Bennett or James. It lowered the tone of the profession. It brought an element of rodeo into the cloistered writing world, and the worst of it all was that in the estimation of James and Conrad, Wells could probably do it better than any of them if only he tried, because he had the finest perceptions about people, overwhelming creative energy, and absolutely no need to drop his characters in exchange for his own ideas about them. Conrad introduced a new note into the elaborate argument, for Conrad took his honour and his writing very seriously as Shaw found out one summer afternoon to Conrad's cost. They first met in Wells' house and almost before the introductions were over Shaw genially announced, with that forthright gaiety which exempted him from normal retaliation, 'You know my dear fellow your books won't *do*.'

Going very white Conrad followed Wells from the room and demanded 'Does that man want to insult me ?' 'The provocation to say yes and assist in the subsequent duel was great.' Wells wrote, 'but I overcame it. " It's humour " I said, and took Conrad to cool off in the garden.' (16)

But Conrad shed his honour and his habits reluctantly. Very soon he shifted his ground and was trying to persuade Hueffer to challenge Wells to a duel, for some article which Wells said was written as though Hueffer were the discharged valet of Hall Caine. 'If Conrad had had his way, either Hueffer's blood or mine would have reddened Dymchurch sands.' (17)

The battle between Wells and James came to a head with the publication of *Boon* (1915), and although there was no sign of anything more lethal than words, both men when they set their minds to it could make the simplest sentence explosive. James was genuinely moved by the earthquake of war and its terrible disruption of individual values, but he never betrayed his artistic faith and believed to the end that we could only come at the inner core of life, at truth, or primal significance, through individual experience. To Wells, riding mightily on the vastness of the upheaval, suddenly a victim of enormous forces he was powerless to control, it was the final absurdity to look inside himself, obsessively, for the key to it all. But *Boon* was unkind. *Boon* was uncalled for. *Boon* revealed yet another streak in the astonishing medley of Wells' make-up. It showed a satirist of no mean order, a satirist who might have become a great one. The main parts of *Boon*— 'The Mind of the Race' and 'The Wild Asses of the Devil'—were written long before, in 1911, in a mood of discomfited belief when the attacks upon himself, his behaviour and his books, had reached a climax. It went further than *The New Machiavelli*. It mocked the precious preoccupations of Henry James and George Moore, it guyed the stylists of the day and even, at bottom, questioned Wells' own ideals and aspirations. In reaction from the mounting tale of horror which the war continued to bring, Wells had found himself unable to complete *The Research Magnificent*, had turned to

*The mature, successful Wells now
become a world figure*

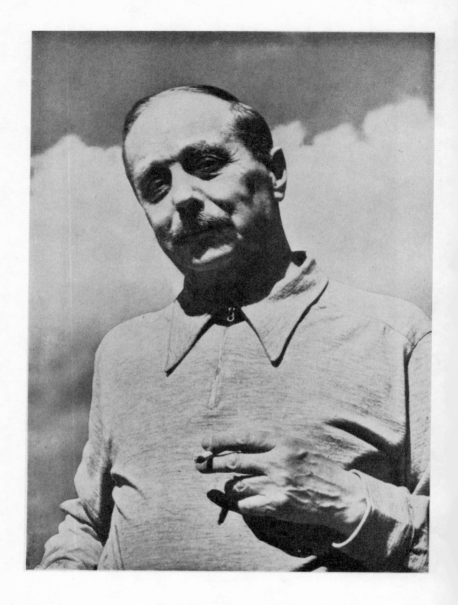

. . . still quizzical in relaxation

the fragmentary papers of *Boon*, added The 'Last Trump'—a sudden cry of despair about the Mind of the Race—and put it all in order for publication. There are few funnier essays in literary caricature than the imaginary conversation between George Moore and Henry James, with the two stylists following totally different paths, treading, with soundless good manners and fine language, through the endless maze of subtle, so subtle experience—or was it really experiences they wanted and not experience—to reach exquisite disagreement. While James is 'labouring through the long cadences of his companion as an indefatigable steam-tug might labour endlessly against a rolling sea,' off-setting everything resembling a statement with closely woven parenthesis, George Moore goes smoothly on, sustained by sheer joy of subtlety to describe 'with an extraordinary and living mastery of detail . . . a glowing little experience that had been almost forced on him at NISMES by a pretty little woman from NEBRASKA, and the peculiar effect it had had and particularly the peculiar effect that the coincidence that both NISMES and NEBRASKA began with N and end so differently had had upon his imagination. . . .' James' style is analysed—'Bare verbs he rarely tolerates. . . . His vast paragraphs sweat and struggle. . . .' And his characters. . . . 'These people cleared for artistic treatment, never make lusty love, never go angry to war, never shout at an election, or perspire at poker. . . .'

It hurt Henry James when it appeared. Nobody was deceived by the sub-title 'Being a First Selection from the Literary Remains of George Boon . . . Prepared for Publication by Reginald Bliss,' because the book carried a transparent introduction by H. G. Wells, and James wrote a pained letter to Wells couched in language which ironically resembled some of the more effective mutterings of Boon. On July 8th, 1915, Wells replied. . . .

'There is of course a real and very fundamental difference in our innate and developed attitudes towards life and literature. To you literature like painting is an end, to me literature like architecture is a means, it has a use. Your view was, I felt, altogether too prominent in the world of criticism and I assailed it in lines of harsh antagonism. And writing that stuff about you was the first escape I had from the obsession of this war. Boon is just a waste-paper basket. Some of it was written before I left my home at Sandgate (1911) and it was while I was turning over some old papers that I came upon it, found it expressive, and went on with it last December. I had rather be called a journalist than an artist, that is the essence of it, and there was no other antagonist possible than yourself. But since it was printed I have regretted a hundred times that I did not express our profound and incurable difference and contrast with a better grace. . . .'

July 10th.   Dictated
21 Carlyle Mansions,
Cheyne Walk, S.W.

My dear Wells,

I am bound to tell you that I don't think your letter makes out any sort of case for the bad manners of Boon, as far as your indulgence in them at the expense of your poor old H. J. is concerned—I say 'your' simply because he has been yours, in the most liberal, continual, sacrificial, the most admiring and abounding critical way, ever since he began to know your writing; as to which you have had copious testimony. . . .

Meanwhile I absolutely dissent from the claim that there are any differences whatever in the amenability to art of forms of literature æsthetically determined, and hold your distinction between a form that is (like) painting and a form that is (like) architecture for wholly null and void . . . There is no sense in which architecture is æsthetically 'for use,' that doesn't leave any other art whatever exactly as much so; and so far from that of literature being irrelevant to the literary report on life, and to its being made as interesting as possible, I regard it as relevant in a degree that leaves everything else behind. It is art that *makes* life, makes interest, makes importance, for our consideration and application of these things, and I know of no substitute whatever for the force and beauty of its process . . . If I were Boon I should say that any pretence of such a substitute is helpless and hopeless humbug; but I wouldn't be Boon for the world, and am only yours faithfully,

HENRY JAMES.

Wells replied on July 13th. . . . 'I don't clearly understand your concluding phrases—which shews no doubt how completely they define our difference. When you say "it is art that *makes* life, makes interest, makes importance," I can only read sense into it by assuming that you are using "art" for every conscious human activity. I use the word for a research and attainment that is technical and special. . . .'

It came in the end to this. Confronted one day with another letter from Henry which read like a missive from the Holy Grail,

Wells brutally declared—and the air about James must have shuddered to his words—'I am a journalist. I refuse to play the artist. If sometimes I am an artist it is a freak of the gods. I am a journalist all the time and what I write *goes now*—and will presently die.' And there for the moment the matter rested. It remains to record that he was sufficiently concerned with these attempts to retrieve his artistic soul to keep every letter James wrote, and before the end there were many.

Chapter Fourteen

HISTORY IS ONE

WELLS the scientist, Wells the artist, Wells the reformer, indissolubly bound by some intangible force which was insufficient to reconcile one with the other and only succeeded in putting now one, now the other in the ascendant. The stresses between the three were enormous. Pushed down, duped, deserted, the artistic sprite would suddenly erupt with volcanic force and upset all the reformer's calculations. Then deeper reverberations of an even older self came up out of the depths and warned him as some corner of his mind glowed bright, that this could no longer be.

But the reformer had things very much his own way in the years which followed the war. Wells came out of the war with one purpose dominating his life. Here was man's great chance. After four years of chaos and destruction and the breaking down of barriers we were faced with a unique opportunity to refashion a new world before everything settled back into its old hide-bound habits. The next ten years, he thought, should be the greatest in history. All those dreams impossible in the unyielding certainty of peace, could flower now amongst the ruins of war, and in the early days of 1919 there seemed more than a glimmer of truth in that. André Maurois has remarked that a society listens more attentively to its artists and prophets in times of disorder and disillusion. Such a time was now and such a hearing about to be granted Wells. Abuse, worship, ridicule, adoration, the reaction varied with different people but everyone had heard of him, felt strongly one way or another about him, and had to admit that he had become a public institution. However one reacted he couldn't be ignored. Wherever he went he was now the centre of correspondence, books, arguments, quarrels from people of every persuasion and nationality. Two secretaries were necessary to cope with the continuous flow pouring in from the outside world and the torrent he sent cascading back again. One month away from home and whole rooms were choked with books, parcels, presents, letters from people he had no chance of knowing or meeting, granted half a dozen lives. Everything he did or said was news. The newspapers kept close check on his whereabouts. Publishers competed fiercely for his next book. Distinguished foreign visitors continually asked whether they could meet Mr. Wells, Mr. H. G. Wells, Mr. Wells the prophet, Mr. Wells the genius.

The League of Nations came first, after the war, to fire his imagination, and in it he saw a draft plan of his New Republic, his organized World State, and for twelve months it seemed to him that all his writing and labour had not been in vain. Then abruptly he changed his mind. The League of Nations was, after all, only a diplomatic expedient to put obstacles in the way of one construc- tive proposal after another and it simply would not do (Geoffrey West). It was old-maidish, diplomatic prudery, it was a stumbling block in the way of progressive ideas. Worse still it had none of the powers which he felt were necessary to enforce its authority, or put down war or suppress insurrection.

The days of his disillusion with the League of Nations marked the beginning of a deep change in his outlook. Again it was in part a reflection of the times. The shadow of disillusion spread across Europe. 'The crudely organised egotisms and passions of national and imperial greed that carried mankind into that tra- gedy, emerged from it sufficiently unimpaired to make some other similar disaster highly probable as soon as the world has a little recovered from its war exhaustion and fatigue.' (1) The Peace Conference had revealed itself as yet another prolonged and pom- pous exercise in the old-fashioned diplomatic conspiracy, Clemen- ceau and Lloyd George had successfully outwitted Wilson and rankling hatred dictated the peace terms where Wells had hoped enlightened rationality might prevail. 'This simulacrum of peace' he called it. There was no end to the duplicity and bluff practised by men believed to be above both. Half the worst elements in Germany were encouraged to recover under the guise of rehabili- tation, Junkerdom rose all over again out of the ruins, and cyni- cism invaded the utterance of people once considered immune to any such shallowness. Presently, as it became very clear that the war to end war had ended nothing and solved nothing, Wells' gloom deepened. It drove him to use every medium for publi- cising his World State, it drove him to insist on the imperative role of a new education for the illiterate masses of the world, it drove him to join the Labour Party, and abandon all hope of finding any real inspiration in the League of Nations. 'For this League of Nations at Geneva,' he wrote in *The Salvaging of Civilisation* (1921) 'this little corner of Balfourean jobs and gentility, no man would dream of fighting. . . .' It was just 'a pedantic bit of stage scenery.'

But if not the League of Nations, what then ? Was there any likelihood of an equivalent body, with different inspirations which might, at some stretch of the imagination, resemble his Utopian Samurai ? Or if these fools and dunderheads did not know their own business, could he, by some sleight of diplomatic hand, teach it them, setting out on a great journey round the world carrying his message to one leader after another, even though that message was full of sounding phrases for which he still had no practical equivalent ? If only the gods had granted H. G. Wells a little more bottom and a little less bounce. Impetuous, fiery, bursting into magnificent rages because the world would not listen, he could convey the spirit of his message in a way which caught your breath because it was full of warmth and beauty and nobility, but ask for the machinery to translate it into action. . . . Machinery ? Anyone could make machinery ! Alas and alack, anyone could not.

When in fact, he went to Russia in September of 1920 it was in response to an invitation from Mr. Kamenev, head of the Russian Trade Delegation in London, and not because he had any hope of persuading Lenin to his own way of thinking. He was excited, eager to see the results of this gigantic upheaval in human affairs, which, whatever other effect it might have, had deeply moved imaginative men and women throughout the world like all vast swarming re-arrangements of the human pattern.

He found Lenin a little man like himself, who when he sat at his great desk in the Kremlin, scarcely touched the ground with his feet. He had a 'pleasant, quick-changing, brownish face, with a lively smile and a habit (due to perhaps some defect in focussing) of screwing up one eye as he pauses in his talk; he is not very like the photographs you see of him because he is one of those people whose change of expression is more important than their features; he gesticulated a little with his hands over the heaped papers as he talked.' (2) Lenin wanted to know what had become of the social revolution in England, what prevented the inevitable overthrow of Capitalism at this stage, why Wells did not work for it ? And automatically Wells required some information about the shape revolutionary Russia was now assuming. He had come through desolated towns where the whole machinery of exchange and living had broken down because they were the negation of Communism, towns where the nature of shopping and marketing determined the character of the city, now irrevocably changed. Did it mean that 'nine-tenths of the buildings in an ordinary town,' would become 'directly or indirectly, unmeaning or useless ?' Did it mean pulling down the adornments of another age, scrapping whole towns and rebuilding them ? Lenin quite cheerfully agreed. Many towns must fall into decay. Russia had to be rebuilt in endless ways, and for the moment they were purely material, very unspiritual ways. There was a sense, at this point in the conversation, of two men having found in each other someone after their own sweeping persuasions, someone able to brush whole towns into oblivion with Olympian detachment. The individual was unimportant; humanity was one. They sat and summoned new cities out of the air while the heritage of another age perished, they moved multitudes as on a chessboard. But when Lenin came to the fairyland of electrification which would revitalize the railways and set a giant pulse stirring in the remotest areas of the steppes, Wells began to wonder whether the dark crystal of Russia held any such future . . . until the little man with the hand going frequently across the defective eye, talked and talked with such deep conviction it almost 'persuaded me to share his vision.'

But whether the end they had in view was the same or not, the approach of these two men differed as the fountain and the spring. Wells had felt himself a Marxist in his teens but had grown out of it. Long before he ever heard of Marx, the boy, humiliated by dreary unending toil in a mean little shop which left him no energy to think of improving himself, would cheerfully have fired the shop and murdered his employers, and it seemed to him then that the privileged and the underprivileged, one class differing widely from another, must remain implacable enemies. He had, with the worker, a common indignation against his lot. (*The Quintessence of Bolshevism.*) But now, in the Kremlin, when the first crusader of the Marxist creed tapped a book by Chiozza Money, *The Triumph of Nationalization*, and said, 'But you see directly you begin to have a good working collectivist organization of any public interest, the Capitalists smash it up again,' Wells nodded thoughtfully and saw it differently. Later he wrote, 'I believe that through a vast sustained educational campaign the existing capitalist system can be *civilized* into a Collectivist world system; Lenin on the other hand tied himself years ago to the Marxist dogmas of the inevitable class war, the downfall of Capitalist order as a prelude to reconstruction, the proletarian dictatorship and so forth. . . .' (*Russia in the Shadow—The Dreamer in the Kremlin*). For the moment he and Lenin talked on. They overrode the diplomatic niceties of a Mr. Rothstein who was present at the interview. They talked freely—to Mr. Rothstein's manifest alarm—of the 'Republican Imperialism that comes to us from America,' they blackguarded and bickered.

Outside in the streets of Moscow and St. Petersburg the promised Russian land seemed far away. The great bazaar-markets of St. Petersburg were closed, the shops dead, with peeling paint, cracked windows and a few fly-blown relics of decaying stock; the roads full of pot-holes eaten out by the frost, and people hurrying in ill-clad streams to and fro, eternally carrying bundles as though 'in readiness for flight.' (3) The population of St. Petersburg had fallen from 1,200,000 to 750,000. Many city dwellers had tried to go back to the land. 'An egg or an apple cost 300 roubles.' Parts of the social apparatus still functioned with an absent automatism, and the brooding sense of destiny, characteristic of the Slav, now seemed to fill the sky.

But Lenin impressed Wells and although he later said of Wells, 'What a bourgeois, what a philistine,' and Wells eventually came away with his mild resistance to Marxism grown into active hostility, he carried with him a sense of noble ferment from which anything might eventually grow. Communism, he felt, could become tremendously creative under Lenin. But he continued to find Marx a Bore. Vast divisions of people into proletariat and bourgeoisie remained 'phantom unrealities' for him, and *Das Kapital* 'a monument of pretentious pedantry,' yet he seems to have forgotten for the moment his own message in the excitement of trying to discover Russia's.

It was only for the moment. Seizing his high eminence to attack or talk to the kings, presidents and dictators who had refused to assimilate his message, was one part of his continuous search to find an answer to the questions—why was it impossible to realize his dream of a scientifically ordered world, why was it that the

Open Conspiracy had not carried the old order away, and why, where it had begun in Russia, had it gone so sadly awry ? Was it lack of knowledge in the ordinary individual, lack of knowing what the world was all about ? If people understood history better would they give him the attention they now squandered on films, race tracks and twopenny fun fairs ? Did the secret of a creative community lie in world education ? His work with the League of Nations had shown him the confusions implicit in history. Nationalist teaching presented not one but a dozen different interpretations of precisely the same episodes with sufficient subtlety to give each at least the semblance of half-truths. 'There can be no common peace and prosperity,' he had written before he went to Russia 'without common historical ideas. Without such ideas to hold them together in harmonious co-operation, with nothing but narrow selfish and conflicting nationalist traditions, races and peoples are bound to drift towards conflict and destruction.' (4) Already in several novels he had brought men together as a species, overruling national divisions, seeing them in the light of a common destiny. The whole conception of One World must be the outcome of one people and one history. Someone, somewhere, must begin to collate, codify and write a World History, which would counteract the insidious influence of national distortions, and make the ordinary person aware of his place in the larger pattern, make him conscious of his destiny as a World Citizen. It would produce a 'mental synthesis and material co-operation from the completely isolated and individual life and death of the primordial animal to the continuing mental life and social organization, now growing to planetary dimensions, of the human species.' (5)

His pamphlet *History is One* was widely read in 1919. He suggested that the Research Committee of the League of Nations Union should organize the writing of an international history. The idea had long simmered at the back of his mind. Early in 1919 it beat to the surface with growing insistence until it blotted out everything else and he had no choice but to plunge in and investigate its possibilities. Who was equipped to do the job ? Who could write it ? Where would the material come from ? How should it be published ? How given the widest publicity ? Put to the test, the scholarly historians shied away from any such crude vigorous task, inevitably entailing some compromise with their delicate instruments of interpretation and definition. One professional historian after another shook his head and smiled at the fatuous optimism of this untrained romanticist who thought he could break all the rules with such impunity. He was asking for the historical moon. He was trying to marry scholarship to a journalistic courtesan. He should be prepared to look at it their way, to recognize a long heart-breaking period of research followed by ten years of writing, collating and checking, with a dozen eminent historians each bound by his own period, each producing a meticulous essay, polished, non-committal and without any common thread, satisfying to the microscopic scruples of the scholarly mind but quite unreadable to the average person. Wells was not prepared. In the end he saw that there was nothing else for it. He saw that if he did not do it himself nobody would.

He brought an almost frantic energy to his approach: as though he knew just how intimidating the task would be and was vaguely afraid that he might not pull it off. It was indeed immense. Like the encyclopædists of old he wanted no less than to grasp the entire panorama of human life from the first mists of our beginnings, to unravel and re-present the story in one monumental book. It took him a little over a year and involved him in a thousand mental and material agonies. A great sweep of reading had to be undertaken, and there were so many gaps in the books available that he constantly turned to one specialist after another for personal talks and interviews, until there were times when it seemed it would never be done. Baffled by the picture of Central Asia and China he wrote to Sir Denison Ross: 'I wish I could tap your knowledge in the matter by half an hour's talk. Could I see you ? If so, I should be very glad.' It was typical of scores of such appeals for help. Chapters were written and rewritten, submitted to accepted authorities, revised from their comments and passed on to final adjudicators.

As the story unfolded he came to see it as a story of increasing interdependence between one part of the world and another, with communications diminishing distance until no one group of people was without contact with another. 'It became an essay on the growth of association since the dawn of animal communities.' The sense of the importance of his subject grew with each chapter. This was the way to present history to the citizen of the modern state, and paradoxically, the very shortcomings from which he suffered gave him special skills for the task. The average historian specialized in a period, steeped himself in one historical age and was hypersensitive to the slightest breath of distortion, apparent or real. He could not move freely with so many subtle steps to take. Wells came to it with a glancing knowledge of archaeology, biology, science and history, with a mind brilliantly equipped to grasp outlines, and without any of the specialist's inhibitions, inevitably he had a much more sweeping sense of the total picture. He could also, most sweetly, most persuasively and lucidly, write.

He did not expect to make money from the History. Indeed he had a very serious talk with Jane about money before he began work on it. She was still, for all the emotional storm and stress, his chief consultant in these matters. Their securities had suffered somewhat in the war, the original £20,000 had fallen to £10,000, and but for the money made by *Mr. Britling Sees It Through*, the History might never have been written. Jane eventually agreed that he could give a year's work to a History Notebook even at the risk of losing his novel-reading public as well as money. His fiction did in fact diminish and change after the History, but never quite died. There was for Jane not only an element of financial and professional risk in the undertaking; it meant a great deal of hard work. She became deeply involved, typing, revising, collating, working sometimes far into the night, quite unaware of the tragedy which waited a few years away. She became the clearing house for a mass of material, books and people all involved in the History. It went on month after month, with mounting intensity. Sometimes it drove Wells close to brain fever, and there were days when a chapter refused to go and it was better not to go near him.

But at last it was done. At last the manuscript went to the printers. It was a brilliant feat if it suffered from certain flaws. It was hastily written, it did not convey half the human story, and the sheer momentum of the book, carrying the reader over many a dangerous gap, made it impossible to be precise about detail. Yet people clamoured in 1920 for a book which unceremoniously rejected all the mumbo-jumbo of school teaching, ignored the pedantry of the professors, insisted that biology must be brought into history, and presented the story of millions of tribes cohering into sixty or so nations over a few thousand years, and now beginning to fuse into a single Olympian unit. It began with the first appearance of life on this planet 1,600,000,000 years ago and reached into the first meetings of the League of Nations in 1920.

'Your cheek,' James had written, 'is the very essence of your genius.' How right he was. Never had anyone so challenged the historians at their own game and made away with it. It was a brilliant condensation and popularization of a mountain of learning. Anthony West has said that when Wells was in the mood of the journalist with a taste for sociology—one of half a dozen selves which he could assume with an almost savage if short-lived dislike of any other incarnation—he talked of the Outline as 'a Hussar-ride round the unprotected rear of the academic world. I gave those stuffy dons oh ! a tremendous shaking-up.' One of the 'stuffy dons' retaliated by saying that it was obvious Mr. Wells had written more history than he had read. And later Hilaire Belloc was driven to retaliate in *The Catholic Universe* with a series of wonderfully ingenious articles which the editor refused to let Wells answer in the same periodical.

Wells turned on him in fury. 'My dear sir, I am sorry to receive your letter of May 19th,' he wrote. 'May I point out to you that Mr. Belloc has been attacking my reputation as a thinker, a writer, an impartial historian and an educated person, four and twenty fortnights in the Universe. He has mis-quoted; he has mis-stated. Will your Catholic public tolerate no reply ?'

Amazingly it would not. Wells promptly burst into another book, *Mr. Belloc Objects* (1926), which drove Belloc back with his own weapons, accused him of insolence and impudence, reduced him to obscurantism, if not blind ignorance, said that he, Belloc, not Wells, imagined his authorities, and distorted—even to the point of sometimes slipping in quotation marks where they did not belong. It was another dazzling explosion.

As a sheer feat of industry alone, the History astonished the most fluent writers of the day, but it was the reception it received which bewildered and buoyed Wells up to consider changing the very roots of his writing. More than two million people bought the book in one edition or another, and what he expected to be something of a philanthropic gesture due to his reading public after years of self-indulgence, made him a rich man on quite a new scale. Before its impetus was quite exhausted it was said to have brought him £60,000.

Enormously excited, he began to explore fresh reaches of the Outline technique—'My self-conceit has always had great recuperative power; it revived bravely now.' (6) If people were so hungry for this vivid simplification of past events, they might be persuaded to follow the fascinating story of biological growth, and perhaps, who knew, they might even squander an hour or two on the less exasperating aspects of economics and the tides of political power. His brain began to teem with the possibilities of a common way of knowledge, a restatement of the broad realities of life and living within a single, cohesive system which anyone could grasp. That was what the world needed. For a new world order there must be first a new world education, with 'a common basis of general ideas.'

Swept along by the success of the History, bubbling with enthusiasm for the new universal education, he was overtaken with the audacious idea that he might single-handed tackle the whole human race, set moving a gigantic one-man system of knowledge capable of establishing the common identity of humanity once and for all. 'God Wells' had momentarily taken charge. It was one of his fire-breathing moments when his torrential vitality boiled over in an irresistible convulsion—like Beethoven shaking his fist at the thunder—and he felt capable of challenging elemental forces themselves, forces as implacable and all-pervading as ignorance. He would take ignorance by the throat. He would wring sense into the dumb world. He would make the universe echo with the voice of reason. But the grandiosity of his vision and the imaginative vigour he brought to it did not deceive him into believing that the *Outline of History* was anything more than a makeshift improvization, shortly to be superseded, and when the omnipotent mood subsided and he saw himself once again in the likeness of a writer struggling against overwhelming odds to make a few simple truths clear, he fell back on the more prosaic conviction that endless argument about the need for a new universal education was far less effective than showing, in however rough and ready a form, what could be done.

Great new books continued to take shape in his mind. There was to be one on biology which would need highly specialized collaborators, great patience, and an artist with rare vision; another on economics and sociology; a third on science. . . . Invited to lecture in the United States he determined to make the lectures the skeleton of one such bible and chose the social, economic and political state of the world, preparing a series of lectures which would shake the complacency of the American continent and clarify his own ideas. They were intended to present American audiences with 'a vision of a European collapse, inevitable if some radical adjustment were not affected, and to urge the idea of working directly for the World State as altogether more hopeful than any project to reform the League of Nations. . . . From this he would pass to the importance of education in the creation of a World State mentality and will.' (7)

But the lectures were never delivered. A month before he should have sailed a cold turned to congestion of the lungs, the trip was postponed and the lectures put aside. Later they appeared in book form—*The Salvaging of Civilization*. Lectures never make very satisfactory reading if they are good lectures, and these were. He went to Italy to convalesce and wrote to Arnold Bennett, 'I am en route for Rome and so far I've done very well—a beautiful crossing and Paris like summer. . . . I'm really going to do nothing unpleasant or laborious for two good months or more. Then I will come back and be a credit to you.' Credit he was but the great four-in-hand books were, for one reason and another delayed. Several years were to pass before he began work on *The Science of Life* and *The Work, Wealth and Happiness of Mankind*.

*   *   *

The battle between the artist and scientist in Wells never entirely died, but he grew so skilled at reconciliation in the second half of his life that once the initial ferment was over he plunged utterly into whatever he was doing, scorned and brushed off the novelist when the World History required a journalist, disowned the scientist when his comedies clamoured for an artist, not only lived nine lives but could become, with steadily diminishing struggle, nine separate people. It was an astounding metamorphosis. It was as if first one, then another, then a third shadow detached itself from the rubicund little man and stalked away with growing solidity to become separate entities, most foully abusing the parent body, returning only with the greatest reluctance to be subdued by the gathering violence of fresh embodiments.

The politician amongst them renewed his cries in 1922. There followed a period noisy with political interest. In the course of various excursions into the Labour Party, Wells had already delivered himself of utterances which might have held some semblance of truth in their day and age but were made absurd by the event.

'The Labour Party is not a party co-extensive with the Liberal and
Conservative parties. These latter fight over practically the whole
country; the former never has and *never will*. . . . Whatever practical legislative work it wants to get done, therefore, must be
done, can only be done, through an understanding with one or
other of the two national parties.' (8) Of course, within the strict
meaning of the word, Wells was never a politician.

But carrying Pater's dictum, that there are times when wisdom
and a change of mind become synonymous, almost to acrobatic
extremes, Wells proceeded to stand on his head before his political
career was out. He applied for membership of the Party which he
had once said had no existence in its own right, and from political
fatuity it suddenly blossomed for him into the last political hope
for Britain. In May 1922, he became Labour candidate for the Lord
Rectorship of Glasgow University and even though he stood no
chance of winning—he wanted to get a strong footing in the
Party best calculated to spread his ideas—he thought for a time of
abandoning his fiction to devote his pen to Labour interests, but
he lost the Lord Rectorship to Lord Birkenhead and failed in two
more attempts on London University. And then, when it seemed
that his sojourn in the political market place was up, with that
special brand of tact which he sometimes exercised so imperiously,
he barely waited for his own defeat to be known before he plunged
in to criticize all over again the Party he had so lately championed,
whirling out a rainbow of words which might have dazzled the
country into belated admiration for the legislator it had lost. He
went on criticizing, he went on demanding radical changes and
presently exchanged some very cross letters with Arthur Hender-
son because the Party refused to endorse birth control (fearing the
Catholic vote) but he never believed that any existing party could
do better. Yet he lost faith in something he called the Labour
Party's creative will. At any rate, when he began preaching the
gospel of the Open Conspiracy it appeared that the Labour Party
would play no very great part.

There was a letter to Sir Richard Gregory which summed up
his attitude to politics and the Labour Party better than all the
speeches and quarrels, the incursions into this organization or
that. . . . 'Science *will endure and rule,* but . . . Labour with
a capital L, as the name of a class of human beings organised for
distinctive class ends, *will pass away.* I am at one with Soddy in

believing that if the spirit of science is carried right through human affairs, it means a complete organization of human society for all common ends, educational and economic, and a common general administration of the whole world and all its resources. In an organized world there will be no organized labour, as such, because everyone will play his or her part in the common task and no one will toil, and there will be no capitalists, because capital, the accumulated resources of mankind, will be administered for the common good. Or if you like to put it in another way, Humanity will be one labour organization and the only capitalist in the world. In such a state questions of wages and dividends disappear. They will give place to the question of the "fair share." Of everyone we shall ask what is the fair share of effort he or she shall contribute to the commonweal and what is the fair share of consumable goods he shall take from the commonweal. The amount of the fair share in each case depends entirely upon the applied science in the world. The more we know, the more developed our science, and in science I include not merely physical and biological science but psychological and educational science, the greater the common product we shall share and the less the exertion needed to produce it. I think the future welfare of mankind depends not at all upon whether labour beats the private capitalist or whether private capitalists get what they think is the better of labour, but upon the supersession of private ownership in economic affairs and of the methods of bargaining and of employment and unemployment, by the infinitely less clumsy ways of co-operation that the social, educational, and physical sciences, as they develop, will render not merely possible but imperative.'

Wells' political pilgrimage is a long story of one instrument after another tried and found wanting because it fell short of his Olympian vision. When the Fabian Society failed him he turned to the Co-efficients, and when they failed, to the League of Nations, and thence on to the Labour Party, only to let out a great cry of baffled rage and despair to a new friend; until *The Open Conspiracy* took possession of him and he at last came to believe that 'a confluent system of trust-owned business organisms and of universities and re-organised military and naval services may presently discover an essential unity of purpose, presently begin thinking a literature and behaving like a State.'

*   *   *

The ageing Wells

H. G. Wells in the last year of his life

1923-4 renewed the symptoms of another self, a restless irritable self, richly endowed with the fugitive impulse, an impulse he had come to see as not uncommon in the life of any intellectual. He suddenly felt 'I must get away from all this and think and then begin again. These daily routines are wrapping me about, embedding me in a mass of trite and habitual responses. . . . I must have the refreshment of new sights, sounds, colours or I shall die away.' (9)

A touch of near hysteria crept in. His wife had met the mood before. It sprang from the same roots which had driven him to escape the draper's shop all those years ago, sent him careering off into the writing wilderness. It expressed itself in many other ways. The symptoms were manifold. Publicly he became irascible and impatient, privately he did hopelessly irrational things. They were small, trivial things which meant very little in their everyday context, but to people who knew what mood was on him . . . His secretary arrived one morning to find him crawling along the floor of his living room followed by several yards of flex, trying to plug in an electric kettle. He had reached a state approaching apoplexy. 'Can I do anything,' the secretary said. 'Yes—get the electrician— No ! Never mind ! I'll write to them. . . . Do they imagine,' he fumed, 'that every time I want a cup of tea I am going to crawl under the sofa trailing half a mile of flex, just to plug in their bloody kettle.' (10) The electric point may have been fitted long before the sofa but that did not interest him. He was restless, craving change from these suffocating surroundings and he must attack something, somebody, even if an innocent electrician and an inanimate kettle became involved.

So there and then, with two secretaries idle and a typewriting agency waiting for his work around the corner, he sat down and wrote a long complaining letter on the imbecility of electricians who should know by instinct where Mr. Wells would be likely to put his sofa. The secretary waited patiently. She was used to these 'difficult days.' He was uneasy, on edge, and had to make himself more so. Distressed enough, he would be forced to take action, forced to break away from the daily routines. And if he came out of the mood suddenly, turned to Miss Hutchinson, the secretary, and said 'Gertrude, it's a lovely day—you ought to be in the park picking flowers—off with you !' the burst of sunshine did not last very long. Back he went to the sofa, lay at full length, and fell to brooding on his next book, until he flung to his feet in a fresh temper and burst out all over again: 'I must get away. I must forget all this—find new sights, sounds, colours. . . .'

In the end, with the connivance of the always understanding Jane, barely four years after his trip to Italy another escape was arranged. Perhaps Jane was more deeply involved that that implies. His relations with her had reached a curious stage. Sometimes it was dull being alone with her, and she was tired of always having to keep him in good conceit. Put another way he constantly needed an audience of people with ideas of their own, people who were not just mirrors. Yet he stuck to his unimpeachable belief of 'never letting the wife down,' and if she had suggested leaving him, he would certainly have dissuaded her. When they were ill together, at considerable risk to himself, he got up, went to her room and implored her, on his knees, to stay alive. The contradictions had multiplied. She was still a vital part of his life.

Now, with Jane's help, he escaped from it all again, took plane to Geneva one day, saw the League of Nations in assembly, and was about to wander off into the wilds in search of spiritual refreshment after the fashion of his Samurai, when he changed his plans, went to Grasse and began to absorb the assuaging scents and sounds of the South of France. Possibly among these gentle hills he could find the refreshment he sought. Possibly sheer sunshine would dissolve this deep-rooted restlessness. Soon he settled to a dual life. Letters flowed through the house at Little Easton in Essex to Lou Bastidon near Grasse, but the mass of correspondence and business was dealt with by Jane and his secretary, leaving him free to distil his thoughts and ideas, to grow gradually at peace with himself until, at length, he would begin to write once more. Some beautifully abusive letters continued to pour out from Lou Bastidon. One postcard to Frank Horrabin began 'What is this bloody Marxist nonsense you talk: there is no proletariat, my dear Horry. . . .' Others to importunate editor-friends—'Stop pestering me. Leave a man alone. I have no desire to decrease your circulation. . . .' And to Gertrude Hutchinson, 'It's not necessary to put South of France on your letters—everybody knows that Grasse is in the South of France,' to be followed not very long afterwards with 'Do not put Grasse A.M. Everybody in France knows that Grasse is in the Alpes Maritimes.' There were vivid telegrams, there were explosive cables to

America, but the fugitive impulse slowly died, the creative surge
took charge once more, and soon he was at work again on a major
novel, the letters became briefer, the postcards less frequent.

It was *William Clissold* which, intermittently, occupied two
winters in that beautiful world of olive terraces and orange trees,
where he sat in the sun, wandered the terraces, and gradually felt
his way towards a fresh realization of the New Republic and of
himself. Those vast intimations of a different brand of civilization
just around the corner had gripped him again, and this time the
effervescent artist went racing away to make another novel about it.

Wells as a thinker is a dubious quantity. In the sense that
Newton was a thinker he does not qualify. In his terms he broke
no new ground. His writings were highly subjective when he
would have liked them to be objective, and 'I have never encountered even a stain on a wall or a glowing cavity in a fire upon
which my mind could not impose a design,' reveals him as an
artist, not a thinker; an artist looking for form in society, which is
odd because he did not gravely care for it in his work. The idea-
novelist had played a big part in the life of the world-maker, and
now culminated in this extraordinary rag-bag of fiction, argument,
and pure Wellsian soliloquy, *The World of William Clissold*. It
marked another crisis in his writing life. He had ventured out
upon those perilous seas where great fiction is born and had all but
surrendered to their mysterious tides. There had been moments of
total intoxication when their beauty and excitement overwhelmed
him, until with *The New Machiavelli* retreat became plain. Now, for
the first time, retreat had become a rout. It was a moving moment.
Great comic characters, beautiful women, many fine spirits had
been his for the asking in those enchanted waters, and given his
undivided attention, who knows what creatures might have been
born beyond the horizons he so far knew. But no. The novelist
had laid about him magnificently and conjured to life some nigh
immortal souls, and his enormous creative gusto was by no means
spent, but great new forces dragged at his attention, forces which
were to take him out again into that objective world from which
for the moment he sought shelter in the sacred places of personality. The universe of Wells began gaseously, full of galaxies and
stars and interstellar space; then it condensed to Mr. Kipps and
Mr. Polly and life was warm for an æon or two. Now, with
William Clissold, everything was about to disintegrate again and

huge movements were ready to remake whole new worlds, and heaven alone knew what ideas would enliven them. The importance of the individual was to wane once again. 'That cherished personal life which men and women struggled to round off and make noble and perfect, disappears from the scheme of things.' The individual turns out after all to be a 'biological device which has served its purpose in evolution and will decline.'

* * *

The World of William Clissold (1926) was far removed from *A Modern Utopia*, but it belonged in direct line of ascent to Wells' World State, and cleared the way for *The Open Conspiracy*. What a figure Clissold was. Another incarnation of Wells, endowed this time with wealth, an industrialist granted the powers of the visionary, a man bewildered by the blindness and deliberate stupidity of humanity, he retreated to the warm backwaters of the South of France and spun a great rambling web of words, inconsistent, discursive, but groping persistently towards the formula which would make palpable his dream world, becoming in the process a mouthpiece for Wells' own melancholy, a way of getting back into shape with himself.

It wasn't in any sense a profound book. It permitted cascades of argument to overwhelm character, it had moments of beautiful nostalgia, it broke all the classic rules of novel writing and involved the reader in long, tedious debates, but it remained a huge, ramshackle feat in the genre of fiction with a purpose, fiction which sought desperately to convey the preliminary conditions of the new society. Perhaps there was a pathetic belief that this laying on of the hands of literature would bring the benediction which escaped the fumbling politicians and the social scientists. Perhaps it was hopeless considered as a straight novel. Perhaps it should have stopped half-way through and permitted most of its characters to die of inanition; but as part of Wells' developing New World Scheme it had a vital place.

'I believe that Dickson and I are not abnormal types. . . . I believe that we industrials and the financiers are beginning to educate ourselves and broaden our outlook as our enterprises grow and interweave. I believe that if we can sufficiently develop the consciousness of contemporary business and associate with it the critical co-operation and the co-operative criticism of scientific and every other sort of able man, we can weave a world system of monetary and economic activities, while the politicians, the diplomatists, and the soldiers are still too busy with their ancient and habitual antics to realise what we are doing. . . . We can build up the monetary and economic world republic in full daylight under the noses of those who represent the old system. For the most part I believe that to understand us will be to be with us, and that we shall sacrifice no advantage and incur no risk of failure in talking out and carrying out our projects and methods quite plainly. That is what I mean by an Open Conspiracy. . . . It is not a project to overthrow existing governments by insurrectionary attacks but to supersede them by disregard. . . .' (11)

Later Wells saw his own biggest mistake. In his usual romantic way he envisaged a handful of industrialists overwhelming the far more powerful financiers. Yet the web of finance held the average industrialist like a fly, and until the banks and the systems of credit were controlled by the State, the world of William Clissold was a remote, rather clumsy fairyland. Nor was Wells entirely fair to the average worker, in *William Clissold*. 'In my reaction against the mass democracy that had produced MacDonald, Snowden, Thomas, Clynes. . . . I underrated the steadily increasing intelligence of the more specialised workers and of the ambitious younger working man. To them at any rate Clissold is an impersonation to apologise for.' (12)

But Clissold led into *The Open Conspiracy* and here, for a time, it was almost as if Wells' feet came within reach of the ground, only to recoil in artistic horror because the ground was liable to prove solid and firm. With *The Open Conspiracy* he wanted a network of groups drawn from all classes and kinds—each devoted to special ends, but all discovering a common purpose—to grow and multiply and spread like Christianity across the world. They would it seems arise spontaneously, or if not spontaneously, largely of their own accord. This was the 'confluent system of trust-owned business organisms and of universities and re-organised military and naval services. . . . It will appear first I believe, as a conscious organisation of intelligent and quite possibly in some cases wealthy men, as a movement having distinct social and political aims, confessedly ignoring most of the existing apparatus of political control.' (13)

A sane and inspiring enough opening. Alas, the message quickly faltered and admitted some confusion of thought. The precise nature of the groups remained indeterminate, a changing mosaic of many-coloured mysteries. They would by some remarkable inversion, repudiate military service without denying 'the need of military action on behalf of the world commonweal for the suppression of nationalist brigandage,' and without preventing 'the military training of Open Conspirators. . . .' Continuing to spread, the groups would absorb one country after another until they had become a force as comprehensive and effective as Socialism or Communism, which they would, very largely, supplant. It would be stronger than they were, having as it were, a streak of religious revelation, and this 'large, loose assimilatory mass of movements, groups and societies' would be 'definitely and obviously attempting to swallow up the entire population of the world' to become 'the new human community.'

It would have seven broad objectives:

'(1) The complete assertion, practical as well as theoretical, of the provisional nature of existing governments and of our acquiescence in them;

'(2) The resolve to minimize by all available means the conflicts of these governments, their militant use of individuals and property, and their interferences with the establishment of a world economic system;

'(3) The determination to replace private, local or national ownership of at least credit, transport, and staple production by a responsible world directorate serving the common ends of the race;

'(4) The practical recognition of the necessity for world biological controls, for example, of population and disease;

'(5) The support of a minimum standard of individual freedom and welfare in the world;

'(6) The supreme duty of subordinating the personal career to the creation of a world directorate capable of these tasks and to the general advancement of human knowledge, capacity, and power; and

'(7) The admission therewith that our immortality is conditional and lies in the race and not in our individual selves.' (14)

The phantoms were very nearly palpable in *The Open Conspiracy*. The glowing cavities of the Wellsian mind echoed to the sound of real hammering, and then, just when the hiss of driving power, the gleam of actual machinery disturbed the air, the very sight and sound seemed to frighten him. He blandly announced that collective action had better for a time—perhaps a long time—be undertaken not through the merging of groups, but through the formation of *ad hoc* associations. 'With the dreadful examples of Christianity and Communism before us, we must insist that the idea of the Open Conspiracy ever becoming a single organization must be dismissed from the mind. It is a movement, yes, a system of purposes, but its end is a free and living if unified, world.'

The clouds rolled in again. It was not, after all, to become a single instrument of action instinct with one underlying purpose. It was to proceed on the curious assumption that the groups would cohere *only when* they had overwhelmed the world. Useless to reason with him, useless to point out that without a party *machine*, a unified organization, centrally inspired and relying on basic identity of action, no group has ever come within a mile of power in this cruelly power-conscious world; useless to say this is beautiful, this is the ideal way to do it, but it won't work. Whoever did so, simply asked for verbal annihilation, for one of those splenetic outbursts which erupted with no regard for reason.

It was a pity. *The Open Conspiracy* began inspiringly. There was a tremendously exciting sense of something *about to happen*, but very soon one was left with the sound of a beautiful sea of words and nothing more. One might have come away from an unsuccessful séance. A message, yes, and voices and strangely moving sensations which carried their own exaltation; but the spirits, if they existed, remained disembodied.

It wasn't quite the end. There was yet to be *The Shape of Things to Come* weighted with more convincing detail, aware of the need for a 'revolutionary' party, admitting the civilized use of force and brilliantly restating the conditions of a Rational World Order where government itself would eventually become quite superfluous. There were yet to be two more sketches of the World State, and a mass of sporadic literature, some of it stirring enough, some lighting up once dark tracts of barren confusion. And, in between, the gloomy admission in *A Forecast of World Affairs* that 'the present system of competing and warring sovereign states may and probably will continue for many generations to come.' But, for the moment, the visions were of the early morning mists and threatened to evaporate. They grew darkly beautiful in the dawn and died under the accomplished day. They were still not—for all his efforts to give them breath, movement, life—practical plans or realities when *The Open Conspiracy* was written. In one sense they were mystical aspirations. In another the ideals of an inspired mechanic. If he was brilliantly before his time in envisaging World Government his visions of its emergence remained impalpable.

Chapter Fifteen

DEATH OF JANE

ON the evidence of the *Autobiography*, there came a time in what were his seasonal retirements to the South of France when a number of small inconveniences about Lou Bastidon began to irritate him. He wanted a better bath, he needed electric light, the garden seemed ill-organized, and the Riviera, aware at last of his presence in the hills began to put out feelers, to send invitations. And then in a moment of sweeping rashness he determined to overcome all this by building his own home amongst the rocks, the vines, jasmine and streams, with a beautiful garden and all the conveniences Lou Bastidon lacked. Lou Pidou it was called when it was half finished. Lou Bastidon, offered to Dorothy Richardson and her husband, was gratefully declined.

But Wells did not set down in the *Autobiography* the story of the woman who enlivened his life in the South of France, the torrential person who delighted and sometimes dismayed him.

They were, it seems, lovers, devouring every second of their devotion, and Lou Pidou, when built, carried the words 'Two Lovers Built This House' inscribed over the big fireplace.

Arnold Bennett went to see them and recorded in his *Journal* for Tuesday, February 22nd, 1927: 'The rendezvous with H. G. was for noon in the Cours at Grasse. We arrived precisely at twelve and he was there signalling, in a big doggy overcoat with the collar turned up in the rain. Plenty of mud. . . . Drive of about ten minutes . . . thoroughly bad little road. . . . We went over to see the new house in process of construction. H. G. designed it himself and got an architect to "re-draw the plans." What he would call a jolly little house. But it wouldn't suit me. Rooms too small and windows too large and no tradition behind the design. . . .' (1)

Bennett could not bear the inscription over the fireplace. It was an inscription said to have saved Wells and Miss Y. from trouble. As the story goes the house was nearing completion when a quarrel suddenly broke out between them. Like most lovers' quarrels it had an irrevocable finality. This was the last revelation. They would neither speak nor meet again. Wells summoned the builder, told him to sell Lou Pidou and went off in a dark eloquent rage. Some time later the builder sought him out again and quietly explained that it was all very well for Wells to say sell the place, but who in the world would buy a half-finished house with 'Built by Two Lovers' inscribed over the fireplace ? It sent Wells into a little delirium of laughter. He rushed off to find Miss Y. They were said to have rocked with merriment, hugged one another, rushed back to the builder and told him to get on with the job and not be so slow.

But they had to break. No two such incandescent souls as Wells and Miss Y. could remain together without consuming each other. They explored a bubbling spring of life full of sparkle and explosion, a spring so vital it would have overwhelmed any two ordinary human beings in half the time. In the end it overwhelmed them.

* * *

Something else occurred meanwhile. In the spring of 1927 Wells was invited to lecture at the Sorbonne and this time went to Paris with Jane. Fully aware that another woman now shared his life in France, Jane gave no sign to the outside world, and indeed, had some correspondence with Miss Y. which was to end on an extraordinary note.

The intellectual, social and political élite turned out to welcome Mr. and Mrs. Wells in Paris, and they seemed very happy together. With no apprehension of approaching tragedy, that curious elasticity of the Latin mind—which understood the subtleties of Wells' Samurai rather better than the Anglo-Saxon—delighted them, and Paris was as enchanting as ever in the spring. Wells delivered a lecture, *Democracy under Revision*, denouncing the current methods of electing the world's leaders as primitive and dangerous, scorning the vote-conscious adventurers attracted by the modern electoral system, asking why the high purposes of government should be given over to noisy, vain, conceited men because we went about electing them in the wrong way. He wanted democracy revised. He wanted the massive force of the base and dull subject to the check of the intelligent minority, and many more changes heretical in the eyes of the modern democrat, but constantly redeemed by the sense of criticism, fierce free criticism, blowing through every scientific pore.

Back in England came the diagnosis which gave Jane six months to live. She had cancer, cancer of the uterus. Its suddenness was terrible. Riddled with endless complaints—weak heart, damaged kidney, diabetes, complications of the liver—Wells sturdily survived them all, but there had seemed every reason to believe that Jane would outlive him, until, abruptly, this thunderbolt came out of the sky and darkened everything. There was something absurd in reversing their expectations of life; absurd and tragic. From the vast abstractions which had absorbed him these past few years, it brought Wells down to the reality of a fatal illness in his own family, an illness involving the one person amongst the very early ties whose affections he still, in his slightly inconsequent way, cherished. It changed him. He lost, for a time, the art of reading. 'I get restless if I read for long,' he told Arnold Bennett. 'Perhaps it's my eyes.' But Bennett knew it wasn't his eyes. When he heard the news, Shaw, astonishingly, said 'Nonsense, there's no such thing as cancer,' and drew a contradictory letter from Mrs. Shaw, full of sympathy for H. G.

His fits of depression deepened. He said to Dorothy Richardson at Easton Glebe one day when the house was packed with visitors as it always was during his visits—'By all means use my garden study. I work upstairs now in my bedroom. Nobody's interested.' The moods when he felt he had failed increased with the news of Jane's imminent death, but it seemed to heighten his perceptions. He became more aware of his immediate surroundings, of the house at Easton Glebe, the flowers his wife so much loved, the lesser lovelinesses which meant more to her than so many other things. And deep down in his heart, it seemed, he rebelled against the idiocy of anything so savage as cancer laying waste this frail form which might have gone down under far less barbarous assault. Somewhere blind nature howled and fastened intolerable pain on the least probable person. It seemed the ultimate cruelty. In the moment of knowing her close to death, the flashes of hostility, the sudden frictions, vanished, her limitations were of no account, and he was warm and close and very much aware of the trials they had survived together, of the affection which still ran deep beneath surface irritabilities.

Their marriage had lasted 33 years. Several crises had come and gone. Once they had nearly broken. Over the last few years they had, in their different ways, lived double lives. Indeed, towards the end, Jane sometimes retired into her own world, where H. G. became a visitor, and at week-ends the house was overrun with a whole medley of guests. But whatever changes had overtaken them, and however important Miss Y. had become to Wells, Jane remained the immensely tolerant, half unreal figure, sometimes away with her other self in the two rooms in Bloomsbury, writing,—rooms which she had taken, and which H. G. never visited—sometimes still the perfect hostess, receiving H. G.'s guests, amongst them women who gave him what it was not in her power to give. She was not blind to their gifts. She was blind to very little which involved her husband. But it was not Jane of the strong character and the careful mask who now ceased to tend her beautiful garden at Easton Glebe, gave up her walks and shopping, stopped bothering with the guests. Something of Catherine came back to die.

The illness developed rapidly. Intolerable to those who loved and watched her, it was made bearable by morphine, as she wasted to impossible frailty. Three entries in Arnold Bennett's *Journal* tell the story: (2)

6th June 1927—Monday.
'I drove off to visit Jane Wells. H. G. opened the door himself. Jane was lying on a broad sofa in the drawing room. She looked ill but not so ill as I had expected. Enlarged eyes. A sort of exhausted but determined wild cheerfulness in her. H. G. kept going in and out.

30th June.
'We left in the car for Easton Glebe at 10.47, 17 minutes late, and got there at 12.40. Jane Wells was in an easy chair and then walking about and she ate lunch with us. Said to be better. But when I asked H. G. privately . . . he said No . . .

27th July.
'Jane had just got downstairs. She is carried down, and wheeled everywhere; but she walks a few steps.'

Until near the end she continued to order new roses for her flower garden, talk to visitors and write letters. One went to Miss ?. I understand it implied what a comfort it was to leave H. G. in her hands. Sometimes when the sun shone, they carried Catherine into the garden which she had made. She was there on September 24, 1927, when a tree which threw the servants' bedrooms in shadow was cut down. As the first rush of the falling branches began she turned away refusing to see the final crash, and she did not go to the garden again. Frank, their son, had arranged to marry a fortnight later, and she hoped she might live to see it through.

Over the next few days she watched that mellow autumn of 1927 ripen through her window, talked occasionally with the family, waited anxiously for her son's wedding day and lived half in a ghost world of the past. But on Sunday, September 25, Arnold Bennett again recorded in his *Journal*: 'We drove down to Easton Glebe to see Jane Wells. Frank Wells was there with fiancée Peggy and Gip with wife Marjorie. Jane was too ill to come down or to see anyone. H. G. was visibly very much upset indeed.' (3) By late September her hold on life relaxed rapidly and she told her husband one evening when the night seemed slow in coming down, 'I am ready to sleep for ever.' The day before her son's wedding day she slipped into unconsciousness, a breathing organism with no cognizance of the outside world. She recovered momentarily to receive Frank when he arrived, but the fluttering consciousness faded again. Her hand was still in Wells' when she ceased to breathe.

They changed the time of the wedding to avoid any possible crowd. At nine o'clock they slipped down through a beautiful morning to the parish church at Dunmow. The ceremony went through smoothly and with music still on the air 'the two young people went off together into the world and I and my elder son and his wife returned to our home. . . . The white and purple Michaelmas daisies were glorious that October morning. It seemed incredible that I could not take in a great armful for her to see.' (4)

*   *   *

Catherine was cremated. As the coffin slid away the words came clearly: 'And may the memory of this gentle, starry spirit be a talisman to hold us to charity, faithfulness and generosity of living. . . .' Wells had helped to write the words, and now as he was about to turn away Bernard Shaw said to him, 'Take the boys and go behind; it's beautiful.' Wells wavered and Shaw added, 'I saw my mother burnt there. You'll be glad if you go.' (5)

They went, and in the furnace room, where the walls rippled with heat they watched the multitudinous flames swarm over the coffin, transforming the dead wood into a living incandescence. 'It was good to think,' Wells wrote, 'that she had gone as a spirit should go.' (6)

* * *

He sold Easton Glebe soon afterwards. It was too big and too empty. 'I couldn't stop there,' he told a friend. 'My life there ended when my wife died; I should soon be an old man there. And I don't want to be old. . . .'

Chapter Sixteen

ENCYCLOPÆDIST

THERE had been periods of disillusion. Sometimes like a spoilt child, he came out of them to write another book infused with something resembling retaliation. Attacked in the public prints by one of his friends, enemies or mistresses for real or imagined grievances, he had an astounding habit of launching another novel in reply. But by the age of sixty-four there were signs and portents to encourage the seeds of disillusion. At sixty-four confronted by what appeared to be impenetrable stupidity and too many deliberately deaf ears, he began at length to lose something of that abounding confidence continually reborn from the ashes of despair. At sixty-four his quarrels multiplied. He had written in 1911: 'When I think of the progress of physical and mechanical science, of medicine and sanitation, during the last century, when I measure the increase in general education and average efficiency, the power now available for human service, the merely physical increment, and compare it with anything that has ever been at man's disposal before, and when I think what a little, straggling, incidental, undisciplined and unco-ordinated minority of inventors, experimenters, educators, writers and organisers has achieved this development of human possibilities, achieved it in spite of the disregard and aimlessness of the huge majority, and the passionate resistance of the active dull, my imagination grows giddy with dazzling intimations of the human splendours the justly organised state may yet attain. I glimpse for a bewildering instant the heights that may be scaled, the splendid enterprises made possible.' (1) And in 1934 . . . 'That universal freedom and abundance dangles within reach of us and is not achieved, and we who are Citizens of the Future wander about this present scene like passengers on a ship overdue, in plain sight of a port which only some disorder in the chart-room prevents us from entering. Though most of the people in the world in key positions are more or less accessible to me, I lack the solvent power to bring them into unison. I can talk to them and even unsettle them, but I cannot compel their brains to see.' (2)

Between these two pronouncements lay a whole world of effort and continuous propaganda in books, articles, lectures and a huge one-man education system designed to do nothing less than prepare the human mind for a universal basis of knowledge and world government. Dejection did not easily overtake him. He was not depressed in these matters without deep and prolonged reason. One burst of optimism sprang from the ashes of the last, the books and ideas went on renewing themselves, he fought back every stupid, ill-phrased pettifogging objection and he did not mind how illiterate the peoples of the world turned out to be: they could still, he believed, learn.

It was this conviction which carried him into another pair of books, two more world encyclopædias which—the *World History* apart—would have satisfied any normal writer as a life's work. For a man who did not believe in continuity of personality there was a curious consistency in the forces which drove him. He had said some years before that he could not convincingly relate himself any longer to a 'certain ill and hungry young man of twenty who lived in 1886. . . . I have photographs of him as he then was; I have stuff that he wrote. And for the life of me I cannot identify my present self with him.' (3) It was not merely that he and other people grew up. They grew into different people. Perhaps everything was implicit from the moment of conception, perhaps the seed sealed one's fate irrevocably at the outset, but the mature man might be utterly alien to the adolescent, and no sign of what eventually flowered appeared in the gangling child. The individual had not one life but many, not one continuous personality but a series of rhythms capable of producing incredibly unlike people. It was the miracle of the phœnix. Whether or not some implicit thread persisted from the moment of birth, Wells could no longer understand the language of the young man of twenty struggling with what he considered unjust hardships. There was no continuity in his personality. But even though he disclaimed that hungry young man, the forces implicit in the struggling student-teacher which had become explicit at thirty, and persisted through middle age, still gripped him at sixty-two. From the time he was thirty he had been subject to certain heroic pressures. They were always there behind him. They drove him now into another huge undertaking. Like all his books, there was no one particular year when it was conceived and written. It was an integral part of the development of his personality and outlook. Each book expressed the different rhythms of his life and one grew into another. Strictly there were no divisions of time. And now, although he came with unbelievable energy, resource and skill after an interval of eight years, to the second of his educational bibles, it had grown in him for years. The *Science of Life* matured slowly. But the widening discovery of his own ignorance, his inability to come to 'proper decisions about a number of urgent matters, from race conflicts, birth control and my private life, to the public control of health and the conservation of natural resources' (4) at last brought it into the open. He realized that he 'did not know enough about the life in my body and its relations to the world of life and matter outside.'

So now he was vouchsafed a wonderful vision of the inner mysteries of living organisms wrested from nature by patient research, building a temple of scientific knowledge painfully, brick by brick, insensible as yet to ordinary touch and known to the scientist alone—a vision which must be brought within reach of the ordinary man if he was to know what the world, life and living were all about. With his son G. P. Wells and Julian Huxley he set out to codify and contain it all in another book *The Science of Life*. From this the average man could find out all he wanted to know about biological discovery, about his body, about the origins of life.

With hardly a pause for breath, he next saw another huge confused landscape to be traversed and charted, and quite undismayed by its complexities or exhausted by what he had already done, he threw himself into the *Work, Wealth and Happiness of Mankind,* a sort of political and economic bible several hundred pages long. This explained the everyday machinery of life, how goods were produced, distributed and sold, just where our money went. 'What,' Wells set himself to answer, 'are the nineteen hundred odd million human beings who are alive to-day doing, and how and why they are doing it ?' (5) A mighty question. Any sort of answer would have fallen short: he contrived an answer which fell less short than most.

These encyclopædias sold in their millions. They were translated into several languages. Men and women in France, Switzerland, Germany, America and the far wastes of Lapland read them. The fecund mind of Wells, comfortably accommodated in London or

France, was reaching out to unfold the human story, for the first time in rational terms, to millions of semi-literate people who had for generations accepted a view of their world which glamorized their own countrymen and damned everyone else. Dimly, at the backs of millions of minds, the rightness of his attitude became apparent. Somewhere the human race was kin, its hopes, sufferings and aspirations granted a common identity. Somewhere a thought sparked native to them all, and H. G. Wells could claim that he had touched it off.

But he did not now sit back, written out, exhausted, with two new books—huge, all-embracing remarkable books—once more accomplished, and wait to see whether his surge of words and prophetic vision would create that light he dreamed of, upon which the waiting darkness could not, this time, close. No. He had grown old and wary. He expected much but would be content with little. Little it was. For although these books reached an enormous public and left a million richly germinating seeds, they still produced no organized movement capable of making the message *real*. That became the trouble. The long and unceasing torrent of his vitality could stir the world from its lethargy, disturb the grossest dullard with a new awareness of his destiny, but it could not inspire the *instruments* of action, as some of his disciples were beginning to see. There were many amongst them touched with the disillusion which began to creep into the master's writing.

His message had quickened millions of minds, established whole new attitudes to life, but he did not so much originate any of this —it was implicit in science, the social fabric and the arts—as bring it out into the light of day, and clothe it in such language that half the world became aware. But after thirty years, the message had reverberated too long, people looked for its translation into something more convincing, and when no evidence of practical *results* came readily to hand, they turned again to their god expecting not reaffirmation and another burst of beautiful language, but *action*, no matter who took it.

*　　*　　*

Until 1933 he continued to winter in France. But Lou Pidou had developed half the troubles of his old home Lou Bastidon. Once identified as Wells' house people sought it out if only to stare at the place where the English genius worked. And the car which he had bought in the hope of moving freely about the country complicated instead of simplified his life, electric light was no longer the boon that he craved, and the voice of London grew steadily more insistent.

Soon everyday affairs found a way into his retreat again, the nerves of new emotional troubles nagged and the hours of sunlit quiet dwindled. Writing fell away, the old irritable symptoms came down on him and presently the restless driving urge to escape once more was raging unchecked. All over again he must find spiritual refreshment and change, all over again he wanted to get away, duck beneath the tyrannous hands of everyday duties and troubles and interferences. For several years he had found quiet for creative work in France. Now it was wrecked again. Now he wrote once more 'I want peace for work. . . . I am in a phase of fatigue and of that discouragement which is a concomitant of fatigue, the petty things of tomorrow skirmish in my wakeful brain, and I find it difficult to assemble my forces to confront this problem which paralyses the proper use of myself.' (6)

He did not any longer see his lot as isolated, or peculiar to himself; he saw it as the common entanglement of men and women with specialized creative work to do, who 'find themselves eaten up by first hand affairs. . . . This is the outcome of a specialization and a sublimation of interests that has become frequent only in the last century or so.' Suddenly self-critical in a strained, desperate way, he decided that a great deal of his work had been slovenly and hurried, with the constant sense of so much more to say and do driving him into slip-shod prose, inadequate research, easy satisfactions. 'I am tormented by a desire for achievement that overruns my capacity, and by a practical incapacity to bring about for myself the conditions under which fine achievement is possible.' (7)

One sleepless night between two and five in the morning he set all this and much more down, pouring out his distress unpremeditated on paper. Expression was often the first way of escape. This time it became the huge *Experiment in Autobiography*. But there was no trace in the *Autobiography* of Miss Y. who had enlivened his life at Lou Pidou and who had such a deep effect on him one way and another. In the end they parted and he decided he must leave Lou Pidou for good, sell the house, break the growing and beautiful ties which threatened to root him in this lovely alien land. It cost him a considerable effort. The house was full of memories, the people and the garden had found a deep place in his affections, but one morning in 1933 he went out into the sunshine to say goodbye to the olive orchard, the rose-beds and the orange trees, and lingered for a while beside his black cat, very much aware that presently he would go down the road to Cannes for the last time. He was a man terribly conscious of the irrevocable finality of the last time.

* * *

Back in England, a handful of people presently accused him of something far more damning than failing to move the world to action. 'When I read, as an adolescent that noble work, *First and Last Things*,' wrote Odette Keun in 1934, 'I sobbed with the ecstasy, the almost intolerable sense of organic liberation that it brought. . . . We were being *delivered*!' (8)

And later 'Alas for me who, my eyes fixed on those agile hands, waited so many years of my life to see them build up salvation. . . . We thought he was a redeemer, when first he rushed upon our sordid scene with the sweep and the urge of a flaring archangel. . . . But he had no vocation to love and lead us. . . . He had found other things to do with his juggler's hands. . . . He was placing and changing, moving and making, shifting and breaking, tossing aside with a violent joy.' (9)

Throughout three articles in *Time and Tide* (1934) the criticism becomes intense. It needs only a slight extension of certain comments to read a devastating message. Oh this monstrous man who had promised so much and done so little! Clear out the lumber room of his mind, show him up for what he really was, make way for the real man Wells skulking underneath the shining knight of rational thinking, a man who turned out to be a sort of sporting sociologist enjoying the shoot.

An authentic note crept into much of it. 'Those temperamental defects which are the cause of his ultimate and irrevocable failure to be great, his self-indulgence, his instability and vanity.' (10) But temperament, high and mettled and forcing out flame on the page, was also the cause of Miss Keun's failure to be—well objective. She admitted 'he was instrumental in bringing about our modern mentality.' (11) She realized that we all absorbed something of what he disseminated, that he wove the intellectual texture of the early 1900's. He was also allowed his infectious vitality, a high place in the world of letters, books of abounding humanity like *Kipps*, others significant in world affairs, a quick resilient enormously receptive brain despite its wilful hasty ways, and unshakable likes as well as dislikes. But from his person she swept on to his later work, and through the steaming clouds of words it became obvious that some of his novels were so much ridiculous romancing. *The Research Magnificent*—a fatuous plea for travel in preference to affection, while one's wife was left in the hands of another man. . . . *The Autocracy of Mr. Parham*—a world enlightened by a fresh sort of Daily Newspaper and Big Business. . . . *The World of William Clissold*—a society made splendid by Big Business, Advertising and the Press. . . . And *The Shape of Things to Come*—the story of an unlucky planet taken over and administered by a band of aviators. What sort of message was this behind the rich style, the unparalleled fancy and the deceptive boyishness of it all ? Was Mr. Wells a cheat ? Had he deliberately used his gifts to inflate a bubble iridescent with his own ridiculous vanity ? Was the man really at heart nothing more than a glorified gamester ? Yes, cried Odette Keun, answering the last question, if she was longer and more vivid and more readable than that.

Why, look at his behaviour in the war. One moment the victim of the worst mass hysteria when he gloried in the death of German sailors, one moment calling Shaw 'an idiot child screaming in a hospital,' and the next, with the war barely finished, 'proclaiming Universal Brotherly Love' all over again. A wanton egotist. An unmannerly exhibitionist. A king of gamesters ! There was an extraordinary tendency in all this to thrust upon poor H. G. some of the worst sins he found in his own public. Odette Keun blamed him for failing to fulfil his mission, for being egotistical, for playing futile games. Wells levelled exactly the same charges at his public. There was some truth in both.

Wells in his 68th year was not only a target for big and small abuse, the inevitable penalty of any public figure; he was now the centre of endless assessment, endless attempts to see what his life, now reaching a rotund Pickwickian fulfilment, amounted to. He was a literary Hitler some people said. He stormed and raged because he and no-one else was right. Possessed by a ruthless passion to save the world, a purblind obstinate world which would not listen, he had endowed himself with the powers of a dictator and had become intolerable in order to *make* it listen. But little Artie Kipps who wept so easily, who hated having sentimental horrors struck from his novels, who burst into tears at the story of infant hardships, who once was so gauche that he could produce nothing but vulgar facetiousness in company, still went skipping along inside the world-maker and the literary Hitler.

Dorothy Richardson saw him as a mass of contradictions: 'Poor little Artie Kipps found his way to the door of the church founded on Huxley's reading of Darwin (in the heyday of Science before her limitations as an explorer of reality became evident) and spent his life there taking notes and writing epistles in all kinds of forms (as a novelist, his characters were devised to illustrate his theories). As a transcendent journalist of science no one could touch him for imaginative power. Largely he transformed the average consciousness of his earlier days and undoubtedly hoped to lead the abstraction labelled "humanity," eager and unanimous, to a new world. Up to a point he was a prophet, but only in regard to things. (Of people he knew relatively nothing.) This planet, he kept saying, is a misfit. We will find our way out, amongst the stars—"beyond our wildest dreams." Enlargement of the premises and improvement of the furniture, leaving individuals unchanged. He tried, in his way, all doors save that of philosophy. *First and Last Things* seemed to suggest a turning-point. But soon, quicker in the uptake than anyone I have ever known, he was chasing after the latest discovery and advertising it in categorical generalisations.'

Odette Keun stuck to her far more personal recipe. She took the outraged ego of a common little boy trapped in a dungeon of lower-class stupidity, remembered his intensities and nerve-endings, hurt if not maimed him with one indignity after another, granted him artistic vision and the gift of tongues, and there were the inevitable roots from which sprang the individualist who brought whole books to bear on gnats, deliberately outraged the conventions, and used up half his energy letting himself go, kicking his skulking *id* out into the light of day, convinced that when it appeared it would resemble—was it Wells or God-Wells? It was all a game, Odette Keun said. A great game. . . . And he's still at it. . . .

But somehow none of this would quite do. Especially if you were a psychologist. For here were some of the stock symptoms of the hopelessly repressed childhood which had twisted his ego for ever. The tempers, games, adolescent quarrellings, might be so many attempts to recover the childhood happiness he had missed. A gap yawned in his life. It had to be filled before he believed himself a full rounded satisfied personality, and to make certain beyond any doubt that he had recovered whatever it was his childhood lacked, he had played the exhibitionist, shown the world the cripple throwing away his crutches, and given society what it had once given him—socks. The stock case-book history of the mother-babe trail was plainly blazed for the least experienced eye to see, and words for Wells had so obviously become a means to power, which granted him in the end verbal omnipotence. He had manipulated people and worlds in writing as he could never manipulate them in real life. Rational analysis had become the big stick for beating the lights out of his enemies, and behind his enemies the society which had forced on him the squalor of his early days.

But if you were a writer it still wouldn't do. Wells was immense. He had in him something of everything and with a dash of ingenuity most things could be proved against him. That he lacked spiritual discipline and was so far emancipated from religious belief as to deny the scientific method. That he did not sift the evidence to the last drop and ask for empirical confirmation, but plunged in, bristling with prejudice, prepared to break down science itself so be it his personal likes and dislikes survived intact. That his 'temperamental ineptitude for abstract truth made greatness impossible.' That humility might have helped to contain the torrential vitality to higher ends. But if you went as far as this, then why not plainly and bluntly call him pathological like the psychologists. Or see him, as Odette Keun saw him, 'established in a state of unconscious personal mental dishonesty.' Or, by all that's holy, carry the lantern into the darkest labyrinth, round the final bend into who knew what black pit where evil itself might lie unadulterated.

But still it left out of account that stream of noble thought and language which time and again lifted his books out of the realm of story-telling into the rare region where high and disinterested purpose holds its own glow of beauty. Or those moments—as it were of revelation—when he grasped the whole range of human endeavour with unparalleled imaginative power and saw from a detachment terrifying in its serenity, the last spark of mind expiring 'in the bleak immensities.' Or the journeys he took into his own brain, returning with strange reports clothed in beautiful language. Or the lyrical phrases poured out on paper with the passionate conviction that men could find in themselves the likeness of gods if only they would listen. To H. G. Wells ? To the self-glorified world-maker ? To the man capable of boundless kindness to strangers, irrepressible fun, generosity with money, great hates and a fountain of compassion for the very snivelling swindlers he most decried; or to one of the many other people he could so easily become ? It was simpler to chart a continent than to find one's way about the diminutive island of Wells.

Chapter Seventeen

DIPLOMAT

THE year 1934 shone not only with Odette Keun's attack in the pages of *Time and Tide*. It took H. G. Wells into the most significant piece of international diplomacy he had yet attempted, and led him into a battle with Stalin, Shaw and Keynes, which finally determined his position among the rosy clouds of Samurai, for ever confusing—with undeniable beauty—practical action. He went to Russia, to the Kremlin, and met Premier Stalin. A similar visit to President Franklin Roosevelt in the United States had persuaded him to travel back across Europe to Moscow in order to compare one man with the other. How far, he wanted to know, were these two brains working towards a Socialist World State which was 'the only hopeful destiny for mankind' ? How far was it true that the end sought—'a progressively more organised big-scale community'—belonged as much to Moscow as to Washington, even though one might be 'a receptive and co-ordinating brain centre, the other a concentrated and personal direction.' It looked for the moment as though he was out to re-affirm what was already a platitude among thinking people, who clearly saw that both communities were becoming more highly organized and big-scale. But when he reached Moscow he carried it into much deeper waters.

The visit dispensed with most of the normal formalities and safeguards. He arrived at the Kremlin and was shown straight to a large and almost empty room where Stalin stood, wearing an embroidered white shirt, dark trousers and boots. Wells saw nothing very fine about the face, as Stalin turned to meet him, and Stalin had none of Lenin's 'boundless curiosity which set him peering at Wells from a dozen different angles, one hand over the defective eye.' Stalin greeted him warmly and shyly. He looked past Wells and not at him. There was something, Wells said later, very commonplace and ordinary about his whole appearance and bearing, and the need for a translator made the atmosphere rather heavy and self-conscious. But a talk scheduled to last three-quarters of an hour lasted for three, perhaps because the two men recited with the unflinching faithfulness of automatons their own creeds, granting as it were suitable pauses for exposition and applause. Mr. Umansky the translator sat alert throughout, making notes, rapidly transcribing, and for Wells, losing something of what he wanted to say with every fresh attempt to say it.

The talk began with a series of old-world pleasantries almost unbelievable in the cold light of dialectical materialism:

WELLS: 'I am very much obliged to you Mr. Stalin for agreeing to see me. I was in the United States recently. I had a long conversation with President Roosevelt, and tried to ascertain what his leading ideas were. Now I have come to you to ask you what you are doing to change the world.'

STALIN: 'Not so very much.'

WELLS: 'I wander around the world as a common man and as a common man observe what is going on around me.'

STALIN: 'Important public men like yourself are not common men. Of course, history alone can show how important this or that public man has been; at all events you do not look at the world as "a common man." ' (1)

To-day, Wells went on, the capitalists have to learn from you to grasp the spirit of Socialism. You and Roosevelt began from two different starting points, but is there not a relation in ideas, a kinship between Washington and Moscow? Their need, like yours, is directive ability.

Stalin replied: No, the aims are different. America is keeping the old basis of economy, although trying to reduce the ruinous basis of the crisis. We have established a new basis of economy. Nor is America a planned economy, because our plan is to reduce unemployment, which is something no capitalist wants to abolish completely.

Wells tried again: I can formulate my point of view in the following way. First I am for order; second I attack the present system in so far as it cannot assure order. Third, I think that class-war propaganda may detach from Socialism just those educated people Socialism needs.

Stalin: I do not stand for any kind of order. I stand for order that corresponds to the interests of the working class.

Wells believed one could have a World State without a revolution, in the Russian sense of the word, which to Stalin was childish nonsense. Wells attacked the class warfare propaganda and clumsy words like bourgeoisie, which brought from Stalin the stock formulas on the proletarian masses. Wells said the proletarian masses were no different from the sovereign peoples that kings had called upon for generations, and Stalin produced another massively inscrutable piece of Marx. It is useless, Wells said, appealing to the men I have in mind—the engineers, airmen, technicians and Clissolds—with class warfare propaganda, or any of the encrusted dogmas of Marx, admirable I don't doubt as political-cum-philosophical analysis, but liable to create unnecessary resistance. 'These people understand the condition of the world. They understand that it is a bloody muddle, but they regard your simple class-war antagonism as nonsense.'

Wells insisted that there were very different kinds of capitalist, with the powerful Morgan on one side devoting his life to the accumulation of wealth, and John D. Rockefeller and Ford on the other, brilliant organizers, men capable of rationalizing production in a quite new way, men from whom the Russians could take a lesson. Why not, Wells seemed to say, call in my old friend Clissold in the likeness of Ford and Rockefeller to help things forward in the Russian state ? Stalin gallantly admitted that Ford and Rockefeller had special skills which were beyond price, but pointed out that even greater skills were called for to organize *them*. Whereupon Wells enigmatically declared, 'It seems to me that I am more to the left than you, Mr. Stalin' and Stalin stared soundlessly back.

So the talk ran on. Wells believed that the country which adopts a planned economy and begins with the state control of banks and heavy industries would come to Socialism in just the same way as Russia had come to it by Revolution. Inspiration would flow from his Clissolds and Fords and permeate the whole society. He instanced America once more—'The effect of the ideas of Roosevelt's New Deal is most powerful and in my opinion they are Socialist ideas.' (2) If I disagree with you, Stalin said, it is for more reasons than one, but how in the first place will your Clissolds and Fords ever *gain political power*, because in politics he who is without power is as sounding brass.

They ran off into sidetracks but never very far. Stalin, cautious, wary, delivered all his answers with the weight of an established gospel, and ever and again it seemed, Wells had to move very quickly and adroitly to avoid being crushed, but just when one felt he must have disappeared under the implacable tread, there he was again, a glinting gnome arguing as persuasively as ever.

They talked of revolution and the Chartists—

WELLS: In England between 1830 and 1870 the aristocracy gave up power to the bourgeoisie without too great struggle.

STALIN: You're talking about reform, not revolution. The Chartists played a great role in the Reforms.

WELLS: The Chartists did little, and left little trace after they were gone.

STALIN: I disagree. They pressed the middle class to action. Generally speaking, it must be said that of all the ruling classes, the ruling classes of England—both the aristocracy and the bourgeoisie—proved to be the cleverest and most flexible from the point of view of their class interests, from the point of view of maintaining their power.

WELLS: You have a higher opinion of the ruling classes in my country than I have. But is there a great difference between a small revolution and a great reform ? Is not a reform a small revolution ?

STALIN: The essence of reform is that the bourgeoisie grant concessions under the pressure of the lower classes in order to stay in power. Revolution means transference of power. (3)

The end was the beginning all over again. Wells believed that a self-dedicated, self-elected Samurai drawn from humanity as a whole and not the proletariat in particular could seep through the social confusion, take control, spread the gospel of rational behaviour and Cosmopolitanism, and create a World Government without any sign of bloody revolution. Stalin believed that the clash between the classes would bring Capitalism to its knees possibly by the use of force, the proletariat then sweeping its Samurai into power, while regular obeisance was still made at the altar of Marx. In their preoccupation with their own creeds, both men completely overlooked the far more practical purposes they might have served by attempting some *modus vivendi* between modified capitalism in the West and Communism in the East. What remained an intellectual exercise could have gone so much deeper. They prepared, and elaborately made, burnt offerings to their own gods. They watched and enjoyed each other's worship. But to open new avenues of understanding between east and west, to discover the formula which might bring them together—no, not before each had justified himself in the eyes of the other, an impossible task from the start. So it remained at the level of the interview, an interchange of ideas, a brouhaha between the crowned heads of the proletariat and the intelligentsia. More's the pity.

Wells returned to England. In London the whole episode had not gone unobserved. The first ambassador to his own world court, Wells could not escape the pursuing finger of the public prints, capable of prising untold treasure from the drabbest chest. He brought back from Russia an agreed text of the Stalin conversation and it was published in *The New Statesman* on November 10th, 1934. Correspondence flowed, but it was Shaw who set off a fine quarrelsome argument, with no quarter asked or given.

'The conversation, or rather collision, between these two extraordinary men has not told us anything we did not know as to their respective views,' Shaw wrote, 'but it is entertaining as a bit of comedy; and I suspect it was not lost as such on Stalin; for he is a man with a keen sense of comedy and a very ready and genial laugh.'

From Shaw's point of view, Stalin had very successfully given Wells a lesson in the political science of Marx, but Wells was a hopeless pupil who had every appearance of being deaf to all but his own voice. Stalin, said Shaw, was a magnificent listener, never in a hurry to talk. 'Wells is a very good talker, but the worst listener in the world. His vision is so wide and assured that the slightest contradiction throws him into a frenzy of contemptuous and eloquently vituperative impatience.' According to Shaw, Wells should have pointed out to Stalin that the Bolsheviks were given power by a soldier peasant class at least as devoted to the laws of private property in the form of peasant proprietorship as any capitalist. He should also have seen that certain Bolsheviks bore some resemblance to the Clissolds of his own imagination. If Stalin could be believed—and Shaw for one was strongly inclined to believe him—the conspiracy which would bring about social salvation needed ruthless men, men with an overwhelming vocation, men who saw Capitalism as 'organized robbery of the proletariat' which they were determined to put down with any other sort of brigandage. Shaw added one last jibe. Wells had suggested that Russian writers should join the intimate circle founded in London under the name of the P.E.N. Club, a circle of international writers, and Shaw commented, 'Mr. Wells, magnificently over-looking the existence of the League of Nations Committee for Intellectual Co-operation, and all the Internationals, first, second and third, offers Russia the P.E.N. Club as a substitute. The offer has struck Russia speechless.'

It would be wrong to say that Wells was roused. He adopted the same patient suffering attitude towards Shaw which had characterized certain parts of his Stalin talk. But asked whether he had anything to add, he said, 'Who can reply to Mr. Bernard Shaw ? He has acquired by habit and prescription the woman's privilege of wanton incoherent assertion. The torrent of fanciful misrepresentation and shrewd insinuation flows, one shrugs one's shoulders. I am Clissold, I am Ponderevo, I am anything but myself; I am mean, I am vain—no gentleman. If it makes Shaw happier, so be it.'

There followed a delicious riposte to Shaw's graceless reference to the P.E.N. Club, with Wells pointing out that it was hardly 'four times as numerous, solvent and well-known as the Fabian Society was thirty years ago.' As to Wells' deafness in the presence of Stalin, 'I may, as he says, be indisposed to listen to what I have heard before, but for all intellectual ends, his touchily defensive egotism and his disposition to dramatise make so brilliant a clamour that he is practically stone deaf !'

Wells now repeated his scorn for the dreary dogma of class warfare and claimed that Shaw could not be unaware of its decline. The human mind was pressing to ends far greater than this 'squabbling legacy' from an age of exploitation, and gigantic possibilities were becoming apparent in the social confusion which would presently infuse a quite new purpose into the whole social fabric, brushing these personal gibes and quarrels and showings-off into the wastepaper basket where they belonged: 'What poor cramped things we shall seem to the generations ahead. Here are Shaw and I nearing the end of our lives, and we can do nothing better with each other than this personal bally-ragging. It is ridiculous to be competitive and personally compara-tive after sixty-five.' Isn't it time, Wells asked uneasily, that we went ? For himself he hung on for one of many reasons: to say to 'this dreary class-war dogma' at the Exit: 'After you.'

It was lordly, it was pontifical, the high priest of Utopia rebuking the unruly apostle who so far forgot his noble calling as to indulge in badinage and bad manners. Shaw should have felt humbled, should have fallen into respectful silence. That was not in his nature. Out it rolled again—the same tide of eloquence, vitality, wit. 'Order gentlemen,' said Shaw. 'Order please. Remember your international manners.' Once more forgetting his own, he plunged on. . . . Would Mr. Wells *never* see that Russia had half realized his own dream by producing a government of the people for the people by 'men and women who care sufficiently about the condition of the people to devote themselves to the work for its own sake. . . .' ? What *had* come over our dear H. G. ? Granted a high privilege which of course he deserved, he 'trots into the Kremlin' and tells Stalin that his head is overstuffed with some absurd nonsense called class-warfare, when it would so much better accommodate the views of Mr. Wells and the P.E.N. whereby Clissolidarity will sanctify the world. 'I ask H. G. whether he is going to leave it like that. . . . Stalin . . . cannot be expected to know what we all know in England—namely that H. G. is just like Marx in refusing to tolerate the existence of any other pebble on the beach.'

And Wells came back: 'Mr. Shaw asks whether I am going to leave it like that. . . . He can have the glory of saying that I "trotted" into the Kremlin, while by implication he and Lady Astor with the utmost grace, strode, swam, stalked, danced, slid, skated or loped in, and conversed in some superior imperial fashion of which no record survives.'

Then out of the blue came a last devastating card which, some weeks later, Wells could not resist playing. Discovering an article which Shaw had written at the time of the Zinovieff letter, he found it so completely reversed Shaw's position as to leave him bereft of any recognizable sense of direction. 'From the point of view of English Socialists,' it said, 'the members of the Third International do not know even the beginnings of their business as Socialists; and the proposition that the world should take its orders from a handful of Russian novices who seem to have gained their knowledge of modern Socialism by sitting over the drawing-room stove and reading the pamphlets of the Liberal

Revolutionists of 1848–70, makes even Lord Curzon and Mr. Winston Churchill seem extreme modernists in comparison.' (4)

As Shaw instantly pointed out, this article was written ten years before, when it seemed impossible for Stalin to deliver the goods, but now he had performed the impossible and 'I take off my hat to him accordingly. . . .'

It still left one dazzling piece of contradiction. 'The Russian writings which make the most favourable impression here,' Shaw had proclaimed in his article, 'are those of Mr. Trotsky, but even he has allowed himself to speak of Mr. H. G. Wells with a contempt which shows that he has not read Wells' *Outline of History*, and has therefore no suspicion of what an enormous advance on *Das Kapital* that work represents.'

Shaw came out of it all with the appearance of a man who might in one breath barter his beliefs for a set of glittering phrases, and in another become a brilliant devotee of Stalin, who worried Wells into a corner from which only lordly declamation offered a way of escape—until *The Daily Herald* article saved him. But Wells . . .?

If Mr. Burnham, who wrote *The Managerial Revolution*, believes in ancestor worship he should bow thrice in the direction of H. G. Wells every morning, for quite clearly he had now blazed the trail which led to this theory. He wanted an open conspiracy, a bloodless revolution led by the airmen, engineers, technicians and thinkers, and Mr. Burnham's position is not so very different.

Sheer pyrotechnics may have overwhelmed the weight of Wells' part in all this. He cared passionately about the interview with Stalin, as he cared passionately about the sorry state of the world. He was desperately concerned to kindle among Russian writers the fierce free criticism which sustained the P.E.N. Club, or if not to kindle, to render it sacrosanct, an inviolable law for all men and women dedicated to the integrity of the written word. And for this and many other reasons, he looked for profound repercussions.

But when it was all over, the Kremlin fifteen hundred miles away, and Shaw settled into chuckling silence, Wells sat back in his study one December day, and wondered once more what it amounted to. The flaring tail of a comet which never came near enough to shake the world? A handful of sputtering phrases dying as they were delivered, without the power to change the scene one whit? For, spectacular though his Stalin talk might be, and however much debated amongst British intellectuals who carried it into endless private and public places, unaccountably the world's problems remained stubbornly the same. Kingsley Martin, editor of *The New Statesman*, suggested printing the whole argument as a pamphlet, to which Wells said, 'Of course it must be a pamphlet. I want it to be in permanent form. Shaw has behaved like a cad and he ought to be exposed.' And Shaw replied: 'Och no. I have a great respect for my old friend H. G. He has made a perfect ass of himself and I would not want it put on permanent record.' (5)

* * *

Literary London arranged an elaborate party to celebrate his 70th birthday. There was some fuss about where a certain titled lady should sit. The old charges of snobbery were revived when Wells wanted her at his table. 'It is a fine thing to be entertained by a great crowd of friends,' he said at the party, 'and I cannot tell you how much I enjoy being praised and having my importance so generously and delightfully exaggerated. I feel uplifted, expanded. . . . Yet all the same I will confess that the mellow brightness of this occasion is not without shadow. I hate being seventy. To make this festival perfect you should have discovered that there had been some mistake and that I was say—forty-five.' He professed a profound faith in the future of 'encyclopædism'. . . . 'Those sketchy outlines and summaries of mine, such as they are, have merely shown what can be done. . . . I believe a new movement on a grand scale towards a comprehensive Encyclopædism is overdue to-day. . . .'

Somerset Maugham wrote of the dinner. . . . 'Hundreds of people came to it. Bernard Shaw, a magnificent figure with his height, his white beard and white hair, his clear skin and bright eyes, made a speech. He stood very erect, his arms crossed, and with his puckish humour said many things highly embarrassing to the guest of the evening. . . . H. G. his nose in the manuscript, read his speech in a high-pitched voice. He spoke peevishly of his age, and not without a natural querulousness protested against the notion any of those present might have that the anniversary, with the attendant banquet, indicated any willingness on his part to set a term to his activities. . . . He protested that he was as ready as ever to set the world to rights. . . .' (6)

But in his seventy-first year Wells felt more than ever like

Roger Bacon of old, settled in his cell, scribbling enormous tracts about a new way of knowledge which never reached the one man who could have given them the sanction they so desperately needed, if he took heart from the memory that Bacon, so shabbily neglected in his day, came most powerfully into his own. Wells had written some time before 'I play at being such a man as he was, a man altogether lonely and immediately futile, a man lit by the vision of a world still some centuries ahead, convinced of its reality and urgency and yet powerless to bring it any nearer. . . .' It rang more poignantly in his seventy-first year. The solver of riddles, the seer and the prophet was sometimes overtaken with the poet's melancholy but the mood had moments of exhilaration. When—Stalin, Shaw and Russia forgotten—he looked out on the world afresh and saw that the processes which might convert man into something more than a dismal accident were still long and painful, he fell into deep glooms. Then the spirit of the poet that was in him prevailed, and some implicit loveliness in the story, a braveness of death, a high melancholy at having come so far to meet no more than futility and extinction, lit his mind with a strange sunlight. The mood became a refuge to him. A refuge against advancing age, unflinching mass ignorance, and a measureless tide of evil arising on the continent of Europe.

Chapter Eighteen

ANCIENT

HIS health did not break down seriously until the last eighteen months, and in his early seventies he continued vigorous, energetic, full of new projects. He was still the same impish, undisciplined, disorderly person, continuing to smite whatever he considered stupid with the same wit and an assurance rather more devastating as death drew nearer, but he grew pathologically sensitive to the lightest breath of criticism, and very very bad-tempered. The habit of pontificating grew on him. At dinner table he was liable to hold forth as the Master, and there were moments of inordinate vanity when he became a little god in his own right, and delivered pronouncements as from the thunderous heights of Olympus. These moods were never sustained. He was still at heart an enchanting person capable of great warmth and understanding, brimming with intelligence. But he contradicted himself rather more often than before and could now say and did say with Walt Whitman, 'Yes, I contradict myself: I am large: I contain multitudes.' He took the Ivy Restaurant by storm, he rounded furiously on half a dozen politicians. 'I am only exceptional,' he said, 'in being exceptionally articulate,' and used that articulation to madden Lord Halifax, challenging in almost the same breath half a dozen other new, and some imaginary, dragons.

Still he dreamed of becoming a Fellow of the Royal Society to the veiled astonishment of that august body. Still he wrote voluminous letters with his son's wife as secretary. One such went to the editor of *Labour Forum*, one-time official quarterly of the Labour Party, sending an article demanding a republic in place of the monarchy and saying—if you do not publish this, I should like to know the reason why. People were still expected to run the gauntlet of his iconoclasm. He suddenly turned on the Secretary of the P.E.N. Club, Hermon Ould, and wrote:

My dear Ould,

What is all this about the P.E.N. hoisting the Red Flag ? Why is a 'left' publisher—a publisher of all things !—taking the chair at *my*

P.E.N. Club and why have you made Maisky the guest of the evening
—when there are real Russian men of letters in the country ? What does
it mean ? The Russians refused to accept a P.E.N. Club in 1934 and
there has been no change in the situation. I shall not be present but I
think I have the right to demand a full report of any speeches that are
made. I must think all this over. My disposition at present—in view of
all I have done to keep the P.E.N. free from partisan bias—is to resign
as publicly as possible all my connections with the Club and to consult
Mrs. Galsworthy about the endowment of the organisation. It was
certainly never in Galsworthy's mind or mine that the P.E.N. should
become an advertisement hoarding for the Left Book Club.
Please communicate this to the Committee.

Yours ever,
H. G.

I take it I have a right to publish a letter in the *P.E.N. News* defining
my position clearly.

To which Ould replied:

My dear H. G.,

Let me explain.

The idea of a Pushkin Centenary Dinner was handed to me by the
Baroness Budberg at Priestley's party at the Ivy. The suggestion was
in the P.E.N. tradition and I said I would do what I could to carry it
out. She offered to try to find a suitable guest of honour, and during
the intervening weeks tried and failed to find one. (Where are the 'real
Russian men of letters '?) The announcement that Alexei Tolstoy was
coming seemed to provide a solution. (He has been prevented at the
last moment by 'flu).

We have had Ibsen and Goethe Centenary Dinners and in the former
case invited the Norwegian Minister and in the latter the German
Ambassador. In inviting the Russian Ambassador to the Pushkin
Dinner we were following the usual P.E.N. tradition.

The Committee suggested Gollancz as Chairman, not because he is a
publisher of 'Left' books, but because he is a P.E.N. member who might
be expected to know something about Pushkin. Both he and Maisky
have been told that they are to talk about Pushkin and Pushkin only,
and are well aware that politics are barred. The Dinner will, indeed, be
in complete accordance with P.E.N. principles and practice. The fact
that it will be rather better attended than usual and will include a number of members whose worst enemies would not accuse them of 'Left'
tendencies, is an indication that your fears are not justified.

You may be interested to know that Ada Galsworthy wrote me last week: 'Best wishes to the next dinner of P.E.N.', and if anybody knows what J. G. would have approved of, she does.

So please, dear H. G., believe that we are not doing the wicked things you accuse us of. If only you had come to the committee meeting at which all these things were arranged!

Yours ever.

Another novel appeared in 1938, a novel in which the possessiveness of women, their emotional greediness, was explored in one envenomed episode after another. It railed against recalcitrant lovers who had to stamp about the ashes of affairs long since dead, praying for a burning spark to torture them afresh, it drew an acid picture of a woman called Dolores.

'Light breaks upon me,' the 'I' of the book wrote. 'Her gestures, her style, her costume, her scent, her accent, her mannerisms, her dogs and decorations, the values she sets upon things, her wildly fluctuating judgments are a jackdaw collection picked up anyhow and gripped and held together with tremendous tenacity.' And later: 'For some years now Dolores has been building up a system of claims upon me and everyone about her, upon the basis that she is sad. She poses more and more definitely as an ailing woman, acutely disappointed by me and the world.'

Dolores disliked his cat as much as he disliked her dog. They came to verbal blows in public, abandoned themselves to bitterness in restaurants, and there was at least one occasion when they both talked at once, heroically resisting the desire to know what the other was saying, rising from a low ebb to shrill crescendo until he got to his feet saying, ' "There is a limit—" ' and knocked over a table. ' "Pouf," she said, for the benefit of the audience. "Quel maladroit! Mon amant! Mais c'est drôle!" '

She had, he wrote, 'a devouring insatiable egotism,' 'a blank craving for notice.' Her excitability made it all so transparent, and 'over everything there hung . . . a faint elusive flavour of incense, of pastilles, of recent battles and duels of perfume.' And her friends! Oh dear, her friends! Immensely worldly women, powerful talkative personalities dressed with 'a chic that hurt,' eternally comparing the relative value of the male lover, whether French, Italian, German or English, running the complete gamut if time and circumstances permitted it from 'the vast but repulsive prowess of le nègre and le gorille' to the gangling young English adolescent. 'They go over this stuff again and again. They roll their imaginations over it. A lover ceases to be a lover; he is a technician. . . . Affection flutters away from this awful stuff in infinite distress.'

But Dolores at her early morning devotions was the final cruelty. 'She practised some marvellous exercises which I gathered were a combination of the best Swedish drill with the finer usages of yoga mysticism. . . . Dolores in a state of nature holding her breath in an effort to send air by some entirely unknown route to her spinal cord, and at the same time bursting to explain the esoteric wonder of it, was an exhilarating spectacle. I would say innocent but provocative things and she would gesticulate fiercely for silence. As if some yogi was listening and might overhear and stop the influence.'

* * *

Still the single, driving purpose which began all those years ago had Wells in its power. Soon it insisted that he make yet another assault on the morass of ignorance and prejudice which had so often swallowed up everything he said, only to smile back complacently, another assault on the stupid, formless resistant mind of half the modern world, hastening to its own destruction under the glorious cloak of scientific discovery and something mistakenly interpreted as progress; another assault before his energies failed him completely, because he still believed the New Jerusalem lay just around the corner.

It was there for all to see, rich, solid, unmistakably real, yet there were still people, numbered in their millions, who smiled when he described it and humoured him as they might a madman listening to his voices. Damnation, devilment and disaster ! Why was it that in a world he took to be rational and free-thinking he must remain for so many, the romantic dreamer, tolerated as a magnificent jester at the court of science, of whom one said 'What would we do without Herbert ?' Yet Socrates and Galileo had suffered a worse fate. He was not yet brought to the hemlock or the gaol. But the jester was growing old. The quips and frolics and gaiety did not come so easily. He knew that the repository of so many full-fledged and incipient illnesses must soon become a worn tired vessel, as the new lines about the face already showed. And now, still under the compulsion of the same heroic pressures, came yet another attempt to cry halt to the heedless drifting ways of modern man.

Some who worked with him on *The Rights of Man* in 1939 say that he no longer concentrated in the same fierce way. Others believed his powers undiminished. Whichever way it went, with the aid of the Sankey Committee—Lord Sankey, Lord Horder, Sir Norman Angell, Miss Margaret Bondfield, Sir Richard Gregory, Mrs. Barbara Wootton, Sir John Orr, Francis Williams and Ritchie Calder—he produced the *Sankey Declaration of the Rights of Man*, as far-reaching a document as any of its kind. It was put together first as a rough draft. 'Mr. Ritchie Calder,' wrote Wells, 'then the able and clear-headed scientific correspondent of *The Daily Herald*, was inspired to take up the matter. He made a very considerable effective newspaper campaign of it.' (1)

But let Calder tell the story. In a letter to me he wrote . . .

'What happened was that Wells called rhetorically for a Great Debate in *The Times*, and I took him at his word. *The Daily Herald* agreed to make available a page a day for a month, with Wells introducing each group of clauses (The Rights of Man) with an article followed by a 'priming' by distinguished people, followed by a free for all for the ordinary men and women.

'In spite of his great cosmic sweep and his timeless interests, Wells paradoxically always reacted to the day's news and in his first article he launched a diatribe against Chamberlain and Halifax —a piece of vituperation which was highly stimulating but quite irrelevant to the Rights of Man.

'I tried, before publication, to persuade him to cut out this irrelevance, but he violently complained that we were trying to interfere with his fundamental right of free speech. I warned him what would happen and it did.

'Wells, at the outset, was chairman of both the Debate and Drafting Committee, on which Sankey had agreed, as an ex-Lord Chancellor to act as the juridical member. When the article appeared, Sankey immediately called me up and said he wanted to resign from the Drafting Committee because, while he agreed with Wells' remarks about Chamberlain and Halifax and was even pre-pared to admit that Wells—as chairman of the Debate—was entitled to make them, he contended that Wells, as Chairman of the Drafting Committee, had prejudged the issues of the discus-sion. The Committee therefore, could not be regarded as objective so long as Wells was chairman, and he (Sankey) as a Law Lord could not serve.

'The situation was serious because, if Sankey had resigned, Lord Horder, Chamberlain's private doctor, would have been forced to follow suit and several other members would have been tempted to do so.

'I saw Sankey on the night of the crisis to ask him to reconsider, but he was adamant until I asked him whether, if I got H. G. to resign as chairman of the Drafting Committee he would agree to continue and to become its chairman to protect it from further "misdemeanours." Sankey was genuinely fond of H. G. and he would hear of nothing likely to distress the Old Man.'

At this point Calder picked up the telephone and to Sankey's manifest alarm addressed Wells in terms which were usually considered the exclusive prerogative of H. G. himself: 'Look,' Calder said, 'you've got to resign your chairmanship of the Drafting Committee!' There was an electric silence. Calder added, 'The Debating Committee is all right but not the Drafting Committee. . . . We're having some trouble.' Wells' normal reaction to strong talk of this kind was a verbal violence which reduced his opponents to silence or flaring rage. Now there came an ominous, high-pitched chuckling at the other end of the line, the squeaky voice asked a number of very nearly normal questions, and then the day was won with no real distress to anyone. Sankey professed astonishment and went away reassured.

'Even after this,' Calder continued, 'behind closed doors, H. G. continually tried to force his point of view and on one occasion "stalled" the Drafting Committee which was meeting at his house by refusing to give them lunch, until at 3 p.m. Lord Horder said it was perfectly obvious that the host was trying to repeat the trial of the seven bishops and moved that the Committee adjourn to the nearest Lyons. Whereupon Wells gave way and lunch. . . .'

Over the next few weeks Wells and Sankey both fell into the habit of enquiring from various people how the Old Boy was to-day, Sankey sometimes conveying the impression of an aged author with slightly homicidal tendencies and Wells a drooling old judge permanently searching for precedents. . . .

'It is an interesting sidelight on human behaviour,' wrote Wells in one of his last books, ('*42 to '44*) 'that the utmost difficulty was experienced in collecting the assent of the drafting committee in order to agree upon the revisions we were finding necessary. . . . These ten people had embarked upon the most important job human beings had ever attempted. . . . Yet, even at our meetings, after an hour or so of discussion, only a novelist could describe how eagerly they adjourned . . . it became plain to one of us at any rate by a feeling of impracticability and unreality in the Declaration upon which we were tinkering. . . .' (2)

It was characteristic of Wells to speak of 'one of us at any rate.' Other members of the committee were not only aware of the same unreality; they felt the atmosphere charged with tensions of another kind. How far age, which gave a new sanction to the streak of egomania in him, and illness, which occasionally fretted and frustrated him, contributed to Wells' fits of lordly irritation—when he delivered himself of another pronouncement to everyone's consternation except his own—it is hard to determine, but the atmospherics were largely of his own creation.

In the end the draft was done. Eleven universal rights of man beginning with the right to live, the right to protection of minors, the right to work or not to work as the individual chose, the right to earn money, to have possessions, to move about freely, to knowledge, to thought, discussion, worship and personal liberty. The eleventh right said 'The rights of man are in his nature and cannot be changed. . . .'

It was a magnificent codification of all those principles within which Man could realize a full, rich, untrammelled way of life, and once released its authors and particularly Wells sat back hopefully.

'The discussion of Wells' articles was taken up in 29 countries,' Calder wrote. 'It even got on the front page of Mussolini's *Popolo d'Italia* and was attacked for a solid week by Fritzsche on Goebbels' radio. It was debated in full in India and had started in Holland the day the Germans marched in. That was why the Great Debate petered out—the phoney war ended and the world had more active preoccupations. To his dying day Wells still clung to the Rights of Man. . . .

'. . . It was proposed to drop [them] as the Wells Debate over Occupied Europe. But H. G. flatly refused to allow his name to be associated with it—saying that it would be "written off as Wellsian" whereas it had now assumed a world impress. Since, if it had gone out anonymously it would have had the weight of a Government statement, and since the Tories had opposed and boycotted the Debate because they said it was a Socialist device, a very great opportunity was lost through Wells' unusual self-abnegation.

'But he was very perturbed about the reactions and to some extent the indifference which it encountered in the East, until he decided, quite rightly, that the translation (done through the School of Oriental Studies) had retained, of course, the idiom of Western parliamentary democracy. He argued that one of the reasons why Sun Yat Sen's 1911 Chinese constitution had failed was because it, too, had tried to translate into the East a Western democracy which had no depth in oriental philosophy.

'Wells therefore sent it out to India, China and elsewhere and had it translated by Eastern philosophers. The results did not change the nature of the fundamental rights but gave them proper Oriental inflection. . . .'

Before the end the Rights of Man were put into Basic English, into Esperanto and translated into many languages; Mass Observation gave their advice, Mr. Harold Keeble made it into a micro-film, and hundreds of people set out voluntarily to spread the gospel. For nearly six months in one way or another the ferment went on. . . . Then it began to subside. By the twelfth month only a few trickles of discussion remained, and as they too evaporated the Rights ceased to be debated, and presently all was quiet again. Wells did not live to see the substance of his Rights translated into the United Nations Human Rights Convention, and now it came as an anti-climax for him. There should have been a great reverberation echoing round the world, reaching a crescendo of many million voices all demanding as one that this noble code be written into the Constitution of every country. There should have been sweeping tides of demonstrators until the earth rang to their feet and presently the Rights of Man, so long implicit in any sane society, became international law. But it amounted to nothing more than a burst of talk and publicity which lost its momentum in mid-Europe and mid-America, to die lamely in the wastes of Lapland and South America twelve months after it began. This had all the appearance of another failure. Wells had called upon the gods of science, invoked the novelist's art, raised his voice in the Fabian Society and the Labour Party, written great educative books, struck a universal note in millions of minds, but the full orchestra he looked for, the great diapason of Humanity, refused to respond, and as the last word of the Rights of Man died away without echo, something of the despair which had pressed on him from time to time, he at last admitted to everyday consciousness. *The Fate of*

Homo Sapiens published in 1939 said 'There is no reason whatever to believe that the order of nature has any greater bias in favour of man than it had in favour of the ichthyosaur or the pterodactyl. In spite of all my disposition to a brave looking optimism I perceive that now the universe is bored with him, is turning a hard face to him, and I see him being carried less and less intelligently, more and more rapidly, suffering as every ill-adapted creature must suffer in gross and detail, along the stream of fate to degradation, suffering and death.'

In the next few years his bouts of gloom deepened. Man, it seemed to him, remained the same feckless unheeding creature, refusing to see that other species had blindly fulfilled their fate and become extinct for the over-riding reason that they were incapable of shaping their own destinies. Man, granted this divine power, chose to ignore it. Given deliberation, the situation might have had the makings of a magnificent martyrdom, but there was no deliberation in the casual drifting of *homo sapiens* towards a brink of which it was either unaware, or did not wish to know.

*　　*　　*

The brink became rather clearer as war broke out again and the long barbarity of bombing began. Mounting in intensity it drove the inhabitants of Hanover Terrace away in ones and twos until the cook, Margaret the maid and H. G. were three of a comparative handful remaining. Several times blast blew in the heavy front door. Still H. G. continued to sleep upstairs. A bomb fell one night almost opposite the house. Wells went out with the help of the servants and put up a huge No. 13 beside the front door. Spectacularly, the dark gods of superstition must be put to the sword. To the glee and profound disturbance of the superstitious, just three years later the self-same gods struck again on the 13th day of the month, after their own highly coincidental fashion. For the moment the war continued to rage about H. G.'s head, and the unreality of a world where people grew accustomed to casual death, and the irrevocable flow of habit absorbed horrors from which the peace-time mind would have recoiled, had its moments of exhilaration.

The ways in which men made war were unendingly fascinating to Wells and there was a diabolic attraction for him in the glares which lit his windows night after night as the planes droned overhead and the scenes he had witnessed in his mind were re-enacted in all reality, until the earth quaked and the house rocked, and one night he was persuaded to stand and cackle at the maniacal mimicry of one bomb launched in answer to another—of Berlin bombed because London had been attacked—an odd shrivelled gnome of a man, evilly lit by the flash of guns. There were also moments of near exaltation. The feverish excitements of war on a scale unmatched in history sometimes carried him over into those higher reaches of personality where intimations of a different level of consciousness troubled him. It was the old detachment all over again. 'I seem to watch it all from outside, from somewhere inconceivably remote, out of time, out of space, out of the stress and tragedy of it all,' he had written in *The War of the Worlds*. In moods like this the grandiose visions returned. One species after another he saw rising and returning to the mud, whole races lifted their faces towards the sun and were obliterated, until he came at last to the end of the earth, when the dying fires of the worn-out sun no longer sustained man, giving giant crustaceans the last inheritance, life ending where it began—in the depths of the sea. But Man was now coming to a testing time of his own making, to an appalling moment of decision, and against the nightmare skies and the guns, doom seemed irrevocably his lot before the solar system had dissipated its energies. The mind of the race, racial consciousness, became 'just a gleam of conscious realization' passing from darkness to darkness. In moods like this Wells still spun beautiful sentences which read like poetry and fell to quoting the most unlikely people. . . . 'And all my thoughts and striving is to compose and gather into one thing what is a fragment and a riddle and a dismal accident. . . . And how could I bear to be man if man was not a poet and a solver of riddles and the saviour of accidents.' (Nietzsche).

1941 took him to the United States for the last time. Somerset Maugham met him and recorded in his *Writer's Notebook*: 'New York. H. G. has been here. He was looking old, tired and shrivelled. He was as perky as he has always been, but with something of an effort. His lectures were a failure. People couldn't hear what he said and didn't want to listen to what they could hear. They left in droves. He was hurt and disappointed. He couldn't understand why they were impatient with him for saying much the same sort of thing as he had been saying for the last thirty years. The river has flowed on and left him high and dry on the bank.' (3) It was true now. Perhaps he had said the same thing for even longer than thirty years. In the days of *A Modern Utopia* and *Anticipations* he could lecture and pontificate with every justification and complete success. In 1941–3 pontification was about to give way to blind anger and dismay. The tragic days were waiting, the days when he was utterly unable to understand why his 'dictatorship' had been refused.

*   *   *

A burst of optimism renewed itself in 1942. *The Conquest of Time* was a restatement of *First and Last Things* (1908) now remote, now considered 'mentally adolescent.' Pavlov, psycho-analysis and infinitely subtle theories of time, unfamiliar in 1908, were introduced into *The Conquest of Time*, and the humanities of *First and Last Things* now admitted a four dimensional universe, rigid, predestined, in some aspects Calvinistic. Our personalities had become 'serviceable synthetic illusions of continuity.' And 'the personal life is not a freedom, though it seems to us to be a freedom; it is a small subjective pattern of freedom in an unchanging all. There is no conflict between fate and free-will; they are major and minor aspects of existence. The major aspect of life is Destiny; the minor, that we do not know our destiny. We struggle because we must; and that struggle *is* life; but the parts of the drama we enact belong to a system that has neither beginning nor end.'

*   *   *

War dragging on interminably and half the peoples of the earth apparently more blind than they were in the beginning, writing become something of an effort, the light trying to the eyes, one's head susceptible to draughts, a brand new complaint threatened. . . . Damaged kidney, diabetes, weak heart, catarrh. Only one whole lung and kidney left to breathe and live by, he would say jokingly. A richly comic act of nature performed under one's very eyes, disintegrating hair, teeth, lungs, kidney, until it seemed in such a farcically crumbling world the head itself could not be long in going. When a friend fell ill now, it became occasion for a burst of bravura. As if these youngsters could hope to beat him at his own game, he who had been at it so long and so skilfully until death itself could hardly match the sustained achievements of sickness to which he laid claim.

He had written his own obituary which began: 'The name H. G. Wells who died yesterday afternoon of heart failure in the Paddington Infirmary at the age of 97 will have few associations for the younger generation. . . . The most interesting thing about Wells was his refusal to accept the social inferiority to which he seemed to have been born and the tenacity with which he insisted upon his role as the free citizen of a new world that was arising out of the débâcle. . . . His keenest feeling seems to have been a cold anger at intellectual and moral pretentiousness. . . .' (4)

In part for the ears of the Royal Society—still steadfastly refusing to entertain him as a Fellow—he plunged into a Thesis for a Doctorate of Science in London University, with the illuminating title: *A Thesis on the Quality of Illusion in the Continuity of the Individual Life in the Higher Metazoa with particular reference to the Species Homo Sapiens*. It was a curious document. It graced the psychology of Jung and Adler in the language of Wells, but added little, if anything, new to their thought. Presented by the average student, any professor would have marvelled at the vivid exposition and found it hard to grant a doctorate, but Wells won his, and now he chuckled in his sun-trap one day: 'That'll show the bastards . . . that'll show them,' referring to the distinguished gentlemen who reached down from the Royal Society clouds to add another to their number.

'An extraordinary amount of unhappiness has been and still is caused in the world by the failure to recognise the fluctuating quality of personality. . . .' (5) Wells wrote in his Thesis and it was as if he said to the Royal Society—don't judge me by my more abandoned moments alone. There is an echo of rationalization about some parts of the document. In place of Freud's ego he has Jung's persona, and the id, prowling in the subconscious, becomes the anima. A stirring and thrusting takes place on the edge of waking life, a number of states of semi-consciousness any of which, catching the persona off its guard, may take possession and taking possession take charge. The frustrated curate constantly dreaming of becoming the rake one day doffs his collar and his persona and plays the part. Wells had never become the rake but his persona willingly surrendered after its own inimitable fashion on several occasions. He was rather more richly endowed with varying states of consciousness than most people and had a considerable gift for giving them their head. He had lived this way many a time, and here was scientific explanation for what had disturbed friends and enemies alike. His persona, the person he pretended and intended to be, sometimes fought a losing battle with a number of 'aberrant drives and impulses' all trying to push the persona out of control, and when one or other of them succeeded, he had rushed off into extraordinarily unconventional antics, mentally slapping the face of his best friend or lifting forbidden skirts and crying—nothing is secret all things are mine ! Always in his life, many states of consciousness had clamoured for attention. At any moment he was likely to enter into one of them with a schoolboy's whoop of release and the beatific zest of the psychologist bent on plundering the subconscious. In part it was Wells and to some extent Jung. I do not pretend to any real knowledge of psychology, but the Thesis, whichever way one looked at it, was obviously something more than an elaborate piece of rationalization. It rang with many other notes, one at least of interest to the Royal Society which turned out to be stone deaf.

Wells was God's gift to psychiatry. He bombinated with complexes, he was loaded with the living lore of half a dozen case-book histories, and he would have detonated under the slightest touch from a tactless analyst, leaving the poor man with little more than the rag of his writing in his hand. That was the extraordinary thing about psychology. By explaining so much it explained so little.

Here it all was according to one psychological interpretation. The man once the boy emotionally malnourished by a mother who had to work, a boy doing outrageous things in his childhood to win the attention which showed that his mother cared; and the boy become the man carrying over his childhood habits into adult life, doing outrageous things to the world to make it take notice. . . . Was there lack of love in his childhood ? Did it explain the man ? A man who sought for the mother he never had in the many women he knew and loved, eternally trying to recover the childhood pattern of family relationships. A man recovering first of all the lawless freedoms of childhood, the irresponsibility, in such excess that even his inflamed ego was overtaken with a sense of guilt, of overdoing it, until he was driven to reconcile it by an overwhelming effort to become a World Citizen, because by becoming the World Citizen or World Scientist he would be absorbed back into the social stream again, a personality at one with cosmic processes. . . . For the last half of his life he was fiercely aware of the need to surrender the conceits of individuality to the larger life, to lose the vanities of self in the sweep of social purpose. 'Religious mystics have long had an apprehension of this ecstasy of self-forgetfulness in complete reunion with a greater being than themselves, but this enlargement comes to those fortunate scientific workers with a power of conviction beyond all precedent and beyond the power of any subsequent doubt . . .' he wrote in the Thesis. Yet psychology and the Thesis left a dark gulf.

The psychological was the pathological approach and where all the extraordinary twists in Herbert G. Wells had their psychopathic explanation, the psychiatrists fell silent when asked to explain his noble language, his vision, his inexhaustible fountain of ideas. . . . It was, anyway, late in the day to ask questions like that. The inexhaustible fountain had slackened. By 1945 there were signs of it running dry. He continued to write and behave as though it were just the same. In a strange, gloomy, rambling book called *Mind at the End of its Tether* (1945) which might have been Wells at the End of His Tether, he wrote. . . . 'The writer sees the world as a jaded world devoid of recuperative power. In the past he has liked to think that man could pull out of his entanglements and start a new creative phase of human living. In the face of our universal inadequacy that optimism has given place to a stoical cynicism. Man must go steeply up or down and the odds seem all in favour of his going down and out. . . .' The same thunder of words distinguishes occasional pages of *Mind at the End of its Tether*, the same serene detachment and moments of majesty; but it was an unhappy book, and illness alone cannot entirely explain its mood.

Wells wrote under sentence of death. The doctors had told him that he could not last another year. He was very frank about the doctors. . . . 'Instead of telling him to get his weight down, walk slowly upstairs, and avoid needless excitement, the excellent but perhaps overworked professional doctors gave alarming instructions to his heirs to prepare to take over at any time. . . .' A scare suddenly developed that his wasting body and other symptoms were possible signs of cancer and his son Gip had to decide whether to tell his father what they suspected. In the end he did and found the old man grateful. To make an obscurantist rite of death would have been the final insult to his slackening mind, dedicated to the high purposes of rational courage. But the scare was without foundation.

He made a will. For a man who had earned as much as £50,000 in one year, who had been paid £600 for one lecture and £333 for a single article, it could be complicated. A large sum of money went to one of his closest friends. Half a year's wages to each domestic servant if more than six months in his service. . . . £500 to his niece Jean Wells. . . . Set legacies for some he had loved and small sums to occasional people who had come in and out of his life. The residue split between his family and close friends.

*   *   *

The General Election came. Wells struggled from his bed to vote Labour. Gip and Marjorie Wells took him in a hired car to the polling booth. The returning officer brought a ballot paper down to him.

Soon there was a nurse and he needed help in half the small necessities of everyday living. Still he went down to the sun parlour, read the papers, played the gramophone, talked at visitors. 'I believe I should have carried out a real experiment or two just to prove . . .' he began one day, and fell asleep groping for the words. He was tired now, terribly tired as a sick child. Sometimes his rages remained undiminished and not his oldest friends were proof against a sudden explosion of temper. Sometimes towards the very end when he realized that all was lost and he could fight no more, he became gentle and more considerate to those surrounding him.

It was an unpleasant death Wells was dying. It wasted his body and sapped his energy. It was painful and mysterious. Any moment he knew the black curtain might descend on the midsummer scene, a sudden cessation probably without his knowledge. They used every trick of modern medicine to stay the day, but as the aches and discomforts grew, and the heart weakened, there were spells when he was infinitely miserable. It wasn't any longer worth it. The outlook for the world was only slightly less black than his own. Sometimes his growing helplessness sent him into swift ineffectual rages, if a wheezy teetering laugh arose as he looked down at his wreck of a body and suddenly found it comic.

Then he would go to the gramophone and play Mozart. There were hours when he sat in a mirthless coma, played out, drained of any reaction whatever, a breathing organism quite withdrawn into his own private world, and Mozart became his only intermediary with this.

He did not help the doctors by having queer ideas on his own body, swearing that there was no such thing as prostatitis, and refusing drugs for a time when they would have brought him rest and refreshment. He wanted no-one's pity and loathed to excite it. He hated admitting that he was so ill he needed a nurse. Still he worked. A scenario *The Way the World is Going* received sporadic attention. But the husk shrank visibly and the light in the eye died and his writing became more rambling, with a glow every now and then of the old glorious language haunting the page.

*　　　*　　　*

The summer of 1946 grew warm and beautiful. There was a lightness in the air as from a liberation to which the world was yet unaccustomed. Two or three times, in the panama hat and dark glasses, he descended the stairs to the garden. He would have liked to have gone more. Marjorie Wells would say to him: 'It would be nice if you could get down into the garden to-day,' and he answered ironically: 'It would be nice. . . .' He went through his letters as usual. He read the newspapers. Sometimes Marjorie read them for him. 'Anything there?' he would say and sometimes meant—'Anything about me?' There rarely was anything.

By July 1946, it seems he should have died months before. By August they wondered sometimes whether he would wake in the morning—the eyes stared out of so shrunken a form, the distress had become so intense—yet there he was, dawn after dawn, dragging on, sometimes quiescent and patient in a new way, sometimes touchily talkative and liable to fire off impossible questions with a glint of humour, sometimes morose, deeply miserable, an old man nodding in the half light of death. . . .

Until one afternoon he slept on. It was August 13th, 1946. He had rung the bell and asked the nurse to remove his pyjama jacket. He sat on the edge of the bed. Then he asked her to put the jacket on again and climbed into bed once more. 'Go away,' he said to the nurse, 'I'm all right.' The nurse went away for ten minutes. In that time, quite alone, he died. The nurse came and found him.

The thunderous news broke for half the world and somewhere out across the earth a shadow flitted, unlike any other in its day and age, and people who had come no closer to him than the pages of his *History*, felt the silence afterwards. Something bigger than H. G. Wells died that day. Something ceased to stir in the blood-stream of the modern mentality.

But it was late in the day for him to die. Fifteen years before when millions listened to his lightest word, there would have been a multitude from half the world to pay him homage. Now a handful of brilliant people went to the funeral at Golders Green Crematorium. No-one wore mourning. J. B. Priestley read the address. . . . 'We have come together to-day to say goodbye to our friend Herbert George Wells. . . . This was a man whose word was light in a thousand dark places. . . . When he was angry it was because he knew far better than we did that life need not be a sordid greedy scramble, and when he was impatient it was because he knew there were glorious gifts of body, mind and spirit only just beyond our present reach. . . .' The faintest movement ran through the small assembly. Death seemed closer to them all at this ceremonial moment of parting and such a death as this there had not been since Dickens vanished from the European scene. Priestley's voice went on '. . . let us say goodbye in his own words and not in ours. . . . "So far and beyond this adventure may continue, and our race survive. The impenetrable clouds that bound our life at last in every direction may hide innumerable trials and dangers, but there are no conclusive limitations even in their deeper shadows, and there are times and seasons, there are moods of exaltation—moments as it were of revelation—when the whole universe about us seems bright with the presence of as yet unimaginable things. . . ." '

APPENDIX

KINGSLEY MARTIN has said that Wells was the logical outcome of the long curve which ran from the Renaissance through the Encyclopædists to Huxley, a curve sustained by the conviction that man was a rational being, that once enlightened education had become universal and scientific techniques widely accepted, hunger, want and war could be controlled. Like Condorcet he wanted One World peopled by a race of cosmopolitans. But he suffered some confusion of identity between himself and the average person. Potentially everyone was Wells for him. Building around himself a world which gave him freedom, enrichment, a wealth of affection, he assumed that this private world could be projected into public affairs with equally happy results.

It was one of endless contradictions. Born into a lower-class background he should have become the rebel with undying faith in class warfare, yet it was a voluntary nobility in which he put his trust in the end. Devoted to the ways of science, his brave new worlds were more mystic than scientific. Impatient when people were not fired to action by his plans, they were plans largely incapable of practical interpretation. A devotee of collectivism, of the group, of the belief that the individual was only a biological device which would decline when it had outlived its use, he stood alone himself against half the world and spectacularly burst out of every group he joined. He was a prophet who expected to be honoured in his own land, a brilliant example of what the ordinary man could become with grave misgivings about the proletariat, an atheist who came close to building his own religion, a man with nine separate lives who wanted a tenth; and yet something there was which held together the whole mass of contradictions, a consistent body of thought illumining many dark corners of the British social scene.

Take the nine lives one by one. . . . As a novelist he brought enlightenment and entertainment to an audience at least as large as Dickens', yet for all his warm, crowded books, his great comic characters, his evocation of every type and kind of scene, he was hopelessly impatient of form, of those subtle patterns of fiction which constitute one part of the novelist's art, not as mere technique forced upon the raw material of life, but as a means of making the written word more real. He threw his people on paper with as much vitality as carelessness, he recorded love and laughter and all the broad experiences, he ran over and away whenever the whim took him, but if every other page was pulsating with life it was more the product of his own gusto than the independent blood of self-sustained characters. There was an unfortunate tendency for his characters to talk not at one another but at the reader, and if you listened sharply enough you would catch a faint squeakiness, somewhere on the air, not difficult to identify. Many of them were very self-conscious characters. They never forgot that they were under observation. Nor could they forget the society to which they belonged. Time and again the roar of the social machinery rose and drowned their voices and it was Wells' peculiar distinction that he encouraged the roar until it vibrated in every voice, and he became the classic example of the novelist who allowed social problems to dominate his novels. It was simple enough for Dickens to reveal the festering slum of Fagin, show the malignant powers of poverty, break open the prisons to the appalled outward eye, evoke the mannerisms of his time in endless and exciting caricature; this was to lift the curtain on dark personal eddies and not to go to the bottom of the pool. It was to dramatize debauchery and squalor, win human pity, and look for some grand gesture from the social gods which would bring harmony and happiness back into a number of broken lives, with all the patronage of high grade charity. It never asked for any essential change in the frame of the society within which such ugly pictures were displayed. With Wells, the frame of the novel, the social values and background, were constantly 'splintering into the picture.' It did not happen by accident. He gave it a deliberate, loudly proclaimed shove. 'We [novelists] are going to deal with political questions and religious questions and social questions. We cannot present people unless we have this free hand, this unrestricted field. What is the good of telling stories about people's lives if one may not deal freely with religious beliefs and organizations that have controlled or failed to control them. . . . The novelist is going to be the most potent of artists because he is going to present conduct, devise conduct, discuss conduct, analyse conduct, suggest conduct, illuminate it through and through. . . .' *The Contemporary Novel* [*1912*.]

Wells loved doing violence to the prevailing literary modes. He kicked against the accepted conventions of the novel as he made the novel kick against society. In his early writing days the scale of social values seemed immutably fixed for all time, fiction was read by people who believed that right would automatically prevail, and it was as well to work within these two accepted formulas, showing, if you must, the ugly twists forced upon certain unstable characters by fortuitous circumstance, but never questioning the stability of the underlying code. Sir Walter Scott flourished against such a background. Salvation was an individual choice open to anyone and no society could, by its own machinations, condemn you to eternal damnation. Dickens accepted this immutability, but rebelled against individual hardship. Thackeray, Trollope and Jane Austen had been more concerned with the inner life of character, and society became a backcloth to be brought artistically alive. Then came Wells to develop the shapeless, exuberant tradition of Smollett, Sterne, Dickens, to insist that nothing was immutable, not even the splendidly embrasured canons of convention which occasionally saluted their own timelessness, or the so long venerated system; to insist that the novel had other purposes than entertainment and enlightenment. Swift and Defoe had used the novel to savagely satirical ends, but it had never, in their day, deeply swayed the ordinary man and woman to action. Richard Henry Dana had written *Two Years Before the Mast* in 1840 and stirred public opinion to soften the seaman's lot. There were many other literary sounding boards. The novel constantly illumined the dark corners of the social scene. But now came Wells to use the novel not only as a sounding board, not only to write a novel with a purpose, openly importunate about the realities of physical love and alive with social implications, but to use it as a means of *action*. Under his hand the novel became the equivalent of the social or political instrument; or far more so than in any novelist before him.

Between them Wells and James profoundly influenced the modern novel. There had been a somnambulistic certainty about its development. Character, form, structure and plot overhung all criticism, the accepted canons of the art, but character grew to overwhelm everything else, and character, as Henry James knew it, had its roots in the Renaissance humanists who pressed forward from man in society to the individual dominating society. An inevitable time-lag between philosophic thought and its effect on society tended to smother their connection, and it was hard to say where the changing conception of man's nature broke into the world of fiction, but break it always did at length. In Shakespeare's day man was supreme, the crowning glory of the universe, quite unchallenged by the immortal protozoa. 'What a piece of work is a man !' By the eighteenth century a new twist appeared in Pope's 'The glory, jest and riddle of the world.' Then the mechanistic philosophies of Huxley rose in the nineteenth century to encourage, still more, eighteenth century doubts, the way was opened for critical questionings of heroism itself, and Wells burst on the scene. He remained for a time the fictional counterpart of T. H. Huxley. It was Man not men that mattered, the race not the individual, but James held up his hands in well-bred horror at any such barbarism and continued to exercise his brilliant gifts on situations which, for Wells, bore all the marks of triviality. The novel divided into two schools, one preoccupied with probing the very ganglia of super-sensitized individuals, deeply imprisoned in the beautiful palaces of their own sensibilities, the other involved with man as part of a community, concerned to interpret one reacting on the other. The novel is still so divided. Somerset Maugham, J. B. Priestley, Joyce Cary and R. C. Hutchinson would be suffocated in the secret places of Proust, Elizabeth Bowen and possibly Sartre. And if there are many average readers to-day, people who make up the bulk of the novel-reading public, who gasp with relief that the old gusto of story-telling, the boisterous and profound moments of conflict between a human being and his environment, and sheer creative exuberance still exist to prevent this tenuous chiselling at the last nerves of introspection from causing a permanent state of literary toothache, Wells was not, in his last years, of their number. He hated intricate investigation of exiguous experiences, but he also abandoned in the end, the story.

In his middle and best years it was different. Let all be simple, frank and without tricks, he cried, let politics and government, gas and gaiters have their full place, and none shall stay the hand of science crying for action. But it all led to a curious disappointment. Action—violent, threatened, or carefully planned—sometimes followed in the wake of his novels, although a burst of conversational bravado more often took its place. The novel itself did not benefit from the method. Instead of giving greater depth to his work, it merely, too often, sent shuddering creaks through the whole structure as the strain of social purpose became more blatant. The dramatic form of the novel was, in one sense, a device for distilling values, social or otherwise, out of character, and reflecting the society which threw them up. It groaned under the unaccustomed weight of a sociological tract. Too often Wells self-consciously portrayed as social background or abstract idea what should have fermented and finally swum to the surface from the primal consciousness of character. By widening his scope he achieved no greater depth of awareness. The result is clear in too many novels.

But he remained, in his early and middle years, a born story-teller, a novelist with moments of original genius, a man with so much teeming literary life, a pen that snapped and sparkled with such vivid observations—like his eyes—he could never be dull. There was also at least one novel rich in all levels of awareness. *Tono-Bungay* is charged with the consciousness of Uncle George caught in a web of destiny, of human beings irrevocably trapped by their own stupidity, struggling to break the order of things to their wills, and occasionally, for a little space, pathetically believing in their success. The struggling fly, wrought upon by the innumerable, conflicting tensions of half the universe, becomes more significant as a writer succeeds in bringing those tensions into his novels. Wells does not really succeed. A hint comes out of the darkness; nothing more. 'The strangeness that is a presence standing by our side,' seldom materialises. Deeper, primal impulses occasionally beat up from the depths in *Tono-Bungay*. There is, towards the end, a sense of man placed not only in the sordid hovel of his own irrational making, but in the stream of life, and the sweep of disillusion eventually carries him over into a new, groping awareness of a level of consciousness beyond the edge of life. This fourth dimension reappears occasionally in other novels, but it is never developed. There are others again—*Mr. Polly* and *Kipps*—guaranteed at least longevity by reason of the special alchemy which finds universality in everyday events, great comic scenes and natural, unstrained life; but what they have to say has long become a cliché. *The Undying Fire*, for some reason obscured by lesser books, remains a noble and profound religious work, and the sudden revival of comic genius in *You Can't Be Too Careful* has never received proper recognition.

Wells had no illusions about the great bulk of his novels. The best works of art he felt were impermanent. 'All art, all science, and still more certainly, all writing are experiments in statement. There will come a time for every work of art when it will have served its purpose.' (1) He thought the waters of oblivion would steadily overwhelm his books, and the first to go would be the novels about love and sex which had served their purpose in their day, and were now interesting as period pieces, as evidence of the pettifogging, self-righteously stupid streak in social codes, and behind the codes, man. They were novels with a purpose and by its very nature that streak doomed them to early decay as the problems each one posed were resolved or proved beyond the power of every literary solvent. *Love and Mr. Lewisham*, *The Sea Lady*, *Marriage*, *The Wife of Sir Isaac Harman* are read with deeply diminished interest to-day. The tide of oblivion creeps up.

With the scientific romances the original freshness of many of them is gone for good as modern knowledge advances, but *The Time Machine* remains as fascinating as ever and it would be a crassly stupid society which did not continue to recognize the macabre power of *The Island of Dr. Moreau* as much for its own good as anything else. No-one has appeared since Wells with anything like his genius for scientific romance.

But the romances, the big novels, the short stories, all the important creative fiction stops short at 1920, with the one exception perhaps of *You Can't Be Too Careful*. 'We should not,' wrote Bagehot of Dickens, 'like to have to speak in detail of [his] later works.' He could have written it of Wells' later fiction. The likeness in temperament, love affairs, humour, gusto and fantastic habits between Dickens and Wells has been richly explored. They shared the same fine indignations, comic effervescence. They were immensely fecund. Something of the untutored genius drove them both, and Dickens' emotional relationships with Maria Beadnell and Ellen Ternan bade fair to outrival Wells', and he was no less skilled in turning women to literary account. But there were many people in Wells unknown to Dickens.

The novelist among them lost his individual life in 1920. A phantom shape resembling the person who had written *Kipps* and

Tono-Bungay sometimes broke out afterwards, but faltered and failed as the world-maker blustered in. Indeed the power to step into life was denied his nine selves, one by one, over the years, until by 1930, only one, or possibly two remained, encrusted with many vestigial remnants long since voiceless, granted a dubious integration under many deaths.

Dragon-slaying became an obsession from then on and for the last part of his life too many of the dragons turned out to be made of paper. If only he had stuck to his novel writing, learnt the patience inseparable from great art, nurtured his natural powers and completely liberated the flashing stream which broke through, with such force, towards the end of *Tono-Bungay*, he might have swept Dickens and half a dozen others to the wall. Or imagine the comic genius in him given its head. Already Artie Kipps, Mr. Hoopdriver and Bert Smallways are acknowledged in the same world as Sam Weller, the Micawbers and Mr. Wemmick, and what Dickens did so well came as naturally to Wells. He could have led the laughter of his generation with a zest and fecundity at least the equal of Dickens—and with more penetration—if Sir Thomas More had not dragged at his shoulders, and the mantle of a major prophet fallen so eloquently into place about him. The compromise did more than suffocate the novelist. By dividing his attention, half of what he did in fiction, prophecy and world-making became second rate. And if his second rate fiction still won him world acclaim, the peculiarly fertile ground of the last decade of the nineteenth century, with Dickens, Meredith, Hardy and Thackeray past their prime, Jane Austen and Trollope ceasing to appeal to the mind of the new reading public created by the Education Act of 1870, and publishers clamouring for new writers as the great Victorian gods declined, was particularly propitious for Wells. There were many lesser lights to satisfy the clamour —Conan Doyle, Mrs. Humphry Ward, Hall Caine, but everything was ripe for the writer with something to say. . . . Wells had everything to say. Very often he said it with distinction. In fiction he might have said it with profound insight. Sometimes he came close to it. One at least of the novels was great. But in the end he threw his genius away.

There were too many dragons waiting to be slain, even if some bore the birth-marks of his own imagination, and there were eight other lives to live and time was short. He must hurry. He might miss something. The world was a hasty place and he the most impulsive of men. The educator, the scientist, the lover, the world-maker, the prophet, all clamoured to be heard, clamoured with the passionate conviction that each one mattered more than the last. He knew very well he could not be first a novelist, first a teacher, first a great comic writer, first a prophet without also being something of a quack. First a prophet. What did he amount to as a prophet? It is one of the legends sustained by the newspaper world that Wells had the gift of second sight or something very close to it. The evidence is not altogether convincing. He foresaw the motor car, the tank, the aeroplane and the atom bomb, he pictured the war in the air and he glimpsed—as no one else—a promised land as rich and full and bountiful as any vision vouchsafed Moses. But how he could blunder. London, Berlin, St. Petersburg would, he wrote, increase their populations to well over 20,000,000; and New York, Philadelphia and Chicago would probably and Hankow almost certainly reach 40,000,000. *Anticipations* implied that 'the struggle between any two naval powers on the high seas . . . will not last more than a week or so. . . .' The main naval manœuvre in the same book seemed to be that of one ironclad ramming another. At one point he had pathetic faith in the balloon as a weapon of war and was inclined to think that 'the many considerations against the successful attack on balloons from the ground, will enormously stimulate enterprise and invention in the direction of dirigible aerial devices that can fight. . . .' (2) In the same period he did not 'think it at all probable that aeronautics will ever come into play as a serious modification of transport and communication. . . .' (3) As for the submarine, 'I must confess that my imagination in spite even of spurring, refuses to see any sort of submarine do anything but suffocate its crew and founder at sea. . . . You may, of course, throw out a torpedo or so, with as much chance of hitting vitally as you would have if you were blindfold. . . .' (4) Russia at one point would never amount to more than another vaster Ireland. Paranoiac leaders like Hitler were dramatically dismissed in *Anticipations* many years before Hitler reached the zenith of his power. . . . 'It is improbable that ever again will any flushed, undignified man with a vast voice, a muscular face in incessant operation, collar crumpled, hair disordered and arms in wild activity talking . . . copiously . . . rise to be the most powerful thing in any democratic state in the world. Continually the individual vocal demagogue dwindles. . . .' (5) In September 1914 he said that this, the greatest of all wars was not just another war—it was a war to end war. In September 1916 he was said to have staked his reputation as a prophet on a declaration that Germany would capitulate in the following June. As to the military power of France. . . . 'I find no reason to doubt the implication of M. Bloch that on land to-day the French are relatively far stronger than they were in 1870, that the evolution of military expedients has been all in favour of the French character and intelligence, and that even single-handed war between France and Germany to-day might have a very different issue from that former struggle. . . .' And civilian morale under bombing. . . . 'Wells imagined cities destroyed and the inhabitants flying in terror. He imagined the soldiers called out to keep order and the conditions of martial law and total anarchy. He imagined mass terror and riot. He did not reckon with the nature, the moral resources, the habits of civilised man.' (V. S. Pritchett: *The Living Novel*.) No, he was a considerable, but not after all divinely inspired prophet.

As a politician he described himself as revealing all the characteristics of a liberal democrat in the sense that he claimed an unlimited right to think and criticize, some meeting place with the Fascists in his desire for domination by a select hierarchy, and Socialist tendencies in his antagonism to what he called 'personal, racial, or national monopolization.' As sociologist he was captivated by the light and colour of the new society, but quite without street names or numbers or machinery. His creative grasp of the possibilities of planning and the implications of scientific data performed brilliant imaginative feats to bring them home to the average man, but he had no notion what to do with the raw material of the new society once he had conjured it out of the air.

As educator ? As educator he outstripped the schools and the pettifogging teachers, and brought enormous panoramas of learning within the grasp of the ordinary individual, making the obscure simple, conveying the sheer excitement of intellectual discovery and doing it all with a disinterested honesty which gave each new book a vivacity quite alien to the schoolroom. It may be true that Wells never influenced the intellectuals or thinkers of his day. Aldous Huxley raised a languid eyebrow and turned to more erudite idols, Einstein applauded and retired to his tower,

Bertrand Russell worshipped similar gods but drew his inspiration from a pool of mathematics, William James waited on logic and psychology, and James Joyce and the Sitwells listened to notes Wells had never even heard. They all thought Wells a little wonder in his way and some envied him the eminence and adoration which went with his work; but he was no pundit in their eyes. It was the masses he touched and moved and perhaps he touched them most deeply as the educator.

There were so many roles. Yet if he succeeded in some and failed in others, he had no driving desire to sustain many of the incarnations he achieved or tried. He could, in the end, have dispensed with the great educator, he did not so fiercely covet the prophet's mantle, and even novel writing, in which profound satisfactions lay, lost some of its colour and attraction. In all these things where popular success came easily, it did not mean half so much to him as failure elsewhere. For at heart it seems Herbert George Wells believed in his Utopia, was prepared to give all the rest to see it realized in his lifetime and had an obsessive desire to become a great scientist in it. These twin urges drove him into great books, the last thesis, abuse of the Royal Society, and occasional moods of choking despair. For the senselessness of a society granted unimaginable powers which it could not bring to heel for its own happiness, finally left him no alternative but despair. And yet . . . having all the appearance of disillusion with the world, it was in part disillusion with himself. Inadequacies in his message grew on him with the years. It should have compelled the world's compliance and did nothing of the kind. Such was his power of evocation that the lightest breath from *The Modern Utopia*, *The New Machiavelli*, or *Clissold* brings the spirit of the thing flooding back and the unseen tide of *The Open Conspiracy* surges up again, but try to immerse yourself in its beautiful waters and they turn to foam and frothing nothingness, and nowhere is there any compulsion to risk the immersion. At touch and sight and smell Wells' world of A.D. 2500 evaporates. Try to grasp the substance and it becomes a shadow. It never really existed. What should have had the weight and measurement and solidity of the scientific method he so dearly loved, turned out to be a mystical aspiration. It did so for two reasons.

Wells had mistaken his vocation. By temperament an artist and by training a scientist, the conflict between the two remained to the end of his days, and it was inevitable that when the artist broke out of his real world into sociology he brought solutions which were intrinsically artistic. They had all the emotional surge of the artist. They had form and colour. They were highly subjective projections of Wells' own way of life, an attempt to make the cold, material outside world—as Scott-James has put it—susceptible to private ideals. One is driven to repeat—if only he had nurtured his genius in its own soil instead of hiring it out to science. But the artist broke into alien territory, and it was typical of the artist turned world-maker that he should brush aside enormous complications with a sweep of words only to leave them firmly in being. . . . Fierce racial differences showed no sign of surrender under his onslaughts. The sanctity of the human person remained without validity for half the world, economic jugglery was only just beginning to look beyond its own frontiers, science steadfastly refused to yield up discoveries for supra-national use and a vast body of people still could not look outside their own narrow interests to the inspiration of wider loyalties. Man was still a jealous creature, driven by cramped motives, conditioned through many years of suffering and deception to ungenerosity and only dimly aware that serenity and happiness did not lie this way. In moments of profounder consciousness the primal impulse prevailed and Man, told by some seventh racial sense that the unsordid act reconciled all the rest, performed it; from which it was clear that one day Wells' noble beliefs would come into their own. They were implicit in mankind. But now he was ten generations before his time and what he saw in a glass he saw darkly. He was a music-maker, a dreamer of sociological dreams. He belonged to the world of Plato and mistook it for the world of Pythagoras. Indeed the Golden Class of Plato's Republic would probably have found Wells' Samurai very palatable people. But modern man, staunchly idolatrous of film stars, equipped with secondary school education and knowing a thing or two about government, had a tendency to sniff. He knew better. He knew and had known for half a generation, that federal control of the air, if not World Government, was desirable. The problem was how to get it.

* * *

When Wells' brain first 'squinted and bubbled at the Universe' 80 years before, the world had been a very different place and it was difficult now to find one in the other. Queen Victoria had been gone half a century. The telephone no longer seemed like sorcery, the stiffness of clothes and conventions had relaxed, the deep division between worker and employer lost its edge. A new morality born of Socialism had redistributed the national income and the great mass structures of rich and poor had virtually vanished. The relations between the sexes were deeply changed. The Hero as a figure had lost much of his appeal, and the old gods of individuality, self-reliance, adventure, were giving place to group loyalty and a social sense. Reason was beginning to take the place of convention as a touchstone, service becoming important alongside self, and if the aristocratic humanities which Wells epitomized in his Samurai were now replaced by the statistical analyses of the social scientists, and there was a tendency for academics and university professors to fill the role once occupied by the Keir Hardies and Cunningham-Grahames, there was no doubt that the release of rational characteristics in the mass mind we know to-day owed more to this than any other single man. Wells 'was one of the creators of modern man.' (6) His flood of words and torrential vitality forced the birth of the modern mentality. He fought passionately for the One World which must, long after our ashes are dust, realize itself. Perhaps, after all, he had not thrown his genius away in vain. Perhaps the sacrifice was worth it, was necessary, was demanded of him. He had taught millions to think. He had influenced three generations. He had cleared great jungles of hypocrisy and cant, and mercilessly reiterated the message which the atom-bomb in one apocalyptic stride finally forced on an unwilling world—that social techniques must be reconciled with scientific techniques. But in the end it was something simpler than any of this by which he would be remembered. His brilliant imaginative powers had unlocked new ways of life hidden in dull, scientific data until we were self-conscious at a profound level of emotional understanding of the greatness within our grasp, and in his own ineffable fashion he had left a glorious sense of expectancy on the air, which remains to-day. We knew now that life need not be like this. We were as impatient as he was because beautiful 'gifts of mind, body and spirit were only just beyond our present reach. . . .' (7) He prepared us for communion with the creative society to come. In the year 2500, some gathering of the Samurai, in a world freed from war, want and frustration, looking out on its sunny spacious life, may remember H. G. Wells as the man who wrote *A Modern Utopia*, *The Time Machine* and *Tono-Bungay*. Some of his books they may continue to read for pleasure. But if they completely fail to see a portrait of themselves in any, they will yet be aware of an indefinable climate in his work, an all-pervading sense as it were of *rational revelation*, familiar to their own highest persuasions.

BIBLIOGRAPHY

EXPERIMENT IN AUTOBIOGRAPHY, H. G. Wells. Victor Gollancz, Cresset Press (1934).
H. G. WELLS, Geoffrey West. Gerald Howe (1930).
PILGRIMAGE (four volumes), Dorothy Richardson. Dent, Cresset Press (1938).

*   *   *

THE RELIGION OF H. G. WELLS, Alexander H. G. Craufurd. T. Fisher Unwin (1909).
THE LIFE OF BENJAMIN DISRAELI, W. F. Monypenny and G. E. Buckle. John Murray (1910–20).
SHOP SLAVERY AND EMANCIPATION, William Paine. King (1912).
PERSONALITY IN LITERATURE, R. A. Scott-James. Secker (1913).
HISTORY OF MIDHURST GRAMMAR SCHOOL, Ernest F. Row. Combridge, Hove (1913).
THE NEW NOVEL, Henry James. Macmillan (1914).
H. G. WELLS, J. D. Beresford. Nisbet (1915).
THE WORLD OF H. G. WELLS, Van Wyck Brooks. Unwin (1915).
HISTORY OF THE FABIAN SOCIETY, Edward R. Pease. Fifield (1916).
SIX MAJOR PROPHETS, E. E. Slosson. Little, Brown & Co. (1917).
LETTERS, William James. Longmans, Green (1920).
H. G. WELLS, Édouard Guyot. Paris (1920).
LETTERS, Henry James. Macmillan (1920).
QUEEN VICTORIA, Lytton Strachey. Chatto & Windus (1921).
LE ROMAN ANGLAIS DE NOTRE TEMPS, Abel Chevalley. Humphrey Milford (1921).
H. G. WELLS, R. T. Hopkins. Cecil Palmer (1922).
UNIVERSITY OF LONDON ELECTION ADDRESS, H. G. Wells. H. Finer (1923)
H. G. WELLS, Ivor Brown. Nisbet (1923)
MEN OF LETTERS, Dixon Scott. Bookman Library (1923).
H. G. WELLS: EDUCATIONALIST, F. H. Doughty. Cape (1926).
CONRAD'S LIFE AND LETTERS, G. Jean-Aubry. Heinemann (1927).
THE BOOK OF CATHERINE WELLS, Introduction, H. G. Wells. Chatto & Windus (1928).
FOUR CONTEMPORARY NOVELISTS, Wilbur L. Cross. Macmillan (1930).
POINTS OF VIEW, Various Authors. Allen & Unwin (1930).
PEN PORTRAITS AND REVIEWS, Bernard Shaw. Constable (1931).
JOURNAL (three volumes), Arnold Bennett. Cassell (1932–33).

THE IDEA IN FICTION, H. W. Leggett. Allen & Unwin (1934).
AUTOBIOGRAPHY, G. K. Chesterton. Hutchinson (1936).
POETS AND PROPHETS, André Maurois. Cassell (1936).
ENGLISH SAGA, Arthur Bryant. Collins; Eyre & Spottiswoode (1940).
MR. CHURCHILL, Philip Guedalla. Hodder & Stoughton (1941).
BRITISH WORKING CLASS POLITICS, G. D. H. Cole. Routledge (1941).
G. K. CHESTERTON, Maisie Ward. Sheed & Ward (1944).
CHARLES DICKENS, Una Constance Birch. Chatto and Windus (1945).
CRITICAL ESSAYS, George Orwell. Secker & Warburg (1946).
LETTERS, Lord Olivier. Allen & Unwin (1948).
THE BOOK OF GREAT CONVERSATIONS, Simon Schuster (1949).
MAKERS OF THE LABOUR MOVEMENT, Margaret Cole. Longmans, Green (1948).
OUR PARTNERSHIP, Beatrice Webb. Longmans, Green (1948).
THE LIVING NOVEL, V. S. Pritchett. Chatto and Windus (1949).
A WRITER'S NOTEBOOK, S. Maugham. Heinemann (1948).

Other Sources

MY OBITUARY—H. G. WELLS, *Coronet Magazine*, 1937.
The Idea of a World Encyclopedia, Lecture, H. G. Wells, Royal Institution, 1936.
Talk by Anthony West, *The Listener*, 1949.
Articles (anonymous) on H. G. Wells, *The Times Literary Supplement*, 1947.
Three Articles by Odette Keun, *Time and Tide*, 1934.
Lecture by Kingsley Martin, Shaw Society, 1949.
THE REDISCOVERY OF THE UNIQUE (H. G. WELLS), *Fortnightly Review*, 1891.
HUXLEY, by H. G. Wells, *Royal College of Science Magazine*, 1901.
MY LUCKY MOMENT (H. G. WELLS), *View*, 1911.
H. G. Wells Confesses to W. R. Titterton, *Daily Herald*, 1930.
WELLS, by Bernard Shaw, *The New Statesman and Nation*, 1946.
Article in *Contact*, (Kingsley Martin), 1946.
A SELECT CONVERSATION, 1911, Ralph Straus.
The Will of H. G. Wells, 1946.

Casual articles in *The Times Literary Supplement, News Chronicle, Daily Express, Evening Standard, Sunday Chronicle*, a large number of obituaries in *The Times, Manchester Guardian*, the *New Statesman and Nation, Daily Graphic, News Chronicle* and many other papers. An excellent and very full dossier on H. G. Wells generously made available to me by a London daily newspaper. A large number of letters and postcards from Edward Pease, Ritchie Calder, Frank Horrabin, Ralph Straus, Dorothy M. Richardson, etc.

People consulted: Fenner Brockway; Baroness Budberg; Ritchie Calder; Colin Coote; Frank Horrabin; Gertrude Hutchinson; Harold J. Laski; H. W. Leggett; Robin Lawrence; Kingsley Martin; Somerset Maugham; Jack Murphy; Hermon Ould; Edward Pease; Hugh Pilcher; Dorothy M. Richardson; Ralph Straus; Eric Trist.

BOOKS AND PAMPHLETS BY H. G. WELLS

TEXT BOOK OF BIOLOGY. The Tutorial Series (1893).
SELECT CONVERSATIONS WITH AN UNCLE. Lane (1895).
THE TIME MACHINE. Heinemann (1895).
THE STOLEN BACILLUS. Methuen (1895).
THE WONDERFUL VISIT. Dent (1895).
THE ISLAND OF DR. MOREAU. Heinemann (1896).
THE WHEELS OF CHANCE. Dent (1896).
THE PLATTNER STORY AND OTHERS. Methuen (1897).
THE INVISIBLE MAN. Pearson (1897).
CERTAIN PERSONAL MATTERS. Lawrence & Bullen (1897).
THE WAR OF THE WORLDS. Heinemann (1898).
WHEN THE SLEEPER WAKES. Harper (1899).
(Revised edition, THE SLEEPER AWAKES. Nelson (1910).)
TALES OF SPACE AND TIME. Harper (1899).
LOVE AND MR. LEWISHAM. Harper (1900).
THE FIRST MEN IN THE MOON. Newnes (1901).
ANTICIPATIONS. Chapman & Hall (1901).
THE DISCOVERY OF THE FUTURE. Unwin (1902).
THE SEA LADY. Methuen (1902).
MANKIND IN THE MAKING. Chapman & Hall (1903).
TWELVE STORIES AND A DREAM. Macmillan (1903).
THE FOOD OF THE GODS. Macmillan (1904).
A MODERN UTOPIA. Chapman & Hall (1905).
KIPPS. Macmillan (1905).
IN THE DAYS OF THE COMET. Macmillan (1906).
THE FUTURE IN AMERICA. Chapman & Hall (1906).
SOCIALISM AND THE FAMILY. Fifield (1906).
THIS MISERY OF BOOTS. Fabian Society (1907).
NEW WORLDS FOR OLD. Constable (1908).
FIRST AND LAST THINGS. Constable (1908).
THE WAR IN THE AIR. Bell (1908).
TONO-BUNGAY. Macmillan (1909).
ANN VERONICA. Unwin (1909).
THE HISTORY OF MR. POLLY. Nelson (1910).
THE NEW MACHIAVELLI. Lane (1911).

THE COUNTRY OF THE BLIND AND OTHER STORIES. Nelson (1911).
FLOOR GAMES. Palmer (1911).
MARRIAGE. Macmillan (1912).
LITTLE WARS. Palmer (1913).
THE PASSIONATE FRIENDS. Macmillan (1913).
AN ENGLISHMAN LOOKS AT THE WORLD. Cassell (1914).
THE WORLD SET FREE. Macmillan (1914).
THE WIFE OF SIR ISAAC HARMAN. Macmillan (1914).
THE WAR THAT WILL END WAR. Palmer (1914).
BOON, THE MIND OF THE RACE, THE WILD ASSES OF THE DEVIL, AND THE LAST TRUMP. Unwin (1915).
BEALBY. Methuen (1915).
THE RESEARCH MAGNIFICENT. Macmillan (1915).
MR. BRITLING SEES IT THROUGH. Cassell (1916).
THE ELEMENTS OF RECONSTRUCTION. Nisbet (1916).
WAR AND THE FUTURE. Cassell (1917).
GOD THE INVISIBLE KING. Cassell (1917).
THE SOUL OF A BISHOP. Cassell (1917).
JOAN AND PETER. Cassell (1918).
THE UNDYING FIRE. Cassell (1919).
THE OUTLINE OF HISTORY. Newnes (1920).
RUSSIA IN THE SHADOWS. Hodder & Stoughton (1920).
THE SALVAGING OF CIVILISATION. Cassell (1921).
WASHINGTON AND THE HOPE OF PEACE. Collins (1922).
THE SECRET PLACES OF THE HEART. Cassell (1922).
A SHORT HISTORY OF THE WORLD. Cassell (1922).
MEN LIKE GODS. Cassell (1923).
THE DREAM. Cape (1924).
THE STORY OF A GREAT SCHOOLMASTER. Chatto & Windus (1924).
CHRISTINA ALBERTA'S FATHER. Cape (1925).
THE WORLD OF WILLIAM CLISSOLD. Benn (1926).
MR. BELLOC OBJECTS. Watts (1926).
MEANWHILE. Benn (1927).
COLLECTED SHORT STORIES. Benn (1927).
MR. BLETTSWORTHY ON RAMPOLE ISLAND. Benn (1928).
THE OPEN CONSPIRACY. Gollancz (1928).
THE AUTOCRACY OF MR. PARHAM. Heinemann (1930).
THE SCIENCE OF LIFE (with Professor J. S. Huxley and G. P. Wells). Cassell (1931).
WHAT ARE WE TO DO WITH OUR LIVES? Heinemann (1931).
AFTER DEMOCRACY. Watts & Co. (1932).
THE WORK, WEALTH AND HAPPINESS OF MANKIND. Heinemann (1932).
THE BULPINGTON OF BLUP. Hutchinson (1932).
THE SHAPE OF THINGS TO COME. Hutchinson (1933).

BIBLIOGRAPHY

STALIN-WELLS TALK, (Pamphlet *New Statesman*), (1934).
EXPERIMENT IN AUTOBIOGRAPHY. Victor Gollancz, Cresset Press (1934).
THE ANATOMY OF FRUSTRATION. Cresset Press (1936).
THE CROQUET PLAYER. Chatto & Windus (1936).
STAR BEGOTTEN. Chatto & Windus (1937).
BRYNHILD. Methuen (1937).
THE CAMFORD VISITATION. Methuen (1937).
THE BROTHERS. Chatto & Windus (1938).
WORLD BRAIN. Methuen (1938).
APROPOS OF DOLORES. Cape (1938).
THE HOLY TERROR. Michael Joseph (1939).
TRAVELS OF A REPUBLICAN RADICAL IN SEARCH OF HOT WATER. Penguin
    (1939).
THE FATE OF HOMO SAPIENS. Secker & Warburg (1939).
THE NEW WORLD ORDER. Secker & Warburg (1940).
THE RIGHTS OF MAN. Penguin (1940).
THE COMMONSENSE OF WAR AND PEACE. Penguin (1940).
BABES IN THE DARKLING WOOD. Secker & Warburg (1940).
ALL ABOARD FOR ARARAT. Secker & Warburg (1940).
GUIDE TO THE NEW WORLD. Victor Gollancz (1941).
YOU CAN'T BE TOO CAREFUL. Secker & Warburg (1941).
THE OUTLOOK FOR HOMO SAPIENS. Secker & Warburg (1942).
SCIENCE AND THE WORLD MIND. New Europe Publishing Co. (1942).
PHŒNIX: A SUMMARY OF THE INESCAPABLE CONDITIONS OF WORLD
    REORGANISATION. Secker & Warburg (1942).
THE CONQUEST OF TIME. Watts (1942).
CRUX ANSATA: AN INDICTMENT OF THE ROMAN CATHOLIC CHURCH.
    Penguin (1943).
'42 TO '44: A CONTEMPORARY MEMOIR. Secker & Warburg (1944).
THESIS ON THE QUALITY OF ILLUSION IN THE CONTINUITY OF THE
    INDIVIDUAL LIFE IN THE HIGHER METAZOA WITH PARTICULAR
    REFERENCE TO THE SPECIES HOMO SAPIENS (1944).
THE HAPPY TURNING. Heinemann (1945).
MIND AT THE END OF ITS TETHER. Heinemann (1945).

SOURCES OF MAIN QUOTATIONS

Unless otherwise specified, the books, pamphlets and articles are by H. G. Wells. The sources of quotations from letters are given in the body of the text.

Page	Reference	Chapter One
3	1	*Coronet Magazine* (1937).
	2	MIND AT THE END OF ITS TETHER (1945).
	3	EXPERIMENT IN AUTOBIOGRAPHY (1934).
4	4	*Time and Tide*—Odette Keun (1934).
	5	*Times Literary Supplement* (1947).
5	6	*New Statesman and Nation*—G. B. Shaw (1946).
	7	PEN PORTRAITS AND REVIEWS—G. B. Shaw (1932).
	8	*New Statesman and Nation*—G. B. Shaw (1946).
6	9	*New Statesman and Nation*—G. B. Shaw (1946).
9	10	EXPERIMENT IN AUTOBIOGRAPHY (1934).
	11	EXPERIMENT IN AUTOBIOGRAPHY (1934).
	12	EXPERIMENT IN AUTOBIOGRAPHY (1934).
10	13	FIRST AND LAST THINGS (1908).

		Chapter Two
18	1	EXPERIMENT IN AUTOBIOGRAPHY (1934).

		Chapter Three
19	1	H. G. WELLS—Geoffrey West (1930).
22	2	EXPERIMENT IN AUTOBIOGRAPHY (1934).
23	3	THE NEW MACHIAVELLI (1911).

		Chapter Four
31	1	TALK TO SHOP ASSISTANTS CONFERENCE (1922).
	2	EXPERIMENT IN AUTOBIOGRAPHY (1934).
32	3	TONO-BUNGAY (1909).
34	4	EXPERIMENT IN AUTOBIOGRAPHY (1934).
35	5	Article on T. H. Huxley—*Royal College of Science Magazine* (1901).
	6	Article on T. H. Huxley—*Royal College of Science Magazine* (1901).
36	7	Article on T. H. Huxley—*Royal College of Science Magazine* (1901).
	8	EXPERIMENT IN AUTOBIOGRAPHY (1934).

Chapter Five

Page	Reference	
46	1	CERTAIN PERSONAL MATTERS (1897).
	2	H. G. WELLS—Geoffrey West (1930).
48	3	CERTAIN PERSONAL MATTERS (1897).
52	4	EXPERIMENT IN AUTOBIOGRAPHY (1934).
53	5	CERTAIN PERSONAL MATTERS (1897).
54	6	THE BOOK OF CATHERINE WELLS (1928).
58	7	THE BOOK OF CATHERINE WELLS (1928).
	8	THE NEW MACHIAVELLI (1911).

Chapter Six

61	1	H. G. WELLS—Geoffrey West (1930).
	2	EXPERIMENT IN AUTOBIOGRAPHY (1934).
62	3	THE TIME MACHINE (1895).
63	4	THE TIME MACHINE (1895).
65	5	COLLECTED SHORT STORIES—INTRODUCTION (1933).
	6	THE LIVING NOVEL—V. S. Pritchett (1946).
	7	THE STAR (1896).

Chapter Seven

67	1	PILGRIMAGE (4 vols.)—Dorothy Richardson (1938).
	2	PILGRIMAGE (4 vols.)—Dorothy Richardson (1938).
68	3	PILGRIMAGE (4 vols.)—Dorothy Richardson (1938).
69	4	A letter from Dorothy Richardson (1949).
	5	Review of Reviews—W. T. Stead (1895).
71	6	THE LIVING NOVEL—V. S. Pritchett (1946).
72	7	WHEN THE SLEEPER WAKES (1899).
74	8	JOURNAL—Arnold Bennett (1932-33).
75	9	MR. BRITLING SEES IT THROUGH (1916).
76	10	EXPERIMENT IN AUTOBIOGRAPHY (1934).
77	11	PILGRIMAGE (4 vols.)—Dorothy Richardson (1938).
	12	PILGRIMAGE (4 vols.)—Dorothy Richardson (1938).
78	13	PILGRIMAGE (4 vols.)—Dorothy Richardson (1938).
79	14	EXPERIMENT IN AUTOBIOGRAPHY (1934).

Chapter Eight

82	1	HISTORY OF THE FABIAN SOCIETY—Edward Pease (1916).
83	2	OUR PARTNERSHIP—Beatrice Webb (1948).
	3	OUR PARTNERSHIP—Beatrice Webb (1948).
84	4	HISTORY OF THE FABIAN SOCIETY—Edward Pease (1916).

Page	Reference	
85	5	*New Statesman*—G. B. Shaw (1946).
	6	*The Christian Commonwealth*—G. B. Shaw (1909).
86	7	PEN PORTRAITS AND REVIEWS—G. B. Shaw (1932).
	8	PEN PORTRAITS AND REVIEWS—G. B. Shaw (1932).
	9	*Fabian News* (1906).

Chapter Nine

| 97 | 1 | EXPERIMENT IN AUTOBIOGRAPHY (1934). |
| | 2 | EXPERIMENT IN AUTOBIOGRAPHY (1934). |

Chapter Ten

101	1	THE WAR OF THE WORLDS (1898).
112	2	LE ROMAN ANGLAIS DE NOTRE TEMPS—A. D. Chevalley (1921).
	3	*The Globe* (1909).
114	4	*View* (1911).
115	5	*View* (1911).

Chapter Eleven

120	1	JAN IN PILGRIMAGE—D. Richardson (1938).
127	2	FIRST AND LAST THINGS (1908).
	3	EXPERIMENT IN AUTOBIOGRAPHY (1934).
	4	FIRST AND LAST THINGS (1908).
	5	EXPERIMENT IN AUTOBIOGRAPHY (1934).
130	6	EXPERIMENT IN AUTOBIOGRAPHY (1934).

Chapter Twelve

133	1	IN THE DAYS OF THE COMET (1906).
	2	OUR PARTNERSHIP—Beatrice Webb (1948).
134	3	OUR PARTNERSHIP—Beatrice Webb (1948).
	4	SOCIALISM AND THE FAMILY.
	5	EXPERIMENT IN AUTOBIOGRAPHY (1934).
135	6	OUR PARTNERSHIP—Beatrice Webb (1948).
	7	OUR PARTNERSHIP—Beatrice Webb (1948).
	8	OUR PARTNERSHIP—Beatrice Webb (1948).
136	9	*Daily Dispatch* (1906).
137	10	MORALS AND MANNERS—Bertrand Russell (1929).
138	11	NEW WORLDS FOR OLD (1908).
	12	EXPERIMENT IN AUTOBIOGRAPHY (1934).
140	13	FIRST AND LAST THINGS (1908).
	14	FIRST AND LAST THINGS (1908).

SOURCES OF MAIN QUOTATIONS

INDEX

251